Laugh with Leacock

An Anthology of the Best Work of Stephen Leacock

McClelland and Stewart Limited
Toronto / Montreal

First paperback publication in Canadian
Best Seller Library, 1968

The Canadian Publishers
McClelland and Stewart Limited
25 Hollinger Road, Toronto 16

Printed and bound in Canada

Dear Professor Leacock:

There is a pretty story which probably comes to us in more languages than most of us read about a captain who is ordered by his superiors to select a number of his men for some extraordinary and hazardous duty. Whereupon, having summoned his company or troop before him, according to the manner which the various times and places where the incident occurs may dictate, the young leader repeats the special orders, and, since the service is not in the regular line of duty, asks for individual volunteers. Immediately, as the old story goes, the entire body steps forward, each man convinced of his own best fitness to represent the others in the special hazard of the moment— a pretty gesture, indeed, but one which leaves the perplexed subaltern in the predicament of making his own choice.

Well, something like that has been our experience in summoning to the desk your score of volumes and selecting therefrom some one thousand words or more, to make this book. We hoped for volunteers, but found the entire contents ready to be chosen. It was not what to include, but what to turn down, that bothered us—and since you cannot possibly telescope a dozen and a half volumes into one, no matter how extensive that one is, the casualties turned out to be numerous. I thought this explanation of the contents of the book should be made to you, the author, by me, the subaltern who had the job of editorial selection. But I should also like to make the point for the sake of those unfortunates who always find in a prize collection of this sort that the judges have left their particular loving-cup just outside the trophy-room door, rendering the whole exhibition for them both null and void.

iii

If anyone in reading this volume should feel that the very cream of your jesting has been omitted, some consolation may be found in the suggestion that a reading of what *is* here will dry up the worst case of lamentation. As a second hint—if one of these unfortunates must have that forgotten *pièce de résistance,* it is still probably available in its original setting, and for him who shall say it alone is not worth the price of the entire volume?

An interesting fact came to notice in the making of this collection of your best work. Before doing so we had written to a dozen or more of the sharpest and wittiest minds of our day, telling them that we were planning this book as a sort of surprise package to you in honor of your twentieth year as an author and your sixtieth as a citizen in a world the happier for your laughter and good fun. We asked each of these distinguished gentlemen, among other things, what his favorite Leacock story or essay might be and, curiously enough, the piece of yours which has been most often requested is not humorous at all but a most shrewd discussion of present-day education, under the caption of "Oxford as I See It." Apparently the old tradition that a humorous man must always be funny has been broken. But not for long; the second most popular sketch you ever wrote is that irresistible account of your first experience in banking. And the most famous single incident in your entire literary career occurs in the story of "Gertrude the Governess,"—more specifically in the description of the phenomenal departure of the disinherited young man and the manner in which he disperses himself from the immediate proximity of his home. All three of these high-spots, of course, will be found in the present volume.

A moment ago I confessed that before making this selection we dropped a hint to some of your friends that this was a jovial occasion in which they might perhaps wish to join. All of what they said in reply may not best be printed for the public eye, as perhaps now and then too intimate and laudatory for anything but a sincere and secret blush; yet never were truer words said than the graceful compliments they have paid you, which we are appending in the order they happened to reach us, and in which these well-wishers of yours are joined by the reader, your devoted publisher, and

THE EDITOR.

IRVIN S. COBB—

"I can't pick out my favorite Leacock story, because all Leacock stories are favorites of mine. How are you going to choose one pearl from a string of perfect pearls? This Leacock is a great humorist, a great person, a great soul and I love him for the laughs he has made."

CHARLES (CHIC) SALE—

"In rounding out the sixtieth year of his varied and remarkable career, Mr. Stephen Leacock deserves the congratulations of a world made happier by his efforts. For a number of years it has been my good fortune to count Stephen Leacock among my closest friends. This personal contact has strengthened my conviction, held for a longer period, that he is one of our greatest humorists. His works are among my prized possessions."

GEORGE ADE—

"Stephen Leacock has achieved the distinction of being a happy combination of the drawing-room Englishman and the liberated and unconventional American. He is a college professor who can be a quizzical fun-maker without sacrificing his dignity as a member of the Faculty. His mortar-board is tilted at just the right angle. He inherits the genial traditions of Lamb, Thackeray and Lewis Carroll and has absorbed, across the Canadian border, the delightful unconventionalities of Oliver Wendell Holmes and Mark Twain, with possibly a slight flavor of Will Rogers. His contributions to current good reading help to

prove that an author may be entertaining without straining for
effects or violating any of the conventions. He is a critic without rancor, a satirist who never loses his temper, and a com-
mentator whose unusual point of view enables him to be amusing at all times and didactic never."

ROBERT BENCHLEY—

"I have just returned from abroad, and I hope that it is not
too late for me to say that I have enjoyed Leacock's works so
much that I have written everything that he ever wrote—anywhere from one to five years after him. In case the proof-reader
thinks that I meant 'I have *read* everything that he ever wrote,'
please tell him that I really meant 'written.'"

HARRY LEON WILSON—

"Your note reminded me that I was late in observing an ancient custom of my house—the annual complete rereading of
Leacock. I began at once with an eye out for my 'favorite'
chapter or story. I haven't found one yet, though if made to
choose it would have to be the Nonsense Novels. My complaint
about Leacock is that his volumes go. Casual book bandits never
molest my set of Plutarch or the works of Herbert Spencer. I
suggest a Leacock edition, the volumes strung on a chain, stout
padlocks at either end. And I wish their author many happy
returns from the years and his publishers."

HOMER CROY—

"Your letter picked me up in Hollywood where I am endeav-
oring to raise the moral tone of the movies. I like it out here,
although there is not as much shooting as I expected. I'll never
forget the day I stumbled onto Stephen Leacock. Well, I've
been spending money on him ever since. He must be a rich
man."

CHRISTOPHER MORLEY—

"I wish I knew how to say, on this sharp spur of the moment,
the just word made perfect in honor of Saint Stephen, LL.D.—
Doctor of Living Laughter. I was never certain whether 1910
should be more famous for the appearance of Halley's Comet,

or the publication of Leacock's first book of irresponsibilities. I can only say that had I been a student at McGill I should have specialized in Political Economy, merely to hear him lecture. I can pay no greater tribute."

ELLIS PARKER BUTLER—

"Stephen Leacock's humor is like a well-woven Scotch plaid— honest and comfortable and satisfying, and all-fired funny when worn as a knee-length kilt for a university professor to do jigs in. Leacock is our premier parodist."

DONALD OGDEN STEWART—

"The only reason that I could not tell you my favorite Leacock story or chapter is that if I started to go back through his works I should probably find so many things that I have since used myself that the blow to my pride would cause me to throw my typewriter out of the window. And if I threw my typewriter out of the window, I should starve. I owe Stephen Leacock a great deal—so does every contemporary American humorist—but I would prefer not to know the exact extent of my debt. Ignorance is golden."

WILL CUPPY—

"He deserves all the laurels and commendations possible right now, when this frightful world is full of imitation, synthetic and otherwise half-witted humorists, and by that I do not mean myself. He is the real grand-daddy of the best ones of the day still. As I remarked, not unsapiently, in my last review of Leacock, 'Any book by Stephen Leacock has the tremendous advantage to start with of being by Stephen Leacock.'"

NUNNALLY JOHNSON—

"I was reading Stephen Leacock when I was in high school and I am still reading him. Writers of humor I have found to be a most poisonous crew, none of them seeming to have anything but loathing and contempt for the stuff of any other. I can think of but two names that are exempt from this harpooning, and Mr. Leacock's is one. Such nonsense as he writes never gets old or outdated to me; it is always fun, great fun to read."

Lawton Mackall—

"Professor Leacock's literary lunacy (equine sagacity in disguise) has been one of the most exhilarating and sanifying influences at large in the universe. As an eminent economist he has shown us the need of better regulation of public futilities. As a philosopher he has tested popular notions by carrying them to their logical confusions. As a critic he has diagnosed the comedy of literary manners. As a man of feeling he has been kind to the balloons he has popped; not pricking them maliciously, nor bashing them with a debunker's axe, but gently fomenting their inflation—till they burst with a spontaneous BANG!"

George S. Chappell—

"Mr. Leacock is so much more than a humorist. He is a searching critic. But for his humor alone he deserves the crown. His work is so robust, so direct, so well-written, so clean, so human and to me so perfect of its kind that I am delighted to have this opportunity of paying my tribute to him. He has brought me much happiness which my one little contact with him at a Coffee House luncheon only enhanced, for he is one of those fine, bluff, jolly men who looks and talks just the way he writes."

Gelett Burgess—

"Though I say it as shouldn't, it takes a fine, scientific mind to write good nonsense, and Stephen Leacock has placed himself in the class of Edward Lear, Dodgson, "Phœnix," Barrie, Oliver Herford and the author of Felix the Cat. I have enjoyed everything that Leacock has written, and I know how rare is the power of dissociation, so to speak, that creates such work. Long may he wave his magic pen!"

Contents

	PAGE
My Financial Career	1
Buggam Grange: A Good Old Ghost Story	5
How We Kept Mother's Day	15
The Laundry Problem	20
The Great Detective	25
The Old, Old Story of How Five Men Went Fishing	45
Guido the Gimlet of Ghent: A Romance of Chivalry	54
The Hallucination of Mr. Butt	62
Cast Up by the Sea	68
How My Wife and I Built Our Home for $4.90	99
Softening the Stories for the Children	106
The Everlasting Angler	112
Love Me, Love My Letters	118
The Golfomaniac	123
Gertrude the Governess: or, Simple Seventeen	128
Letters to the New Rulers of the World	140
The Marine Excursion of the Knights of Pythias	157
My Lost Dollar	180
Personal Experiments with the Black Bass	183
The Restoration of Whiskers a Neglected Factor in the Decline of Knowledge	189
Old Junk and New Money	200
Oxford as I See It	205

	PAGE
The Snoopopaths or Fifty Stories in One	226
My Affair with My Landlord	237
The Give and Take of Travel	242
The Retroactive Existence of Mr. Juggins	247
Homer and Humbug, an Academic Discussion	252
"We Have with Us To-night"	259
Caroline's Christmas: or, The Inexplicable Infant	276
Father Knickerbocker—A Fantasy	289
Simple Stories of Success or How to Succeed in Life	301
Historical Drama	309
Humour as I See It	326
L'Envoi	337

LAUGH WITH LEACOCK

My Financial Career

WHEN I go into a bank I get rattled. The clerks rattle me; the wickets rattle me; the sight of the money rattles me; everything rattles me.

The moment I cross the threshold of a bank and attempt to transact business there, I become an irresponsible idiot.

I knew this beforehand, but my salary had been raised to fifty dollars a month and I felt that the bank was the only place for it.

So I shambled in and looked timidly round at the clerks. I had an idea that a person about to open an account must needs consult the manager.

I went up to a wicket marked "Accountant." The accountant was a tall, cool devil. The very sight of him rattled me. My voice was sepulchral.

"Can I see the manager?" I said, and added solemnly, "alone." I don't know why I said "alone."

"Certainly," said the accountant, and fetched him.

The manager was a grave, calm man. I held my fifty-six dollars clutched in a crumpled ball in my pocket.

"Are you the manager?" I said. God knows I didn't doubt it.

"Yes," he said.

"Can I see you," I asked, "alone?" I didn't want to say "alone" again, but without it the thing seemed self-evident.

The manager looked at me in some alarm. He felt that I had an awful secret to reveal.

"Come in here," he said, and led the way to a private room. He turned the key in the lock.

"We are safe from interruption here," he said; "sit down."

We both sat down and looked at each other. I found no voice to speak.

"You are one of Pinkerton's men, I presume," he said.

He had gathered from my mysterious manner that I was a detective. I knew what he was thinking, and it made me worse.

"No, not from Pinkerton's," I said, seeming to imply that I came from a rival agency.

"To tell the truth," I went on, as if I had been prompted to lie about it, "I am not a detective at all. I have come to open an account. I intend to keep all my money in this bank."

The manager looked relieved but still serious; he concluded now that I was a son of Baron Rothschild or a young Gould.

"A large account, I suppose," he said.

"Fairly large," I whispered. "I propose to deposit fifty-six dollars now and fifty dollars a month regularly."

The manager got up and opened the door. He called to the accountant.

"Mr. Montgomery," he said unkindly loud, "this gentleman is opening an account, he will deposit fifty-six dollars. Good morning."

I rose.

A big iron door stood open at the side of the room.

"Good morning," I said, and stepped into the safe.

"Come out," said the manager coldly, and showed me the other way.

I went up to the accountant's wicket and poked the ball of money at him with a quick convulsive movement as if I were doing a conjuring trick.

My face was ghastly pale.

"Here," I said, "deposit it." The tone of the words seemed to mean, "Let us do this painful thing while the fit is on us."

He took the money and gave it to another clerk.

He made me write the sum on a slip and sign my name in a book. I no longer knew what I was doing. The bank swam before my eyes.

"Is it deposited?" I asked in a hollow, vibrating voice.

"It is," said the accountant.

"Then I want to draw a cheque."

My idea was to draw out six dollars of it for present use. Someone gave me a cheque-book through a wicket and someone else began telling me how to write it out. The people in the bank had the impression that I was an invalid millionaire. I wrote something on the cheque and thrust it in at the clerk. He looked at it.

"What! are you drawing it all out again?" he asked in surprise. Then I realised that I had written fifty-six instead of six. I was too far gone to reason now. I had a feeling that it was impossible to explain the thing. All the clerks had stopped writing to look at me.

Reckless with misery, I made a plunge.

"Yes, the whole thing."

"You withdraw your money from the bank?"

"Every cent of it."

"Are you not going to deposit any more?" said the clerk, astonished.

"Never."

An idiot hope struck me that they might think something had insulted me while I was writing the cheque and that I had changed my mind. I made a wretched attempt to look like a man with a fearfully quick temper.

The clerk prepared to pay the money.

"How will you have it?" he said.

"What?"

"How will you have it?"

"Oh"—I caught his meaning and answered without even trying to think—"in fifties."

He gave me a fifty-dollar bill.

"And the six?" he asked dryly.

"In sixes," I said.

He gave it me and I rushed out.

As the big door swung behind me I caught the echo of a roar of laughter that went up to the ceiling of the bank. Since then I bank no more. I keep my money in cash in my trousers pocket and my savings in silver dollars in a sock.

Buggam Grange: A Good Old Ghost Story

THE evening was already falling as the vehicle in which I was contained entered upon the long and gloomy avenue that leads to Buggam Grange.

A resounding shriek echoed through the wood as I entered the avenue. I paid no attention to it at the moment, judging it to be merely one of those resounding shrieks which one might expect to hear in such a place at such a time. As my drive continued, however, I found myself wondering in spite of myself why such a shriek should have been uttered at the very moment of my approach.

I am not by temperament in any degree a nervous man, and yet there was much in my surroundings to justify a certain feeling of apprehension. The Grange is situated in the loneliest part of England, the marsh country of the fens to which civilization has still hardly penetrated. The inhabitants, of whom there are only one and a half to the square mile, live here and there among the fens and eke out a miserable existence by frog fishing and catching flies. They speak a dialect so broken as to be practically unintelligible, while the perpetual rain which falls upon them renders speech itself almost superfluous.

Here and there where the ground rises slightly above the level of the fens there are dense woods tangled with parasitic creepers and filled with owls. Bats fly from wood to wood. The air on the lower ground is charged with the poisonous gases which exude from the marsh, while in the

woods it is heavy with the dank odors of deadly nightshade
and poison ivy.

It had been raining in the afternoon, and as I drove up
the avenue the mournful dripping of the rain from the
dark trees accentuated the cheerlessness of the gloom. The
vehicle in which I rode was a fly on three wheels, the fourth
having apparently been broken and taken off, causing the
fly to sag on one side and drag on its axle over the muddy
ground, the fly thus moving only at a foot's pace in a way
calculated to enhance the dreariness of the occasion. The
driver on the box in front of me was so thickly muffled
up as to be indistinguishable, while the horse which drew
us was so thickly coated with mist as to be practically in-
visible. Seldom, I may say, have I had a drive of so mournful a character.

The avenue presently opened out upon a lawn with over-
grown shrubberies and in the half darkness I could see the
outline of the Grange itself, a rambling, dilapidated building. A dim light struggled through the casement of a
window in a tower room. Save for the melancholy cry of
a row of owls sitting on the roof, and croaking of the
frogs in the moat which ran around the grounds, the place
was soundless. My driver halted his horse at the hither
side of the moat. I tried in vain to urge him, by signs,
to go further. I could see by the fellow's face that he was
in a paroxysm of fear and indeed nothing but the extra
sixpence which I had added to his fare would have made
him undertake the drive up the avenue. I had no sooner
alighted than he wheeled his cab about and made off.

Laughing heartily at the fellow's trepidation (I have a
way of laughing heartily in the dark), I made my way
to the door and pulled the bell-handle. I could hear the
muffled reverberations of the bell far within the building.
Then all was silent. I bent my ear to listen, but could

hear nothing except perhaps the sound of a low moaning as of a person in pain or in great mental distress. Convinced, however, from what my friend Sir Jeremy Buggam had told me, that the Grange was not empty, I raised the ponderous knocker and beat with it loudly against the door.

But perhaps at this point I may do well to explain to my readers (before they are too frightened to listen to me) how I came to be beating on the door of Buggam Grange at nightfall on a gloomy November evening.

A year before I had been sitting with Sir Jeremy Buggam, the present baronet, on the verandah of his ranch in California.

"So you don't believe in the supernatural?" he was saying.

"Not in the slightest," I answered, lighting a cigar as I spoke. When I want to speak very positively, I generally light a cigar as I speak.

"Well, at any rate, Digby," said Sir Jeremy, "Buggam Grange is haunted. If you want to be assured of it go down there any time and spend the night and you'll see for yourself."

"My dear fellow," I replied, "nothing will give me greater pleasure. I shall be back in England in six weeks, and I shall be delighted to put your ideas to the test. Now tell me," I added somewhat cynically, "is there any particular season or day when your Grange is supposed to be specially terrible?"

Sir Jeremy looked at me strangely. "Why do you ask that?" he said. "Have you heard the story of the Grange?"

"Never heard of the place in my life," I answered cheerily, "till you mentioned it to-night, my dear fellow, I hadn't the remotest idea that you still owned property in England."

"The Grange is shut up," said Sir Jeremy, "and has been for twenty years. But I keep a man there—Horrod—he was butler in my father's time and before. If you care to go, I'll write him that you're coming. And since you are taking your own fate in your hands, the fifteenth of November is the day."

At that moment Lady Buggam and Clara and the other girls came trooping out on the verandah, and the whole thing passed clean out of my mind. Nor did I think of it again until I was back in London. Then by one of those strange coincidences or premonitions—call it what you will—it suddenly occurred to me one morning that it was the fifteenth of November. Whether Sir Jeremy had written to Horrod or not, I did not know. But none the less nightfall found me, as I have described, knocking at the door of Buggam Grange.

The sound of the knocker had scarcely ceased to echo when I heard the shuffling of feet within, and the sound of chains and bolts being withdrawn. The door opened. A man stood before me holding a lighted candle which he shaded with his hand. His faded black clothes, once apparently a butler's dress, his white hair and advanced age left me in no doubt that he was Horrod of whom Sir Jeremy had spoken.

Without a word he motioned me to come in, and, still without speech, he helped me to remove my wet outer garments, and then beckoned me into a great room, evidently the dining room of the Grange.

I am not in any degree a nervous man by temperament, as I think I remarked before, and yet there was something in the vastness of the wainscotted room, lighted only by a single candle, and in the silence of the empty house, and still more in the appearance of my speechless attendant which gave me a feeling of distinct uneasiness. As Horrod moved to and fro I took occasion to scrutinize his face more narrowly. I have seldom seen features more calculated to inspire a nervous dread. The pallor of his face and the whiteness of his hair (the man was at least seventy), and still more the peculiar furtiveness of his eyes, seemed to mark him as one who lived under a great terror. He moved with a noiseless step and at times he turned his head to glance in the dark corners of the room.

"Sir Jeremy told me," I said, speaking as loudly and as heartily as I could, "that he would apprise you of my coming."

I was looking into his face as I spoke.

In answer Horrod laid his finger across his lips and I knew that he was deaf and dumb. I am not nervous (I think I said that), but the realization that my sole companion in the empty house was a deaf mute struck a cold chill to my heart.

Horrod laid in front of me a cold meat pie, a cold goose, a cheese, and a tall flagon of cider. But my appetite was gone. I ate the goose, but found that after I had finished the pie I had but little zest for the cheese, which I finished without enjoyment. The cider had a sour taste, and after having permitted Horrod to refill the flagon twice, I found that it induced a sense of melancholy and decided to drink no more.

My meal finished, the butler picked up the candle and beckoned to me to follow him. We passed through the empty corridors of the house, a long line of pictured Buggams looking upon us as we passed, their portraits in the flickering light of the taper assuming a strange and lifelike appearance as if leaning forward from their frames to gaze upon the intruder.

Horrod led me upstairs and I realized that he was taking me to the tower in the east wing in which I had observed a light.

The rooms to which the butler conducted me consisted of a sitting room with an adjoining bedroom, both of them fitted with antique wainscotting against which a faded tapestry fluttered. There was a candle burning on the table in the sitting room but its insufficient light only rendered the surroundings the more dismal. Horrod bent down in front of the fireplace and endeavoured to light a fire there. But the wood was evidently damp, and the fire flickered feebly on the hearth.

The butler left me, and in the stillness of the house I could hear his shuffling step echo down the corridor. It may have been fancy, but it seemed to me that his departure was the signal for a low moan that came from somewhere behind the wainscot. There was a narrow cupboard door at one side of the room, and for the moment I wondered whether the moaning came from within. I am not as a rule lacking in courage (I am sure my reader will be decent enough to believe this), yet I found myself entirely unwilling to open the cupboard door and look within. In place of doing so I seated myself in a great chair in front of the feeble fire. I must have been seated there for some time when I happened to lift my eyes to the mantel above and saw, standing upon it, a letter addressed to myself. I knew the handwriting at once to be that of Sir Jeremy Buggam.

I opened it, and spreading it out within reach of the feeble candle light, I read as follows:

"*My dear Digby,*
In our talk that you will remember I had no time to finish telling you about the mystery of Buggam Grange. I take for granted, however, that you will go there and

that Horrod will put you in the tower rooms, which are the only ones that make any pretense of being habitable. I have, therefore, sent him this letter to deliver at the Grange itself. The story is this:

On the night of the fifteenth of November, fifty years ago, my grandfather was murdered in the room in which you are sitting, by his cousin Sir Duggam Buggam. He was stabbed from behind while seated at the little table at which you are probably reading this letter. The two had been playing cards at the table and my grandfather's body was found lying in a litter of cards and gold sovereigns on the floor. Sir Duggam Buggam, insensible from drink, lay beside him, the fatal knife at his hand, his fingers smeared with blood. My grandfather, though of the younger branch, possessed a part of the estates which were to revert to Sir Duggam on his death. Sir Duggam Buggam was tried at the Assizes and was hanged. On the day of his execution he was permitted by the authorities, out of respect for his rank, to wear a mask to the scaffold. The clothes in which he was executed are hanging at full length in the little cupboard to your right, and the mask is above them. It is said that on every fifteenth of November at midnight the cupboard door opens and Sir Duggam Buggam walks out into the room. It has been found impossible to get servants to remain at the Grange, and the place —except for the presence of Horrod—has been unoccupied for a generation. At the time of the murder Horrod was a young man of twenty-two, newly entered into the service of the family. It was he who entered the room and discovered the crime. On the day of the execution he was stricken with paralysis and has never spoken since. From that time to this he has never consented to leave the Grange where he lives in isolation.

Wishing you a pleasant night after your tiring journey,
I remain,
Very faithfully,
JEREMY BUGGAM."

I leave my reader to imagine my state of mind when I completed the perusal of the letter.

I have as little belief in the supernatural as anyone, yet I must confess that there was something in the surroundings in which I now found myself which rendered me at least uncomfortable. My reader may smile if he will, but I assure him that it was with a very distinct feeling of uneasiness that I at length managed to rise to my feet, and, grasping my candle in my hand, to move backward into the bedroom. As I backed into it something so like a moan seemed to proceed from the closed cupboard that I accelerated my backward movement to a considerable degree. I hastily blew out the candle, threw myself upon the bed and drew the bed clothes over my head, keeping, however, one eye and one ear still out and available.

How long I lay thus listening to every sound, I cannot tell. The stillness had become absolute. From time to time I could dimly hear the distant cry of an owl and once far away in the building below a sound as of someone dragging a chain along a floor. More than once I was certain that I heard the sound of moaning behind the wainscot. Meantime I realized that the hour must now be drawing close upon the fatal moment of midnight. My watch I could not see in the darkness, but by reckoning the time that must have elapsed I knew that midnight could not be far away. Then presently my ear, alert to every sound, could just distinguish far away across the fens the striking of a church bell, in the clock tower of Buggam village church, no doubt, tolling the hour of twelve.

On the last stroke of twelve, the cupboard door in the next room opened. There is no need to ask me how I knew it. I couldn't, of course, see it, but I could hear, or sense in some way, the sound of it. I could feel my hair, all of it, rising upon my head. I was aware that there was a *presence* in the adjoining room, I will not say a person, a living soul, but a *presence*. Anyone who has been in the next room to a presence will know just how I felt. I could hear a sound as of someone groping on the floor and the faint rattle as of coins.

My hair was now perpendicular. My reader can blame it or not, but it was.

Then at this very moment from somewhere below in the building there came the sound of a prolonged and piercing cry, a cry as of a soul passing in agony. My reader may censure me or not, but right at this moment I decided to beat it. Whether I should have remained to see what was happening is a question that I will not discuss. My one idea was to get out and to get out quickly. The window of the tower room was some twenty-five feet above the ground. I sprang out through the casement in one leap and landed on the grass below. I jumped over the shrubbery in one bound and cleared the moat in one jump. I went down the avenue in about six strides and ran five miles along the road through the fens in three minutes. This at least is an accurate transcription of my sensations. It may have taken longer. I never stopped till I found myself on the threshold of the Buggam Arms in Little Buggam, beating on the door for the landlord.

I returned to Buggam Grange on the next day in the bright sunlight of a frosty November morning, in a seven cylinder motor car with six local constables and a physician. It makes all the difference. We carried revolvers, spades, pickaxes, shotguns and a ouija board.

What we found cleared up forever the mystery of the Grange. We discovered Horrod the butler lying on the dining room floor quite dead. The physician said that he had died from heart failure. There was evidence from the marks of his shoes in the dust that he had come in the night to the tower room. On the table he had placed a paper which contained a full confession of his having murdered Jeremy Buggam fifty years before. The circumstances of the murder had rendered it easy for him to fasten the crime upon Sir Duggam, already insensible from drink. A few minutes with the ouija board enabled us to get a full corroboration from Sir Duggam. He promised moreover, now that his name was cleared, to go away from the premises forever.

My friend, the present Sir Jeremy, has rehabilitated Buggam Grange. The place is rebuilt. The moat is drained. The whole house is lit with electricity. There are beautiful motor drives in all directions in the woods. He has had the bats shot and the owls stuffed. His daughter, Clara Buggam, became my wife. She is looking over my shoulder as I write. What more do you want?

How We Kept Mother's Day

As Related by a Member of the Family

OF all the different ideas that have been started lately, I think that the very best is the notion of celebrating once a year "Mother's Day." I don't wonder that May the eleventh is becoming such a popular date all over America and I am sure the idea will spread to England too.

It is especially in a big family like ours that such an idea takes hold. So we decided to have a special celebration of Mother's Day. We thought it a fine idea. It made us all realize how much Mother had done for us for years, and all the efforts and sacrifice that she had made for our sake.

So we decided that we'd make it a great day, a holiday for all the family, and do everything we could to make Mother happy. Father decided to take a holiday from his office, so as to help in celebrating the day, and my sister Anne and I stayed home from college classes, and Mary and my brother Will stayed home from High School.

It was our plan to make it a day just like Xmas or any big holiday, and so we decided to decorate the house with flowers and with mottoes over the mantelpieces, and all that kind of thing. We got Mother to make mottoes and arrange the decorations, because she always does it at Xmas.

The two girls thought it would be a nice thing to dress in our very best for such a big occasion, and so they both got new hats. Mother trimmed both the hats, and they looked fine, and Father had bought four-in-hand silk ties for himself and us boys as a souvenir of the day to remem-

ber Mother by. We were going to get Mother a new hat
too, but it turned out that she seemed to really like her
old grey bonnet better than a new one, and both the girls
said that it was awfully becoming to her.

Well, after breakfast we had it arranged as a surprise
for Mother that we would hire a motor car and take her
for a beautiful drive away into the country. Mother is
hardly ever able to have a treat like that, because we can
only afford to keep one maid, and so Mother is busy in the
house nearly all the time. And of course the country is so
lovely now that it would be just grand for her to have a
lovely morning, driving for miles and miles.

But on the very morning of the day we changed the
plan a little bit, because it occurred to Father that a thing
it would be better to do even than to take Mother for a
motor drive would be to take her fishing. Father said that
as the car was hired and paid for, we might just as well
use it for a drive up into hills where the streams are. As
Father said, if you just go out driving without any object,
you have a sense of aimlessness, but if you are going to
fish, there is a definite purpose in front of you to heighten
the enjoyment.

So we all felt that it would be nicer for Mother to have
a definite purpose; and anyway, it turned out that Father
had just got a new rod the day before, which made the
idea of fishing all the more appropriate, and he said that
Mother could use it if she wanted to; in fact, he said it was
practically for her, only Mother said she would much
rather watch him fish and not try to fish herself.

So we got everything arranged for the trip, and we
got Mother to cut up some sandwiches and make up a sort
of lunch in case we got hungry, though of course we were
to come back home again to a big dinner in the middle
of the day, just like Xmas or New Year's Day. Mother

packed it all up in a basket for us ready to go in the motor.

Well, when the car came to the door, it turned out that there hardly seemed as much room in it as we had supposed, because we hadn't reckoned on Father's fishing basket and the rods and the lunch, and it was plain enough that we couldn't all get in.

Father said not to mind him, he said that he could just as well stay home, and that he was sure that he could put in the time working in the garden; he said that there was a lot of rough dirty work that he could do, like digging a trench for the garbage, that would save hiring a man, and so he said that he'd stay home; he said that we were not to let the fact of his not having had a real holiday for three years stand in our way; he wanted us to go right ahead and be happy and have a big day, and not to mind him. He said that he could plug away all day, and in fact he said he'd been a fool to think there'd be any holiday for him.

But of course we all felt that it would never do to let Father stay home, especially as we knew he would make trouble if he did. The two girls, Anne and Mary, would gladly have stayed and helped the maid get dinner, only it seemed such a pity to, on a lovely day like this, having their new hats. But they both said that Mother had only to say the word, and they'd gladly stay home and work. Will and I would have dropped out, but unfortunately we wouldn't have been any use in getting the dinner.

So in the end it was decided that Mother would stay home and just have a lovely restful day round the house, and get the dinner. It turned out anyway that Mother doesn't care for fishing, and also it was just a little bit cold and fresh out of doors, though it was lovely and sunny, and Father was rather afraid that Mother might take cold if she came.

He said he would never forgive himself if he dragged

Mother round the country and let her take a severe cold at a time when she might be having a beautiful rest. He said it was our duty to try and let Mother get all the rest and quiet that she could, after all that she had done for all of us, and he said that that was principally why he had fallen in with this idea of a fishing trip, so as to give Mother a little quiet. He said that young people seldom realize how much quiet means to people who are getting old. As to himself, he could still stand the racket, but he was glad to shelter Mother from it.

So we all drove away with three cheers for Mother, and Mother stood and watched us from the verandah for as long as she could see us, and Father waved his hand back to her every few minutes till he hit his hand on the back edge of the car, and then said that he didn't think that Mother could see us any longer.

Well, we had the loveliest day up among the hills that you could possibly imagine, and Father caught such big specimens that he felt sure that Mother couldn't have landed them anyway, if she had been fishing for them, and Will and I fished too, though we didn't get so many as Father, and the two girls met quite a lot of people that they knew as we drove along, and there were some young men friends of theirs that they met along the stream and talked to, and so we all had a splendid time.

It was quite late when we got back, nearly seven o'clock in the evening, but Mother had guessed that we would be late, so she had kept back the dinner so as to have it just nicely ready and hot for us. Only first she had to get towels and soap for Father and clean things for him to put on, because he always gets so messed up with fishing, and that kept Mother busy for a little while, that and helping the girls get ready.

But at last everything was ready, and we sat down to the

grandest kind of dinner—roast turkey and all sorts of things like on Xmas Day. Mother had to get up and down a good bit during the meal fetching things back and forward, but at the end Father noticed it and said she simply mustn't do it, that he wanted her to spare herself, and he got up and fetched the walnuts over from the sideboard himself.

The dinner lasted a long while, and was great fun, and when it was over all of us wanted to help clear the things up and wash the dishes, only Mother said that she would really much rather do it, and so we let her, because we wanted just for once to humor her.

It was quite late when it was all over, and when we all kissed Mother before going to bed, she said it had been the most wonderful day in her life, and I think there were tears in her eyes. So we all felt awfully repaid for all that we had done.

The Laundry Problem

A Yearning for the Good Old Days of the Humble Washerwoman

A LONG time ago, thirty or forty years ago, there used to exist a humble being called a Washerwoman. It was her simple function to appear at intervals with a huge basket, carry away soiled clothes, and bring them back as snow-white linen.

The washerwoman is gone now. Her place is taken by the Amalgamated Laundry Company. She is gone but I want her back.

The washerwoman, in fact and in fiction, was supposed to represent the bottom end of everything. She could just manage to exist. She was the last word. Now the Amalgamated Laundry Company uses hydro-electric power, has an office like a bank, and delivers its goods out of a huge hearse driven by a chauffeur in livery. But I want that humble woman back.

In the old days any woman deserted and abandoned in the world took in washing. When all else failed there was at least that. Any woman who wanted to show her independent spirit and force of character threatened to take in washing. It was the last resort of a noble mind. In many of the great works of fiction the heroine's mother almost took in washing.

Women whose ancestry went back to the crusades *very nearly*, though never quite, started to wash when the discovery of the missing will saved them from the suds. But nowadays if a woman exclaimed, "What shall I do? I am alone in the world! I will open an Amalgamated Laundry!"—it would not sound the same.

The operation of the old system—as I recall it from the days of forty years ago—was very simple. The washerwoman used to call and take away my shirt and my collar and while she washed them I wore my other shirt and my other collar. When she came back we changed over. She always had one and I had one. In those days any young man in a fair position needed two shirts.

Where the poor washerwoman was hopelessly simple was that she never destroyed or injured the shirt. She never even thought to bite a piece out with her teeth. When she brought it back it looked softer and better than ever. It never occurred to her to tear out one of the sleeves. If she broke out a button in washing, she humbly sewed it on again.

When she ironed the shirt it never occurred to the simple soul to burn a brown mark right across it. The woman lacked imagination. In other words, modern industrialism was in its infancy.

I have never witnessed at first hand the processes of a modern incorporated laundry company using up-to-date machinery. But I can easily construct in my imagination a vision of what is done when a package of washing is received. The shirts are first sorted out and taken to an expert who rapidly sprinkles them with sulphuric acid.

They then go to the coloring room where they are dipped in a solution of yellow stain. From this they pass to the machine-gun room where holes are shot in them and from there by an automatic carrier to the hydraulic tearing room where the sleeves are torn out. After that they are squeezed absolutely flat under enormous pressure which puts them into such a shape that the buttons can all be ripped up at a single scrape by an expert button ripper.

The last process is altogether handwork and accounts, I am informed, for the heavy cost. A good button-ripper with an expert knowledge of the breaking strain of material, easily earns fifty dollars a day. But the work is very exacting, as not a single button is expected to escape his eye. Of late the big laundries are employing new chemical methods, such as mustard gas, tear bombs, and star shells.

Collars, I understand, are treated in the same way, though the process varies a little according as the aim is to produce the Fuzzled Edge Finish or the Split Side Slit. The general idea, of course, in any first class laundry, is to see that no shirt or collar ever comes back twice. If it should happen to do so, it is sent at once to the Final Destruction Department, who put gun cotton under it and blow it into six bits. It is then labelled *"damaged"* and sent home in a special conveyance with an attendant in the morning.

Had the poor washerwoman kept a machine-gun and a little dynamite, she could have made a fortune. But she didn't know it. In the old days a washerwoman washed a shirt for ten-twelfths of a cent—or ten cents a dozen pieces. The best laundries, those which deny all admission to their offices and send back their laundry under an armed guard, now charge one dollar to wash a shirt, with a special rate of twelve dollars a dozen.

On the same scale the washerwoman's wages would be multiplied by a hundred and twenty. She really represented in value an income of fifty dollars a year. Had it been known, she could have been incorporated and dividends picked off her like huckleberries.

Now that I think of it, she was worth even more than that. With the modern laundry a shirt may be worn twice, for one day each time. After that it is blown up. And it costs four dollars to buy a new one. In the old days a shirt lasted till a man outgrew it. As a man approached middle life he found, with a certain satisfaction, that he had outgrown his shirt. He had to spend seventy-five cents on a new one, and that one lasted till he was buried in it.

Had some poor woman only known enough to pick up one of these shirts and bite the neck out of it, she might have started something really big.

But even when all this has been said there remains more yet. In the old days if you had a complaint to make to the washerwoman you said it to her straight out. She was *there*. And she heard the complaint and sneaked away with tears in her eyes to her humble home where she read the Bible and drank gin.

But now if you have a complaint to make to an Amalgamated Laundry Corporation, you can't find it. There is no use complaining to the chauffeur in livery. He never saw a shirt in his life.

There is no use going to the office. All you find there are groups of lady employees sheltered behind a cast iron grating. They never saw your shirt. Don't ask them. They have their office work and in the evening they take extension lectures on the modern drama. They wouldn't know a shirt if they saw it.

Nor can you write to the company. I speak here of what I know for I have tried to lay a complaint before a laundry company in writing, and I know the futility of it. Here is the letter I wrote:

To the Board of Directors,

  The Amalgamated Universal Laundry Company

Gentlemen:—

  I wish you would try to be a little more careful with my shirt. I mean the pink one. I think you put a little more starch in the neck last time than you intended and it all seems stuck together.

Very faithfully yours —

But the only answer I got was a communication in the following terms:

Dear Sir,

  Folio 110,615. Department 0412. Received February 19th, 9.26 A.M. Read March 19, 8.23 A.M. Sent down April 19th, 4.01 A.M. Sent up May 19th, 2 A.M.

  We beg to inform you that your communication as above will be laid before the shareholders at the next general meeting. In answering kindly indicate folio, department, street, age and occupation. No complaints received under names or in words.

Yours,
Folio 0016.

After that I felt it was hopeless to go on. My only chance for the future is that I may get to know some beautiful rich woman and perhaps her husband will run away and leave her weeping and penniless and drinking gin, and then I will appear in the doorway and will say, "Dry your tears, dear, dear friend; there is prosperity for you yet; you shall wash my shirt."

The Great Detective

I

" 'Ha!' exclaimed the Great Detective, raising himself from the resilient sod on which he had lain prone for half an hour, 'what have we here?'

"As he spoke, he held up a blade of grass he had plucked.

" 'I see nothing,' said the Poor Nut.

" 'No, I suppose not,' said the Great Detective; after which he seated himself on a stone, took out his saxophone from its case, and for the next half hour was lost in the intricacies of Gounod's 'Sonata in Six Flats with a Basement.' "

—*Any Detective Story.*

————

The publishers tell us that more than a thousand detective stories are sold every day—or is it every hour? It does not matter. The point is that a great many are sold all the time, and that there is no slackening of the appetite of the reading public for stories of mysterious crime.

It is not so much the crime itself that attracts as the unraveling of the mystery by the super-brain of the Great Detective, as silent as he is efficient. He speaks only about once a week. He seldom eats. He crawls around in the grass picking up clews. He sits upside down in his armchair forging his inexorable chain of logic.

But when he's done with it, the insoluble mystery is solved, justice is done, the stolen jewels are restored, and the criminal is either hanged or pledges his word to go and settle on a ranch in Saskatchewan; after which the Great

25

Detective takes a night off at the Grand Opera, the only thing that really reaches him.

The tempting point about a detective story—both for the writer and the reader—is that it is so beautifully easy to begin. All that is needed is to start off with a first-class murder.

"Mr. Blankety Blank sat in his office in the drowsy hour of a Saturday afternoon. He was alone. Work was done for the day. The clerks were gone. The building, save for the janitor, who lived in the basement, was empty.

"As he sat thus, gazing in a sort of reverie at the papers on the desk in front of him, his chin resting on his hand, his eyes closed and slumber stole upon him."

Quite so. Let him feel just as drowsy as ever he likes. The experienced reader knows that now is the very moment when he is about to get a crack on the nut. This drowsy gentleman, on the first page of a detective story, is not really one of the characters at all. He is cast for the melancholy part that will presently be called The Body. Some writers prefer to begin with The Body itself right away—after this fashion:

"The Body was that of an elderly gentleman, upside down, but otherwise entirely dressed."

But it seems fairer to give the elderly gentleman a few minutes of life before knocking him on the head. As long as the reader knows that there is either a Body right away, or that there is going to be one, he is satisfied.

Sometimes a touch of terror is added by having the elderly gentleman killed in a country house at night. Most readers will agree that this is the better way to kill him.

"*Sir Charles Althorpe sat alone in his library at Althorpe Chase. It was late at night. The fire had burned low in the grate. Through the heavily curtained windows no sound came from outside. Save for the maids, who slept in a distant wing, and save for the butler, whose room was under the stairs, the Chase, at this time of the year, was empty. As Sir Charles sat thus in his arm-chair, his head gradually sank upon his chest and he dozed off into slumber.*"

Foolish man! Doesn't he know that to doze off into slumber in an isolated country house, with the maids in a distant wing, is little short of madness? Apparently he doesn't, and his fate, to the complete satisfaction of the reader, comes right at him.

Let it be noted that in thus setting the stage for a detective story, the Body selected is, in nine cases out of ten, that of an "elderly gentleman." It would be cowardly to kill a woman, and even our grimmest writers hesitate to kill a child. But an "elderly gentleman" is all right, especially when "fully dressed" and half asleep. Somehow they seem to invite a knock on the head.

After such a beginning, the story ripples brightly along with the finding of the Body, and with the Inquest, and with the arrest of the janitor, or the butler, and the usual details of that sort.

Any trained reader knows when he sees that trick phrase, "*save for the janitor, who lived in the basement,*" or "*save for the butler, whose room was under the stairs,*" that the janitor and the butler are to be arrested at once.

Not that they really did commit the murder. We don't believe they did. But they are suspected. And a good writer in the outset of a crime story throws suspicion around like pepper.

In fact, the janitor and the butler are not the only ones. There is also, in all the stories, a sort of Half Hero (he can't be a whole hero, because that would interfere with the Great Detective), who is partly suspected, and sometimes even arrested. He is the young man who is either heir to the money in the story, or who had a "violent quarrel" with the Body, or who was seen "leaving the premises at a late hour" and refuses to say why.

Some writers are even mean enough to throw a little suspicion on the Heroine—the niece or ward of the elderly gentleman—a needless young woman dragged in by convention into this kind of novel. She gets suspected merely because she bought half a gallon of arsenic at the local chemist shop. They won't believe her when she says, with tears in her eyes, that she wanted it to water the tulips with.

The Body being thus completely dead, Inspector Higginbottom of the local police having been called in, having questioned all the maids, and having announced himself "completely baffled," the crime story is well set and the Great Detective is brought into it.

Here, at once, the writer is confronted with the problem of how to tell the story, and whether to write it as if it were told by the Great Detective himself. But the Great Detective is above that. For one thing, he's too silent. And in any case, if he told the story himself, his modesty might hold him back from fully explaining how terribly clever he is, and how wonderful his deductions are.

So the nearly universal method has come to be that the story is told through the mouth of an Inferior Person, a friend and confidant of the Great Detective. This humble associate has the special function of being lost in admiration all the time.

In fact, this friend, taken at his own face value, must be regarded as a Poor Nut. Witness the way in which his

brain breaks down utterly and is set going again by the
Great Detective. The scene occurs when the Great Detective begins to observe all the things around the place
that were overlooked by Inspector Higginbottom.

" 'But how,' I exclaimed, 'how in the name of all that is
incomprehensible, are you able to aver that the criminal
wore rubbers?'

"My friend smiled quietly.

" 'You observe,' he said, 'that patch of fresh mud about
ten feet square in front of the door of the house. If you
would look, you will see that it has been freshly walked
over by a man with rubbers on.'

"I looked. The marks of the rubbers were there plain
enough—at least a dozen of them.

" 'What a fool I was!' I exclaimed. 'But at least tell me
how you were able to know the length of the criminal's
foot?'

"My friend smiled again, his same inscrutable smile.

" 'By measuring the print of the rubber,' he answered
quietly, 'and then subtracting from it the thickness of the
material multiplied by two.'

" 'Multiplied by two!' I exclaimed. 'Why by two?'

" 'For the toe and the heel.'

" 'Idiot that I am,' I cried, 'it all seems so plain when
you explain it.' "

In other words, the Poor Nut makes an admirable narrator. However much fogged the reader may get, he has
at least the comfort of knowing that the Nut is far more
fogged than he is. Indeed, the Nut may be said, in a way,
to personify the ideal reader, that is to say the stupidest—
the reader who is most completely bamboozled with the
mystery, and yet intensely interested.

Such a reader has the support of knowing that the police are entirely "baffled"—that's always the word for them; that the public are "mystified"; that the authorities are "alarmed"; the newspapers "in the dark"; and the Poor Nut, altogether up a tree. On those terms, the reader can enjoy his own ignorance to the full.

A first-class insoluble crime having thus been well started, and with the Poor Nut narrating it with his ingenuous interest, the next stage in the mechanism of the story is to bring out the personality of the Great Detective, and to show how terribly clever he is.

II

When a detective story gets well started—when the "body" has been duly found—and the "butler" or the "janitor" has been arrested—when the police have been completely "baffled"—then is the time when the Great Detective is brought in and gets to work.

But before he can work at all, or at least be made thoroughly satisfactory to the up-to-date reader, it is necessary to touch him up. He can be made extremely tall and extremely thin, or even "cadaverous." Why a cadaverous man can solve a mystery better than a fat man it is hard to say; presumably the thinner a man is, the more acute is his mind. At any rate, the old school of writers preferred to have their detectives lean. This incidentally gave the detective a face "like a hawk," the writer not realizing that a hawk is one of the stupidest of animals. A detective with a face like an ourang-outang would beat it all to bits.

Indeed, the Great Detective's face becomes even more important than his body. Here there is absolute unanimity. His face has to be "inscrutable." Look at it though you will, you can never read it. Contrast it, for example, with the face of Inspector Higginbottom, of the local police force. Here is a face that can look "surprised," or "relieved," or, with great ease, "completely baffled."

But the face of the Great Detective knows of no such changes. No wonder the Poor Nut, as we may call the person who is supposed to narrate the story, is completely mystified. From the face of the great man you can't tell whether the cart in which they are driving jolts him or whether the food at the Inn gives him indigestion.

To the Great Detective's face there used to be added the old-time expedient of not allowing him either to eat or drink. And when it was added that during this same period of about eight days the sleuth never slept, the reader could realize in what fine shape his brain would be for working out his "inexorable chain of logic."

But nowadays this is changed. The Great Detective not only eats, but he eats well. Often he is presented as a connoisseur in food. Thus:

"'Stop a bit,' thus speaks the Great Detective to the Poor Nut and Inspector Higginbottom, whom he is dragging round with him as usual; 'we have half an hour before the train leaves Paddington. Let us have some dinner. I know an Italian restaurant near here where they serve frogs' legs à la Marengo better than anywhere else in London.'

"A few minutes later we were seated at one of the tables of a dingy little eating-place whose signboard with the words 'Restauranto Italiano' led me to the deduction that it was an Italian restaurant. I was amazed to observe that my friend was evidently well known in the place, while his order for 'three glasses of Chianti with two drops of vermicelli in each,' called for an obsequious bow from the *appreciative padrone. I realized that this amazing man knew as much of the finesse of Italian wines as he did of playing the saxophone."*

We may go further. In many up-to-date cases the detective not only gets plenty to eat, but a liberal allowance of strong drink. One generous British author of to-day is never tired of handing out to the Great Detective and his friends what he calls a "stiff whiskey and soda." At all moments of crisis they get one.

For example, when they find the Body of Sir Charles Althorpe, late owner of Althorpe Chase, a terrible sight, lying on the floor of the library, what do they do? They reach at once to the sideboard and pour themselves out a "stiff whiskey and soda." Or when the heroine learns that her guardian Sir Charles is dead and that she is his heiress and when she is about to faint, what do they do? They immediately pour "a stiff whiskey and soda" into her. It is certainly a great method.

But in the main we may say that all this stuff about eating and drinking has lost its importance. The great detective has to be made exceptional by some other method.

And here is where his music comes in. It transpires—not at once but in the first pause in the story—that this great man not only can solve a crime, but has the most extraordinary aptitude for music, especially for dreamy music of the most difficult kind. As soon as he is left in the Inn room with the Poor Nut out comes his saxophone and he tunes it up.

" 'What were you playing?' I asked, as my friend at last folded his beloved instrument into its case.

" 'Beethoven's Sonata in Q,' he answered modestly.

" 'Good Heavens!' I exclaimed."

Another popular method of making the Great Detective a striking character is to show him as possessing a strange and varied range of knowledge. For example, the Poor Nut is talking with a third person, the Great Detective being apparently sunk in reveries. In the course of the conversation the name of Constantinople is mentioned.

"*I was hardly aware that my friend was hearing what was said.*

"*He looked up quietly.*

" *'Constantinople?' he said. 'That was the capital of Turkey, was it not?'*

"*I could not help marveling again how this strange being could have acquired his minute and varied knowledge.*"

The Great Detective's personality having been thus arranged, he is brought along with the Poor Nut and Inspector Higginbottom to Althorpe Chase and it is now up to him to start to "solve" the mystery. Till a little while ago, the favorite way of having him do this was by means of tracks, footprints, and other traces. This method, which has now worn threadbare, had a tremendous vogue. According to it, the Great Detective never questioned anybody.

But his real work was done right at the scene of the crime, crawling round on the carpet of the library, and wriggling about on the grass outside. After he has got up after two days of crawling, with a broken blade of grass, he would sit down on a stone and play the saxophone and then announce that the mystery is solved and tell Inspector Higginbottom whom to arrest. That was all. He would not explain anything but what the Poor Nut, half crazy with mystification, begged him to do.

" 'The case,' he at last explained very airily, 'has been a simple one, but not without its features of interest.'

" 'Simple!' I exclaimed.

" 'Precisely,' said he; 'you see this blade of grass. You tell me that you see nothing. Look at it again under this lense. What do you see? The letters ACK clearly stamped, but in reverse, on the soft green of the grass. What do they mean?'

" 'Nothing,' I groaned.

" 'You are wrong,' he said, 'they are the last three letters of the word DACK, the name of a well-known shoemaker in Market Croydon four miles west of the Chase.'

" 'Good Heavens,' I said.

" 'Now look at this soft piece of mud which I have baked and which carries a similar stamp—ILTON.'

" 'Ilton, Ilton,' I repeated, 'I fear it means less than ever.'

" 'To you,' he said. 'Because you do not observe. Did you never note that makers of trousers nowadays stamp their trouser buttons with their names? These letters are the concluding part of the name BILTON, one of the best-known tailors of Kings Croft, four miles east of the Chase.'

" 'Good Heavens!' I cried, 'I begin to see.'

" 'Do you?' he said drily. 'Then no doubt you can piece together the analysis. Our criminal is wearing a pair of trousers, bought in Kings Croft, and a shoe bought in Market Croydon. What do you infer as to where he lives?'

" 'Good Heavens,' I said, 'I begin to see it!'

" 'Exactly,' said the Great Detective. 'He lives halfway between the two!"

" 'At the Chase itself!' I cried. 'What a fool I have been.'

" 'You have,' he answered quietly."

· · · · · · ·

But unfortunately the public has begun to find this method of traces and tracks a "bit thick." All these fond old literary fictions are crumbling away.

THE METHOD OF RECONDITE KNOWLEDGE

In fact, they are being very largely replaced by the newer and much more showy expedient that can be called the Method of Recondite Knowledge. The Great Detective is equipped with a sort of super-scientific knowledge of things, materials, substances, chemistry, actions, and reactions that would give him a Ph.D. degree in any school of applied science.

Some of the best detectives of the higher fiction of to-day even maintain a laboratory and a couple of assistants. When they have this, all they need is a little piece of dust or a couple of micrometer sections and the criminal is as good as caught.

Thus, let us suppose that in the present instance Sir Charles Althorpe has been done to death—as so many "elderly gentlemen" were in the fiction of twenty years ago—by the intrusion into his library of a sailor with a wooden leg newly landed from Java. Formerly the crime would have been traced by the top heaviness of his wooden leg—when the man drank beer at the Althorpe Arms, his elbow on the side away from his leg would have left an impression on the bar, similar to the one left where he climbed the window sill.

But in the newer type of story the few grains of dust found near the Body would turn out to be specks from the fiber of Java cocoanut, such as is seen only on the decks of ships newly arrived from Java, and on the clothes of the sailors.

But, by the one method or the other method, the "in-

exorable chain of logic" can be completed to the last link.
The writer can't go on forever; sooner or later he must
own up and say who did it. After two hundred pages, he
finds himself up against the brutal necessity of selecting his
actual murderer.

So, now then, who did it? Which brings us to the final
phase of the Detective Story. Who really killed Sir
Charles?

III

THE TRAMP SOLUTION

According to one very simple expedient, the murder was
not committed by any of the principal characters at all.
It was committed *by a tramp*. It transpires that the tramp
was passing the Chase late that night and was attracted by
the light behind the curtain (as tramps are apt to be), and
came and peered through the window (as tramps love to
do), and when he saw Sir Charles asleep in his chair with
the gold watch on the table beside him, he got one of
those sudden impulses (such as tramps get when they see
a gold watch), and, before he knew what he had done, he
had lifted the window and slipped into the room.

Sir Charles woke—and there you are. All quite simple.
Indeed, but for the telltale marks on the grass, or the telltale fiber on the carpet, or the tell tale something, the
murderer would never have been known.

And yet the solution seems paltry. It seems a shame to
drag in the poor tattered creature at the very end and
introduce and hang him all in one page.

So we have to look round for some other plan.

THE MURDER WAS COMMITTED BY SOMEBODY ELSE
ALTOGETHER DIFFERENT

A solution, which is a prime favorite with at least one very distinguished contemporary author, is to have it turn out that the murder has been *committed by somebody else altogether different.* In other words, it was committed by some casual person who just came into the story for about one half a second.

Let us make up a simple example. At the Althorpe Arms Inn where the Great Detective and the Poor Nut are staying while they investigate the death of Sir Charles, we bring in, just for one minute, *"a burly-looking man in a check suit drinking a glass of ale in the bar."* We ask him quite casually, if he can tell us anything about the state of the road to Farringham. He answers in a surly way that he's a stranger to these parts and knows nothing of it. That's all. He doesn't come in any more till the very end.

But a really experienced reader ought to guess at once that he committed the murder. Look at it: he's burly; and he's surly; and he has a check suit; and he drinks ale; and he's a stranger; that's enough. Any good law court could hang him for that—in a detective story, anyway.

When at last the truth dawns on the Poor Nut.

" 'Great Heavens,' I exclaimed, 'the man in the check suit!'

"The Great Detective nodded.

" 'But how on earth!' I exclaimed, more mystified than ever, 'were you ever led to suspect it?'

" 'From the very first,' said my friend, turning to Inspector Higginbottom, who nodded in confirmation, 'we had a strong clew.'

"*A clew!*" *I exclaimed.*

" '*Yes, one of the checks on his coat had been cached.*'

" '*Cashed,*' *I cried.*

" '*You misunderstand me; not "cashed," CACHED. He had cut it out and hidden it. A man who cuts out a part of his coat and hides it on the day after a crime is probably concealing something.*"

" '*Great Heavens!*" *I exclaimed,* '*how obvious it sounds when you put it that way. To think that I never thought of it!*' "

THE SOLUTION OF THE THOROUGHLY DANGEROUS WOMAN

According to this method, the crime was committed by a thoroughly bad, thoroughly dangerous woman, generally half foreign—which is supposed to account for a lot. She has just come into the story casually—as a nurse, or as an assistant bookkeeper, or, more usual and much better, as a "discarded flame" of somebody or other.

These discarded flames flicker all through detective literature as a terrible warning to persons of a fickle disposition. In any case, great reliance is placed on foreign blood as accounting for her. For Anglo-Saxon readers, if you put a proper quantity of foreign blood into a nurse and then discard her, that will do the trick every time.

To show how thoroughly bad she is, the Dangerous Woman used to be introduced by the writers of the Victorian age as smoking a cigarette. She also wore "high-heeled shoes and a skirt that reached barely to her ankles." In our time, she would have to do a little better than that. In short, as the key to a murder, we must pass her by. She would get acquitted every time.

Let us try something else.

THE SOLUTION THAT THE MURDER WAS COMMITTED BY BLUE EDWARD

According to this explanation of the mysterious crime, it turns out, right at the end of the story, that the murder was not done by any of the people suspected—neither by the Butler, nor the Half Hero, nor the Tramp, nor the Dangerous Woman. Not at all. It was the work of one of the most audacious criminals ever heard of (except that the reader never heard of him till this second), the head and brain of a whole gang of criminals, ramifying all over Hades.

This head criminal generally goes under some such terrible name as Black Pete, or Yellow Charlie, or Blue Edward. As soon as his name is mentioned, then at once not only the Great Detective but everybody else knows all about him—except only the reader and the Nut, who is always used as a proxy for the reader in matters of astonishment or simplicity of mind.

At the very height of the chase, a new murder, that of a deputy police inspector (they come cheap; it's not like killing one of the regular characters), is added to the main crime of killing Sir Charles. The manner of the murder —by means of a dropping bullet fired three miles away with its trajectory computed by algebra—has led to the arrest. The Great Detective, *calculating back the path of the bullet*, has ordered by telephone the arrest of a man three miles away. As the Detective, the Nut, and the police stand looking at the body of the murdered policeman, word comes from Scotland Yard that the arrest is made:

"The Great Detective stood looking about him, quietly shaking his head. His eye rested a moment on the pros-

trate body of Sub-Inspector Bradshaw, then turned to scrutinize the neat hole drilled in the glass of the window.

" 'I see it all now,' he murmured. 'I should have guessed it sooner. There is no doubt whose work this is.'

" 'Who is it?' I asked.

" 'Blue Edward,' he announced quietly.

" 'Blue Edward!' I exclaimed.

" 'Blue Edward,' he repeated.

" 'Blue Edward!' I reiterated, 'but who then is Blue Edward?' "

.   .   .   .

This, of course, is the very question that the reader is wanting to ask. Who on earth is Blue Edward? The question is answered at once by the Great Detective himself.

" 'The fact that you have never heard of Blue Edward merely shows the world that you have lived in. As a matter of fact, Blue Edward is the terror of four continents. We have traced him to Shanghai, only to find him in Madagascar. It was he who organized the terrible robbery at Irkutsk in which ten mujiks were blown up with a bottle of Epsom salts.

" 'It was Blue Edward who for years held the whole of Philadelphia in abject terror, and kept Oshkosh, Wisconsin, on the jump for even longer. At the head of a gang of criminals that ramifies all over the known globe, equipped with a scientific education that enables him to read and write and use a typewriter with the greatest ease, Blue Edward has practically held the police of the world at bay for years.

" 'I suspected his hand in this from the start. From the very outset, certain evidences pointed to the work of Blue Edward.' "

After which all the police inspectors and spectators keep shaking their heads and murmuring, "Blue Edward, Blue Edward," until the reader is sufficiently impressed.

IV

The writing of a detective story, without a doubt, gets harder and harder towards the end. It is not merely the difficulty of finding a suitable criminal; there is added the difficulty of knowing what to do with him. It is a tradition of three centuries of novel writing that a story ought to end happily. But in this case, how end up happily?

For example, here we have Blue Edward, caught at last, with handcuffs on his wrists—Blue Edward, the most dangerous criminal that ever interwove the underworld into a solid mesh; Blue Edward, who—well, in fact, the whole aim of the writer only a little while before was to show what a heller Blue Edward was. True, we never heard of him until near the end of the book, but when he *did* get in we were told that his Gang had ramified all the way from Sicily to Oklahoma. Now, what are we to do?

If it is not Blue Edward, then we've got to hang the Tramp—the poor tattered creature who fried potatoes by the hedge. But we are called upon to notice that now he has "a singularly vacant eye." You can hardly hang a man with a vacant eye. It doesn't do.

What if we send him to prison for life? But that's pretty cold stuff, too—sitting looking at four stone walls with a vacant eye for forty years. In fact, the more we think of it, the less satisfied we are with hanging the Tramp. Personally I'd rather hang Meadows the Butler, as we first set out to do, or I'd hang the Nut or the Thoroughly Bad Woman, or any of them.

In the older fiction, they used to face this problem fairly

and squarely. They hanged them,—and apparently they liked it. But nowadays we can't do it. We have lost the old-fashioned solid satisfaction in it, so we have to look round for another solution. Here is one, a very favorite one with our sensitive generation. If I had to give it a name, I would call it—

THE CRIMINAL WITH THE HACKING COUGH

The method of it is very simple. Blue Edward, or whoever is to be "it," is duly caught. There's no doubt of his guilt. But at the moment when the Great Detective and the Ignorant Police are examining him he develops a "hacking cough." Indeed, as he starts to make his confession, he can hardly talk for hacks.

" 'Well,' says the criminal, looking round at the little group of police officers, 'the game is up—hack! hack!— and I may as well make a clean breast of it—hack, hack, hack.' "

Any trained reader when he hears these hacks knows exactly what they are to lead up to. The criminal, robust though he seemed only a chapter ago when he jumped through a three-story window after throttling Sub-Inspector Juggins half to death, is a dying man. He has got one of those terrible diseases known to fiction as a "mortal complaint." It wouldn't do to give it an exact name, or somebody might get busy and cure it. The symptoms are a hacking cough and a great mildness of manner, an absence of all profanity, and a tendency to call everybody "you gentlemen." Those things spell finis.

In fact, all that is needed now is for the Great Detective himself to say, *"Gentlemen"* (they are all gentlemen at this stage of the story), "*a higher conviction than any earthly law has, et cetera, et cetera.*" With that, the curtain is dropped, and it is understood that the criminal made his exit the same night.

That's better, decidedly better. And yet, lacking in cheerfulness, somehow.

It is just about as difficult to deal with the Thoroughly Bad woman. The general procedure is to make her raise a terrible scene. When she is at last rounded up and caught, she doesn't "go quietly" like the criminal with the hacking cough or the repentant tramp. Not at all. She raises —in fact, she is made to raise so much that the reader will be content to waive any prejudice about the disposition of criminals, to get her out of the story.

"*The woman's face as Inspector Higginbottom snapped the handcuffs on her wrists was livid with fury.*
"*'Gur-r-r-r-r!' she hissed.*"

(This is her favorite exclamation, and shows the high percentage of her foreign blood.)

"*'Gur-r-r-r-r! I hate you all. Do what you like with me. I would kill him again a thousand times, the old fool.'*
"*She turned furiously towards my friend (the Great Detective).*
"*'As for you,' she said, 'I hate you. Gur-r-r! See, I spit at you. Gur-r-r-r!'*"

In that way, the Great Detective gets his, though, of course, his impassive face never showed a sign. Spitting on him doesn't faze him. Then she turns on the Heroine and gives her what's coming to her.

"'*And you! Gur-r-r! I despise you, with your baby face! Gur-r-r! And now you think you will marry him! I laugh at you! Ha! Ha! Hahula!*'"

And after that she turns on the Nut and gives him some, and then some for Inspector Higginbottom, and thus with three "Gur-r-r's" for everybody and a "Ha! ha!" as a tiger, off she goes.

. . . .

But, take it which way you will, the ending is never satisfactory. Not even the glad news that the Heroine sank into the Poor Nut's arms, never to leave them again, can relieve the situation. Not even the knowledge that they erected a handsome memorial to Sir Charles, or that the Great Detective played the saxophone for a week can quite compensate us.

The Old, Old Story of How Five Men Went Fishing

THIS is a plain account of a fishing party. It is not a story. There is no plot. Nothing happens in it and nobody is hurt. The only point of this narrative is its peculiar truth. It not only tells what happened to us—the five people concerned in it—but what has happened and is happening to all the other fishing parties that at the season of the year, from Halifax to Idaho, go gliding out on the unruffled surface of our Canadian and American lakes in the still cool of early summer morning.

We decided to go in the early morning because there is a popular belief that the early morning is the right time for bass fishing. The bass is said to bite in the early morning. Perhaps it does. In fact the thing is almost capable of scientific proof. The bass does *not* bite between eight and twelve. It does *not* bite between twelve and six in the afternoon. Nor does it bite between six o'clock and midnight. All these things are known facts. The inference is that the bass bites furiously at about daybreak.

At any rate our party were unanimous about starting early. "Better make an early start," said the Colonel when the idea of the party was suggested. "Oh, yes," said George Popley, the Bank Manager, "we want to get right out on the shoal while the fish are biting."

When he said this all our eyes glistened. Everybody's do. There's a thrill in the words. To "get right out on the shoal at daybreak when the fish are biting," is an idea that goes to any man's brain.

If you listen to the men talking in a Pullman car, or a

hotel corridor, or better still, at the little tables in a first-class bar, you will not listen long before you hear one say—"Well, we got out early, just after sunrise, right on the shoal." . . . And presently, even if you can't hear him you will see him reach out his two hands and hold them about two feet apart for the other men to admire. He is measuring the fish. No, not the fish they caught; this is the big one that they lost. But they had him right up to the top of the water: Oh, yes, he was up to the top of the water all right. The number of huge fish that have been heaved up to the top of the water in our lakes is almost incredible. Or at least it used to be when we still had bar rooms and little tables for serving that vile stuff Scotch whiskey and such foul things as gin Rickeys and John Collinses. It makes one sick to think of it, doesn't it? But there was good fishing in the bars, all winter.

But, as I say, we decided to go early in the morning. Charlie Jones, the railroad man, said that he remembered how when he was a boy, up in Wisconsin, they used to get out at five in the morning—not get up at five but be on the shoal at five. It appears that there is a shoal somewhere in Wisconsin where the bass lie in thousands. Kernin, the lawyer, said that when he was a boy—this was on Lake Rosseau—they used to get out at four. It seems there is a shoal in Lake Rosseau where you can haul up the bass as fast as you can drop your line. The shoal is hard to find—very hard. Kernin can find it, but it is doubtful —so I gather—if any other living man can. The Wisconsin shoal, too, is very difficult to find. Once you find it, you are all right; but it's hard to find. Charlie Jones can find it. If you were in Wisconsin right now he'd take you straight to it, but probably no other person now alive could reach that shoal. In the same way Colonel

Morse knows of a shoal in Lake Simcoe where he used to fish years and years ago and which, I understand, he can still find.

I have mentioned that Kernin is a lawyer, and Jones a railroad man and Popley a banker. But I needn't have. Any reader would take it for granted. In any fishing party there is always a lawyer. You can tell him at sight. He is the one of the party that has a landing net and a steel rod in sections with a wheel that is used to wind the fish to the top of the water.

And there is always a banker. You can tell him by his good clothes. Popley, in the bank, wears his banking suit. When he goes fishing he wears his fishing suit. It is much the better of the two, because his banking suit has ink marks on it, and his fishing suit has no fish marks on it.

As for the Railroad Man,—quite so, the reader knows it as well as I do,—you can tell him because he carries a pole that he cut in the bush himself, with a ten cent line wrapped round the end of it. Jones says he can catch as many fish with this kind of line as Kernin can with his patent rod and wheel. So he can, too. Just the same number.

But Kernin says that with his patent apparatus if you get a fish on you can *play* him. Jones says to Hades with *playing* him: give him a fish on his line and he'll haul him in all right. Kernin says he'd lose him. But Jones says *he* wouldn't. In fact he *guarantees* to haul the fish in. Kernin says that more than once (in Lake Rosseau) he has played a fish for over half an hour. I forget now why he stopped; I think the fish quit playing.

I have heard Kernin and Jones argue this question of their two rods, as to which rod can best pull in the fish, for half an hour. Others may have heard the same question debated. I know no way by which it could be settled.

Our arrangement to go fishing was made at the little golf club of our summer town on the verandah where we sit in the evening. Oh, it's just a little place, nothing pretentious: the links are not much good for *golf;* in fact we don't play much *golf* there, so far as golf goes, and of course, we don't serve meals at the club, it's not like that, —and no, we've nothing to drink there because of prohibition. But we go and *sit* there. It's a good place to *sit,* and, after all, what else can you do in the present state of the law?

So it was there that we arranged the party.

The thing somehow seemed to fall into the mood of each of us. Jones said he had been hoping that some of the boys would get up a fishing party. It was apparently the one kind of pleasure that he really cared for. For myself I was delighted to get in with a crowd of regular fishermen like these four, especially as I hadn't been out fishing for nearly ten years: though fishing is a thing I am passionately fond of. I know no pleasure in life like the sensation of getting a four pound bass on the hook and hauling him up to the top of the water, to weigh him. But, as I say, I hadn't been out for ten years: Oh, yes, I live right beside the water every summer, and yes, certainly,—I am saying so,—I am passionately fond of fishing, but still somehow I hadn't been *out.* Every fisherman knows just how that happens. The years have a way of slipping by. Yet I must say I was surprised to find that so keen a sport as Jones hadn't been out,—so it presently appeared,—for eight years. I had imagined he practically lived on the water. And Colonel Morse and Kernin,—I was amazed to find,—hadn't been out for twelve years, not since the day (so it came out in conversation) when they went out together in Lake Rosseau and Kernin landed a perfect monster, a regular corker, five pounds and a half,

they said: or no, I don't think he *landed* him. No, I remember he didn't *land* him. He caught him,—and he
could have landed him,—he should have landed him,—but
he *didn't* land him. That was it. Yes, I remember Kernin
and Morse had a slight discussion about it,—oh, perfectly
amicable,—as to whether Morse had fumbled with the net
—or whether Kernin—the whole argument was perfectly
friendly—had made an ass of himself by not "striking"
soon enough. Of course the whole thing was so long ago
that both of them could look back on it without any bitterness or ill nature. In fact it amused them. Kernin said
it was the most laughable thing he ever saw in his life to
see poor old Jack (that's Morse's name) shoving away with
the landing net wrong side up. And Morse said he'd never
forget seeing poor old Kernin yanking his line first this
way and then that and not knowing where to try to haul
it. It made him laugh to look back at it.

They might have gone on laughing for quite a time but
Charlie Jones interrupted by saying that in his opinion a
landing net is a piece of darned foolishness. Here Popley
agrees with him. Kernin objects that if you don't use a
net you'll lose your fish at the side of the boat. Jones says
no: give him a hook well through the fish and a stout line
in his hand and that fish has *got* to come in. Popley says
so too. He says let him have his hook fast through the
fish's head with a short stout line, and put him (Popley)
at the other end of that line and that fish will come in.
It's *got* to. Otherwise Popley will know why. That's the
alternative. Either the fish must come in or Popley must
know why. There's no escape from the logic of it.

But perhaps some of my readers have heard the thing
discussed before.

So as I say we decided to go the next morning and to

make an early start. All of the boys were at one about that. When I say "boys," I use the word, as it is used in fishing, to mean people from say forty-five to sixty-five. There is something about fishing that keeps men young. If a fellow gets out for a good morning's fishing, forgetting all business worries, once in a while—say once in ten years —it keeps him fresh.

We agree to go in a launch, a large launch,—to be exact, the largest in the town. We could have gone in row boats, but a row boat is a poor thing to fish from. Kernin said that in a row boat it is impossible properly to "*play*" your fish. The side of the boat is so low that the fish is apt to leap over the side into the boat when half "played." Popley said that there is no *comfort* in a row boat. In a launch a man can reach out his feet, and take it easy. Charlie Jones said that in a launch a man could rest his back against something and Morse said that in a launch a man could rest his neck. Young inexperienced boys, in the small sense of the word, never think of these things. So they go out and after a few hours their necks get tired; whereas a group of expert fishers in a launch can rest their backs and necks and even fall asleep during the pauses when the fish stop biting.

Anyway all the "boys" agreed that the great advantage of a launch would be that we could get a *man* to take us. By that means the man could see to getting the worms, and the man would be sure to have spare lines, and the man would come along to our different places,—we were all beside the water,—and pick us up. In fact the more we thought about the advantage of having a "man" to take us the better we liked it. As a boy gets old he likes to have a man around to do the work.

Anyway Frank Rolls, the man we decided to get, not only has the biggest launch in town, but what is more

Frank *knows* the lake. We called him up at his boat house over the phone and said we'd give him five dollars to take us out first thing in the morning provided that he knew the shoal. He said he knew it.

I don't know, to be quite candid about it, who mentioned whiskey first. In these days everybody has to be a little careful. I imagine we had all been *thinking* whiskey for some time before anybody said it. But there is a sort of convention that when men go fishing they must have whiskey. Each man makes the pretence that the one thing he needs at six o'clock in the morning is cold raw whiskey. It is spoken of in terms of affection. One man says the first thing you need if you're going fishing is a good "snort" of whiskey: another says that a good "snifter" is the very thing and the others agree, that no man can fish properly without "a horn," or a "bracer" or an "eye-opener." Each man really decides that he himself won't take any. But he feels that in a collective sense, the "boys" need it.

So it was with us. The Colonel said he'd bring along "a bottle of booze." Popley said, no, let *him* bring it; Kernin said let him; and Charlie Jones said no, he'd bring it. It turned out that the Colonel had some very good Scotch at his house that he'd like to bring: oddly enough Popley had some good Scotch in *his* house too; and, queer though it is, each of the boys had Scotch in his house. When the discussion closed we knew that each of the five of us was intending to bring a bottle of whiskey. Each of the five of us expected the others to drink one and a quarter bottles in the course of the morning.

I suppose we must have talked on that verandah till long after one in the morning. It was probably nearer two than one when we broke up. But we agreed that that made no difference. Popley said that for him three hours' sleep, the right kind of sleep, was far more refreshing than ten. Kernin said that a lawyer learns to snatch his sleep when he can, and Jones said that in railroad work a man pretty well cuts out sleep.

So we had no alarms whatever about not being ready by five. Our plan was simplicity itself. Men like ourselves in responsible positions learn to organise things easily. In fact Popley says it is that faculty that has put us where we are. So the plan simply was that Frank Rolls should come along at five o'clock and blow his whistle in front of our places, and at that signal each man would come down to his wharf with his rod and kit and so we'd be off to the shoal without a moment's delay.

The weather we ruled out. It was decided that even if it rained that made no difference. Kernin said that fish bite better in the rain. And everybody agreed that a man with a couple of snorts in him need have no fear of a little rain water.

So we parted, all keen on the enterprise. Nor do I think even now that there was anything faulty or imperfect in that party as we planned it.

I heard Frank Rolls blowing his infernal whistle opposite my summer cottage at some ghastly hour in the morning. Even without getting out of bed, I could see from the window that it was no day for fishing. No, not raining exactly. I don't mean that, but one of those peculiar days —I don't mean *wind*—there was no wind, but a sort of feeling in the air that showed anybody who understands bass fishing that it was a perfectly rotten day for going out. The fish, I seemed to know it, wouldn't bite.

When I was still fretting over the annoyance of the disappointment I heard Frank Rolls blowing his whistle in front of the other cottages. I counted thirty whistles altogether. Then I fell into a light doze—not exactly sleep, but a sort of *doze*,—I can find no other word for it. It was clear to me that the other "boys" had thrown the thing over. There was no use in my trying to go out alone. I stayed where I was, my doze lasting till ten o'clock.

When I walked up town later in the morning I couldn't help being struck by the signs in the butchers' shops and the restaurants, FISH, FRESH FISH, FRESH LAKE FISH.

Where in blazes do they get those fish anyway?

Guido the Gimlet of Ghent: A Romance of Chivalry

It was in the flood-tide of chivalry. Knighthood was in the pod.

The sun was slowly setting in the east, rising and falling occasionally as it subsided, and illuminating with its dying beams the towers of the grim castle of Buggensberg.

Isolde the Slender stood upon an embattled turret of the castle. Her arms were outstretched to the empty air, and her face, upturned as if in colloquy with heaven, was distraught with yearning.

Anon she murmured, "Guido"—and bewhiles a deep sigh rent her breast.

Sylph-like and ethereal in her beauty, she scarcely seemed to breathe.

In fact she hardly did.

Willowy and slender in form, she was as graceful as a meridian of longitude. Her body seemed almost too frail for motion, while her features were of a mould so delicate as to preclude all thought of intellectual operation.

She was begirt with a flowing kirtle of deep blue, bebound with a belt bebuckled with a silvern clasp, while about her waist a stomacher of point lace ended in the ruffled farthingale at her throat. On her head she bore a sugar-loaf hat shaped like an extinguisher and pointing backward at an angle of 45 degrees.

"Guido," she murmured, "Guido."

And erstwhile she would wring her hands as one distraught and mutter, "He cometh not."

The sun sank and night fell, enwrapping in shadow the frowning castle of Buggensberg, and the ancient city of Ghent at its foot. And as the darkness gathered, the windows of the castle shone out with fiery red, for it was Yuletide, and it was wassail all in the Great Hall of the castle, and this night the Margrave of Buggensberg made him a feast, and celebrated the betrothal of Isolde, his daughter, with Tancred the Tenspot.

And to the feast he had bidden all his liege lords and vassals—Hubert the Husky, Edward the Earwig, Rollo the Rumbottle, and many others.

In the meantime the Lady Isolde stood upon the battlements and mourned for the absent Guido.

The love of Guido and Isolde was of that pure and almost divine type, found only in the middle ages.

They had never seen one another. Guido had never seen Isolde, Isolde had never seen Guido. They had never heard one another speak. They had never been together. They did not know one another.

Yet they loved.

Their love had sprung into being suddenly and romantically, with all the mystic charm which is love's greatest happiness.

Years before, Guido had seen the name of Isolde the Slender painted on a fence.

He had turned pale, fallen into a swoon and started at once for Jerusalem.

On the very same day Isolde in passing through the streets of Ghent had seen the coat of arms of Guido hanging on a clothes line.

She had fallen back into the arms of her tirewomen more dead than alive.

Since that day they had loved.

Isolde would wander forth from the castle at earliest

morn, with the name of Guido on her lips. She told his name to the trees. She whispered it to the flowers. She breathed it to the birds. Quite a lot of them knew it. At times she would ride her palfrey along the sands of the sea and call "Guido" to the waves! At other times she would tell it to the grass or even to a stick of cordwood or a ton of coal.

Guido and Isolde, though they had never met, cherished each the features of the other. Beneath his coat of mail Guido carried a miniature of Isolde, carven on ivory. He had found it at the bottom of the castle crag, between the castle and the old town of Ghent at its foot.

How did he know that it was Isolde?

There was no need for him to ask.

His *heart* had spoken.

The eye of love cannot be deceived.

And Isolde? She, too, cherished beneath her stomacher a miniature of Guido the Gimlet. She had it of a travelling chapman in whose pack she had discovered it, and had paid its price in pearls. How had she known that he it was, that is, that it was he? Because of the Coat of Arms emblazoned beneath the miniature. The same heraldic design that had first shaken her to the heart. Sleeping or waking it was ever before her eyes: A lion, proper, quartered in a field of gules, and a dog, improper, three-quarters in a field of buckwheat.

And if the love of Isolde burned thus purely for Guido, the love of Guido burned for Isolde with a flame no less pure.

No sooner had love entered Guido's heart than he had determined to do some great feat of emprise or adventure, some high achievement of deringdo which should make him worthy to woo her.

He placed himself under a vow that he would eat nothing, save only food, and drink nothing, save only liquor, till such season as he should have performed his feat.

For this cause he had at once set out for Jerusalem to kill a Saracen for her. He killed one, quite a large one. Still under his vow, he set out again at once to the very confines of Pannonia determined to kill a Turk for her. From Pannonia he passed into the Highlands of Britain, where he killed her a Caledonian.

Every year and every month Guido performed for Isolde some new achievement of emprise.

And in the meantime Isolde waited.

It was not that suitors were lacking. Isolde the Slender had suitors in plenty ready to do her lightest hest.

Feats of arms were done daily for her sake. To win her love suitors were willing to vow themselves to perdition. For Isolde's sake, Otto the Otter had cast himself into the sea. Conrad the Cocoanut had hurled himself from the highest battlement of the castle head first into the mud. Hugo the Hopeless had hanged himself by the waistband to a hickory tree and had refused all efforts to dislodge him. For her sake Siegfried the Susceptible had swallowed sulphuric acid.

But Isolde the Slender was heedless of the court thus paid to her.

In vain her stepmother, Agatha the Angular, urged her to marry. In vain her father, the Margrave of Buggensberg, commanded her to choose the one or the other of the suitors.

Her heart remained unswervingly true to the Gimlet.

From time to time love tokens passed between the lovers. From Jerusalem Guido had sent to her a stick with a notch in it to signify his undying constancy. From Pannonia he sent a piece of board, and from Venetia about two feet of scantling. All these Isolde treasured. At night they lay beneath her pillow.

Then, after years of wandering, Guido had determined to crown his love with a final achievement for Isolde's sake.

It was his design to return to Ghent, to scale by night the castle cliff and to prove his love for Isolde by killing her father for her, casting her stepmother from the battlements, burning the castle, and carrying her away.

This design he was now hastening to put into execution. Attended by fifty trusty followers under the lead of Carlo the Corkscrew and Beowulf the Bradawl, he had made his way to Ghent. Under cover of night they had reached the foot of the castle cliff; and now, on their hands and knees in single file, they were crawling round and round the spiral path that led up to the gate of the fortress. At six of the clock they had spiralled once. At seven of the clock they had reappeared at the second round, and as the feast in the hall reached its height, they reappeared on the fourth lap.

Guido the Gimlet was in the lead. His coat of mail was hidden beneath a parti-coloured cloak and he bore in his hand a horn.

By arrangement he was to penetrate into the castle by the postern gate in disguise, steal from the Margrave by artifice the key of the great door, and then by a blast of his horn summon his followers to the assault. Alas! there was no need for haste, for at this very Yuletide, on this very night, the Margrave, wearied of Isolde's resistance, had determined to bestow her hand upon Tancred the Tenspot.

It was wassail all in the great hall. The huge Margrave, seated at the head of the board, drained flagon after flagon of wine, and pledged deep the health of Tancred the Ten-spot, who sat plumed and armoured beside him.

Great was the merriment of the Margrave, for beside him, crouched upon the floor, was a new jester, whom the seneschal had just admitted by the postern gate, and the novelty of whose jests made the huge sides of the Margrave shake and shake again.

"Odds Bodikins!" he roared, "but the tale is as rare as it is new! and so the wagoner said to the Pilgrim that sith he had asked him to put him off the wagon at that town, put him off he must, albeit it was but the small of the night —by St. Pancras! whence hath the fellow so novel a tale? —nay, tell it me but once more, haply I may remember it"—and the Baron fell back in a perfect paroxysm of merriment.

As he fell back, Guido—for the disguised jester was none other than he, that is, than him—sprang forward and seized from the girdle of the Margrave the key of the great door that dangled at his waist.

Then, casting aside the jester's cloak and cap, he rose to his full height, standing in his coat of mail.

In one hand he brandished the double-headed mace of the Crusader, and in the other a horn.

The guests sprang to their feet, their hands upon their daggers.

"Guido the Gimlet!" they cried.

"Hold," said Guido, "I have you in my power!!"

Then placing the horn to his lips and drawing a deep breath, he blew with his utmost force.

And then again he blew—blew like anything.

Not a sound came.

The horn wouldn't blow.

"Seize him!" cried the Baron.

"Stop," said Guido, "I claim the laws of chivalry. I am

here to seek the Lady Isolde, betrothed by you to Tancred. Let me fight Tancred in single combat, man to man."

A shout of approbation gave consent.

The combat that followed was terrific.

First Guido, raising his mace high in the air with both hands, brought it down with terrible force on Tancred's mailed head. Then Guido stood still, and Tancred raising his mace in the air brought it down upon Guido's head. Then Tancred stood still and turned his back, and Guido, swinging his mace sideways, gave him a terrific blow from behind, midway, right centre. Tancred returned the blow. Then Tancred knelt down on his hands and knees and Guido brought the mace down on his back. It was a sheer contest of skill and agility. For a time the issue was doubtful. Then Tancred's armour began to bend, his blows weakened, he fell prone. Guido pressed his advantage and hammered him out as flat as a sardine can. Then placing his foot on Tancred's chest he lowered his vizor and looked around about him.

At this second there was a resounding shriek.

Isolde the Slender, alarmed by the sound of the blows, precipitated herself into the room.

For a moment the lovers looked into each other's faces.

Then with their countenances distraught with agony they fell swooning in different directions.

There had been a mistake!

Guido was not Guido, and Isolde was not Isolde. They were wrong about the miniatures. Each of them was a picture of somebody else.

Torrents of remorse flooded over the lovers' hearts.

Isolde thought of the unhappy Tancred, hammered out as flat as a picture-card and hopelessly spoilt; of Conrad the Cocoanut head first in the mud, and Sickfried the Susceptible coiled up with agonies of sulphuric acid.

Guido thought of the dead Saracens and the slaughtered Turks.

And all for nothing!

The guerdon of their love had proved vain. Each of them was not what the other had thought. So it is ever with the loves of this world, and herein is the medieval allegory of this tale.

The hearts of the two lovers broke together.

They expired.

Meantime Carlo the Corkscrew and Beowulf the Bradawl, and their forty followers, were hustling down the spirals as fast as they could crawl, hind end uppermost.

The Hallucination of Mr. Butt

It is the hallucination of Mr. Butt's life that he lives to do good. At whatever cost of time or trouble to himself, he does it. Whether people appear to desire it or not, he insists on helping them along.

His time, his company and his advice are at the service not only of those who seek them but of those who, in the mere appearances of things, are not asking for them.

You may see the beaming face of Mr. Butt appear at the door of all those of his friends who are stricken with the minor troubles of life. Whenever Mr. Butt learns that any of his friends are moving house, buying furniture, selling furniture, looking for a maid, dismissing a maid, seeking a chauffeur, suing for plumber or buying a piano —he is at their side in a moment.

So when I met him one night in the cloak room of the club putting on his raincoat and his galoshes with a peculiar beaming look on his face, I knew that he was up to some sort of benevolence.

"Come upstairs," I said, "and play billiards." I saw from his general appearance that it was a perfectly safe offer.

"My dear fellow," said Mr. Butt, "I only wish I could. I wish I had the time. I am sure it would cheer you up immensely if I could. But I'm just going out."

"Where are you off to?" I asked, for I knew he wanted me to say it.

"I'm going out to see the Everleigh-Joneses,—you know them? no?—just come to the city, you know, moving into their new house, out on Seldom Avenue."

"But," I said, "that's away out in the suburbs, is it not, a mile or so beyond the car tracks?"

"Something like that," answered Mr. Butt.

"And it's going on for ten o'clock and it's starting to rain—"

"Pooh, pooh," said Mr. Butt, cheerfully, adjusting his galoshes. "I never mind the rain—does one good. As to their house. I've not been there yet but I can easily find it. I've a very simple system for finding a house at night by merely knocking at the doors in the neighborhood till I get it."

"Isn't it rather late to go there?" I protested.

"My dear fellow," said Mr. Butt warmly, "I don't mind that a bit. The way I look at it is, here are these two young people, only married a few weeks, just moving into their new house, everything probably upside down, no one there but themselves, no one to cheer them up"—he was wriggling into his raincoat as he spoke and working himself into a frenzy of benevolence—"good gracious, I only learned at dinner time that they had come to town, or I'd have been out there days ago—days ago—"

And with that Mr. Butt went bursting forth into the rain, his face shining with good will under the street lamps.

The next day I saw him again at the club at lunch time.

"Well," I asked, "did you find the Joneses?"

"I did," said Mr. Butt, "and, by George, I was glad that I'd gone—quite a lot of trouble to find the house (though I didn't mind that; I expected it)—had to knock at twenty houses at least to get it—very dark and wet out there—no street lights yet—however I simply pounded at the doors until someone showed a light—at every house I called out the same things, 'Do you know where the Everleigh-Joneses live?' They didn't. 'All right,' I said, 'go back to bed. Don't bother to come down.'

"But I got to the right spot at last. I found the house all dark. Jones put his head out of an upper window. 'Hullo,' I called out; 'it's Butt.' 'I'm awfully sorry,' he said, 'we've gone to bed.' 'My dear boy,' I called back, 'don't apologize at all. Throw me down the key and I'll wait while you dress. I don't mind a bit.'

"Just think of it," continued Mr. Butt, "those two poor souls going to bed at half past ten, through sheer dullness! By George, I was glad I'd come. 'Now then,' I said to myself, 'let's cheer them up a little, let's make things a little brighter here.'

"Well, down they came and we sat there on furniture cases and things and had a chat. Mrs. Jones wanted to make me some coffee. 'My dear girl,' I said (I knew them both when they were children) 'I absolutely refuse. Let *me* make it.' They protested. I insisted. I went at it— kitchen all upset—had to open at least twenty tins to get the coffee. However, I made it at last. 'Now,' I said, 'drink it.' They said they had some an hour or so ago. 'Nonsense,' I said, 'drink it.' Well, we sat and chatted away till midnight. They were dull at first and I had to do all the talking. But I set myself to it. I can talk, you know, when I try. Presently about midnight they seemed to brighten up a little. Jones looked at his watch. 'By Jove,' he said, in an animated way, 'it's after midnight.' I think he was pleased at the way the evening was going; after that we chatted away more comfortably. Every little while Jones would say, 'By Jove, it's half past twelve,' or 'it's one o'clock,' and so on.

"I took care, of course, not to stay too late. But when I left them I promised that I'd come back to-day to help straighten things up. They protested, but I insisted."

That same day Mr. Butt went out to the suburbs and put the Joneses' furniture to rights.

"I worked all afternoon," he told me afterwards—"hard at it with my coat off—got the pictures up first—they'd been trying to put them up by themselves in the morning. I had to take down every one of them—not a single one right. 'Down they come,' I said, and went at it with a will."

A few days later Mr. Butt gave me a further report. "Yes," he said, "the furniture is all unpacked and straightened out but I don't like it. There's a lot of it I don't quite like. I half feel like advising Jones to sell it and get some more. But I don't want to do that till I'm quite certain about it."

After that Mr. Butt seemed much occupied and I didn't see him at the club for some time.

"How about the Everleigh-Joneses?" I asked. "Are they comfortable in their new house?"

Mr. Butt shook his head. "It won't do," he said. "I was afraid of it from the first. I'm moving Jones in nearer to town. I've been out all morning looking for an apartment; when I get the right one I shall move him. I like an apartment far better than a house."

So the Joneses in due course of time were moved. After that Mr. Butt was very busy selecting a piano, and advising them on wall paper and woodwork.

They were hardly settled in their new home when fresh trouble came to them.

"Have you heard about Everleigh-Jones?" said Mr. Butt one day with an anxious face.

"No," I answered.

"He's ill—some sort of fever—poor chap—been ill three days, and they never told me or sent for me—just like their grit—meant to fight it out alone. I'm going out there at once."

From day to day I had reports from Mr. Butt of the progress of Jones's illness.

"I sit with him every day," he said. "Poor chap—he was very bad yesterday for a while—mind wandered—quite delirious—I could hear him from the next room—seemed to think some one was hunting him—'Is that damn old fool gone,' I heard him say.

"I went in and soothed him. 'There is no one here, my dear boy,' I said, 'no one, only Butt.' He turned over and groaned. Mrs. Jones begged me to leave him. 'You look quite used up,' she said. 'Go out into the open air.' 'My dear Mrs. Jones,' I said, 'what *does* it matter about me?'"

Eventually, thanks no doubt to Mr. Butt's assiduous care, Everleigh-Jones got well.

"Yes," said Mr. Butt to me a few weeks later, "Jones is all right again now, but his illness has been a long hard pull. I haven't had an evening to myself since it began. But I'm paid, sir, now, more than paid for anything I've done—the gratitude of those two people—it's unbelievable—you ought to see it. Why do you know that dear little woman is so worried for fear that my strength has been overtaxed that she wants me to take a complete rest and go on a long trip somewhere—suggested first that I should go south. 'My dear Mrs. Jones,' I said laughing, 'that's the *one* place I will not go. Heat is the one thing I *can't* stand.' She wasn't nonplussed for a moment. 'Then go north,' she said. 'Go up to Canada, or better still go to Labrador'—and in a minute that kind little woman was hunting up railway maps to see how far north I could get by rail. 'After that,' she said, 'you can go on snow-shoes.' She's found that there's a steamer to Ungava every spring and she wants me to run up there on one steamer and come back on the next."

"It must be very gratifying," I said.

"Oh, it is, it is," said Mr. Butt warmly. "It's well worth anything I do. It more than repays me. I'm alone in the world and my friends are all I have. I can't tell you how it goes to my heart when I think of all my friends, here in the club and in the town, always glad to see me, always protesting against my little kindnesses and yet never quite satisfied about anything unless they can get my advice and hear what I have to say.

"Take Jones for instance," he continued. "Do you know, really now as a fact,—the hall porter assures me of it,—every time Everleigh-Jones enters the club here the first thing he does is to sing out, 'Is Mr. Butt in the club?' It warms me to think of it." Mr. Butt paused, one would have said there were tears in his eyes. But if so the kindly beam of his spectacles shone through them like the sun through April rain. He left me and passed into the cloak room.

He had just left the hall when a stranger entered, a narrow, meek man with a hunted face. He came in with a furtive step and looked about him apprehensively.

"Is Mr. Butt in the club?" he whispered to the hall porter.

"Yes, sir, he's just gone into the cloak room, sir, shall I—"

But the man had turned and made a dive for the front door and had vanished.

"Who is that?" I asked.

"That's a new member, sir, Mr. Everleigh-Jones," said the hall porter.

Cast Up by the Sea

A Sea Coast Melodrama (As Thrown up for 30 cents)—
Period, 1880

EVERYBODY who has reached or passed middle age looks
back with affection to that splendid old melodrama *Cast
Up by the Sea*. Perhaps it wasn't called exactly that. It
may have been named *Called Back from the Dead*, or
Broken Up by the Wind, or *Buried Alive in the Snow*,
or anything of the sort. In fact I believe it was played
under about forty different names in fifty different forms.
But it was always the same good old melodrama of the
New England Coast, with the farmhouse and the yellow
fields running down to the sea, and the lighthouse right at
the end of the farm with the rocks and the sea beyond,
looking for trouble.

Before the cinematograph had addled the human brain
and the radio broadcast had disintegrated the human mind,
you could go and see *Cast Up by the Sea* any Saturday
afternoon in any great American City for thirty cents;
you got a thrill from it that lasted twenty years. For
thirty cents you had an orchestra chair on the ground floor
where you could sit and eat peanuts and study the program
till the play began. After it had begun you couldn't eat
any more; you were too excited.

The first thing everybody used to do in studying the
program was to see how many years elapsed between the
acts; because in those days everybody used to find it wiser
to go out between the acts—for air. And the more years
that elapsed and the more acts there were, the more air

they could get. Some of the plays used to have ten acts and the people got out nine times. Nowadays this is all changed. People talk now of the unity of the drama, and in some of the plays to-day there is a deliberate announcement on the program that reads "Between Acts II and III the curtain will be merely lowered and raised again." We wouldn't have stood for that in 1880. We needed our two years between the acts. We had a use for it.

As I say, it was necessary to study the program. Nobody had yet invented that system of marking the characters "in the order of their appearance." You had to try and learn up the whole lot before the play began. You couldn't really. But you began conscientiously enough. Hiram Haycroft, a farmer; Martha, his wife; Hope, their daughter; Phœbe, a girl help; Zeke, a hired man,—Rube also a hired man,—and by that time you had just forgotten the farmer's own name and looked back for it when just then—

Up went the curtain with a long stately roll, two men at the side hoisting it, and there you were looking at the farmstead by the sea.

Notice how quick and easy and attractive that old fashioned beginning was. One minute you were eating peanuts and studying the program and the next minute the play had begun. There was none of that agonizing stuff that precedes the moving pictures of to-day: No "*Authorized by the Board of Census of the State of New York.*" The world, even New York State, was so good in 1880 that it had never heard of a censor. Nor was there any announcement of something else altogether heralded as "*A Great Big Compelling Life Drama—Next Week.*"

If the moving picture people could have been in control (forty years before their time) they would have announced the farm and lighthouse play with a written panegyric on what they were going to show—"a gripping heart-drama in which the foam of the sea and the eerie of the spindrift carry to the heart a tale of true love battled by the wind next Thursday."

But if they had worked that stuff on an audience of 1880 it would have gone out and taken another drink, and never come back until next Thursday.

So the play began at once. There was the farmhouse, or at least the porch and door, at the right hand side of the stage, all bathed in sunlight (yellow gas) and the grass plot and the road in the centre, and the yellow wheat (quite a little bunch of it) at the left, and the fields reaching back till they hit the painted curtain with the lighthouse and the rocks and the sea.

Everybody who looked at that painted curtain and saw that lighthouse knew it wasn't there for nothing. There'd be something doing from that all right, and when they looked back at the program and saw that Act IV was marked *In the Lighthouse Tower—Midnight*, they got the kind of a thrill that you can never get by a mere announcement that there is going to be a "gripping heart-drama next Tu., Thurs., and Sat."

Surely enough there would be something doing with that lighthouse. Either the heroine thrown off it, or the hero thrown over it—anyway something good.

But for the moment all is peace and sunlight, on the seashore farm. There is no one on the stage but two men on the left, evidently Zeke and Rube, the hired men. They've got scythes and they are cutting the little patch of wheat over at the edge of the stage. Just imagine it, *real* wheat, they're actually cutting it! Upon my word those stage effects of 1880 were simply wonderful. I do wish that "Doug" Fairbanks and those fellows who work so hard to give us thrills could realize what we used to get in 1880 by seeing Zeke and Rube cutting real wheat on the left hand side of the stage.

Then they speak. You can't really hear what they say —but it sounds like this:

Zeke says, "I swan b'gosh heck b'gosh gum yak! yak!"

And Rube answers: "Heck gosh b'gum, yes, yak! yak!"

And they both laugh.

These words probably have a meaning, but you don't need it. The people are still moving into their seats and this is just the opening of the play. It's a mere symbol. It stands for New England dialect, farm life, and honesty of character. Presently Rube gets articulate. He quits reaping and he says:

"So Miss Hope'll be coming back this morning."

"Yes, sir, that she will. A whole year now it'll be that she's been to boarding school."

And Rube says:

"Yup, a whole yer come Gurdlemas."

Rube and Zeke have a calendar all their own.

"She'll be a growd up lady now all right."

"Yes, sir, and as purty as a pitcher, I'll be bound, by heck."

They whet their scythes with a clang and out comes Martha, the farmer's wife, and Phœbe, the help, from the porch on the right. With them comes a freckled boy, evidently the younger son of the farm family. This freckled boy is in all the melodramas. It is his business to get his ears boxed, mislay the will, lose the mortgage, forget to post the letters and otherwise mix up the plot.

"Do you see the buggy yet, Rube? Can you see them coming yet, Zeke?"

Zeke and Rube hop about making gestures of looking down the road, their hands up over their eyes.

"Not yet, Missus, but they'll be along right soon now."

"There they are," calls Phœbe, "coming along down in the hollow."

There is great excitement at once. Martha cries, "Land's sake, if it ain't Hope all right," and boxes the freckled boy's ears. The others run to and fro saying, "Here they come!" so as to get the audience worked up with excitement, at the height of which there comes the actual clatter of the horse's hoofs and the next moment a horse and buggy, a real horse and buggy, drive on to the stage. That clattering horse coming on to the stage was always one of the great effects in 1880,—a real horse with real harness and with added anxiety for fear that the horse would misbehave himself when he came on.

The buggy stops with a lot of shouting of "Whoa there"—intended to keep the horse lively. If they didn't shout at it this stage horse was apt to subside into a passive melancholy not suited for the drama.

So here is the farmer sitting in the buggy in a suit of store clothes and a black slouch hat, and beside him is Hope, his daughter, just home from boarding school. How sweet and fresh she looks in her New England sun hat with the flowers on it. I don't know what they did to the girls in the boarding schools in 1880—some line of algebra perhaps—to make them look so fresh. There are none like them now.

Hope leaps out in one spring and kisses her mother in one bound and she cries, "Well, Mother! Well, Phœbe! Why, Zeke! Why, Rube!" They all circulate and hop and dance about saying, "Well, Miss Hope, well, I never!" And all the while there's the sunshine in the yellow fields and the red hollyhocks beside the porch, and light and happiness everywhere.

You'd think, would you not, that that old homestead represented the high water mark of happiness? And so it does. But wait a bit. Before long they'll start trouble enough. All the audience know in advance that that farm will be mortgaged and the farmer ruined and Hope driven from home,—oh, there's lots of trouble coming. Trouble was the proper business of the melodrama. So presently they all get through their congratulations and Hope has embraced everybody, and the farmer's wife has got off two jokes about the size of Boston and then the freckled boy wants to take Hope away to see the brindle cow, and they all fade away off the stage except the farmer and his wife.

And right away the whole tone of the play changes, just like that.

The farmer stands alone with his wife.

And Martha comes over to him and puts her hand timidly on his shoulder. The joy has gone out of her face.

"Hiram," she says, "Lawyer Ellwood's agent was here this morning."

The farmer fairly humps into his shoulders with anger.

"Ay," he snarls.

"And, Hiram, Lawyer Ellwood wants his money."

"Ay! he wants his money, does he? Curse him!"

The farmer's fist is clenched and there's a scowl on his face.

"He says, Hiram, that it's got to be paid to-morrow. Oh, Hiram, we can't never pay it."

Martha puts her apron up to her face and sobs.

The farmer turns and shakes his clenched fist at the scenery away off to the left.

"Curse him!" he rages. "Ay, curse him. This three years he has thrown a blight across our life."

"You was friends oncet, Hiram," sobs Martha again, "years ago before he went to the city you was friends."

"Friends!" raves the farmer, "a fine friend, drawing

me on with his schemes of money and profit. 'To make my fortune,' he said—a fine fortune—ruin, ruin it meant —till I had signed this and signed that, till it was all mortgaged away and till he held me, as he thought, in the hollow of his hand. Martha, if that man stood before me now, by the God that lives, I could choke him with these hands."

Hiram makes a gesture so terrible and yet so passionate that the one hope of the audience in the top gallery is that Lawyer Ellwood will happen along right now and get choked.

Martha tries to dry her eyes.

"Nay, Hiram, you mustn't talk like that. Those are evil thoughts. It is God's will, Hiram, and it must be right. But we can't never pay."

"Not pay," shouts Hiram, "who says I can't pay? I *can* pay and when that man comes to-morrow I can throw the money in his face. Look, Martha, there it is!"

Hiram Haycroft draws a great wallet from his pocket and slaps it down on the palm of his hand.

"Two thousand dollars, every cent of his accursed debt. Martha, it will mean poverty and hard times for us where all was plenty, but, thank God! it can be paid."

"Why, Hiram!"

"I've raised it, Martha. I've sold the stock, I've parted with this and I've pledged that—everything but the roof above our heads is sold or pledged. But this accursed mortgage can be paid."

"Oh, Hiram!"

"It will mean hard times again, hard and bitter times—"

"I don't mind that, Hiram"—and Martha puts her hands up to her husband's neck—"we've borne it together before and we can bear it together again— But oh, Hiram, if only our boy Jack had been spared to us, I could have borne it so easily then."

Martha begins to cry.

"There, there, Martha," says the farmer, "you mustn't lay it so to heart. The sea has taken him, Mother, as it has taken many a brave lad before him—"

"The sea, the sea—" groans Martha, "I see it there so bright and calm in the sunlight. But will it give me back my boy? Three years this day, Hiram since he left us. I can feel his good-bye kiss still on my cheek. And since then no word, never a word."

Hiram draws his wife to him to comfort her.

"Come, Mother, come into the house; we mustn't show sad faces for Hope's home coming—come—"

They go in through the wooden porch under the flowers on the right, leaving the audience sad and disturbed. That infernal lawyer! But they were all alike in 1880. Show them a sun-lit farm and a happy family and they clap a mortgage on it at sight. And to think that farmer Haycroft and his wife had lost their only son at sea—that calm blue sea in the back curtain with the sunlight on it.

In fact the play is getting too sad; so it has to be relieved and Rube and Phœbe are brought on to the stage again and go through one of those rural love scenes that were used to ease the strain of the melodrama. Rube shambles over to her in a sheepish way, evidently proposing to kiss her, and says:

"Ain't you got nothing for me this morning, Phœbe?"

And Phœbe says:

"Go along, you big thing, I've got *that* for you," and swats him over the face with a thistle. The audience roar with laughter, the strain is removed and they're ready to get on with the play when Phœbe disappears with Rube in pursuit.

"Why, Mother,"—it is Hope calling—"where are you, Mother?"

"I'm here, daughter," says Martha, reappearing out of the porch.

"I was looking for you all over, Mother," says Hope, coming over to her coyly. "I have been wanting so much to talk to you all by ourselves."

"Ah! And I think I can guess something of what that's about." Martha has taken Hope's hand in hers and is patting it and Hope is looking at the ground and swinging herself about on one heel in a way that in a New England play always symbolized the approach of love.

"—and now Hope tell me all about it," says the farmer's wife.

"You remember, Mother, that I wrote and told you that I had a secret—"

"Yes, dearie, a *great* secret, you said—"

"—a secret that I didn't want to put on paper and didn't want to tell to anybody till I could tell it to you first, Mother dear."

Hope has snuggled up close to her mother, who is patting her on the shoulder and repeating. "Ay, lass a great secret, and I'll be bound I can guess a little of what it is—I suppose it means that there is someone—that my little girl—"

She whispers into Hope's ear.

"Oh, Mother," Hope goes on, "it's even greater than that. Look, Mother, see what's on my hand."

Hope holds out her hand, her face downcast and not only her mother but even the girls in the gallery can see the plain gold ring that's on her finger. The men in the audience don't get it, but the girls and women explain to them what it is.

"Why Hope, darling," says Martha, all in a tremble, "what does it mean?"

"Why, Mother, it means—it means," Hope takes a flying leap into her mother's arms—"it means, Mother, that I'm married."

"Married!"

"Yes, married, Mother, last Saturday in Boston at eleven o'clock in the morning."

"Married, my little girl married!"

Martha has to be terribly astonished so as to keep the audience in the same frame of mind: not at Hope being married the very day she left her finishing school. That was nothing.—That was a favourite way of getting married in 1880—but at the fact that she hadn't told her mother about it. So Martha keeps repeating—

"Married! My little girl married!"

"It was all in such a hurry, Mother—I couldn't tell you. It all came so sudden—"

Hope is half crying, half smiling.

"But I shouldn't cry, Mother, because really I'm so happy—"

"That's right, darling, and now tell me all about it."

"We were married in Boston last Saturday, Mother. And, oh, I did so want you to be there, only it couldn't be. It was all in such a hurry—because Ned was offered a new ship—just think, Mother, captain of a ship at twenty-one."

"Not a sailor, dearie," says Martha Haycroft in evident agitation, "don't tell me that your man is a sailor."

"Why, yes, Mother, Ned's been at sea ever since he was fifteen."

"The sea, the sea," groans the farmer's wife. "I see it flying there in the sunlight. I hear it roaring in the winter wind. When will it give me back my boy?"

"Mother, you mustn't cry. It was years ago and it was God's will, and Mother, Ned will only be at sea a little while longer now—just this one voyage in his new ship, and listen, Mother, Ned's new ship (it's a schooner, Mother, and it's Ned's father who owns it and it's called the *Good Hope,* after me)—will be off the coast here this evening, and if Ned can manage it he'll come ashore and see us all, and his father—though I've never seen *him*—will be with Ned. And Ned is to settle down and be a farmer, Mother, on a farm beside the sea. His father is a rich lawyer in Boston, Mother, and Ned says that his father has a mortgage on a farm right on the seashore just like this, and after this one voyage—"

"A lawyer, a rich lawyer!"

"Yes, Mother, a rich lawyer in Boston, but he once lived in the country, near here I think, years ago."

"His name? What name?"

"Ellwood, Mother, Lawyer Ephraim Ellwood."

Martha breaks from her daughter in alarm.

"No, no, not that, don't say it's that name—Hope, it couldn't be, it can't be."

And at that moment the farmer, Hiram Haycroft, steps on to the stage.

"Why, Mother! Why, Hope! What's—what's all this?"

Hope (tearfully)—"I don't know, Father; I only began to tell Mother a secret—"

"Yes, daughter!"

"That I—that we—that I am married, Father."

"Married, my little girl married! That don't seem possible. But what's all this ado about, Mother, and who's the lucky man that's gone and taken my little girl?"

Hiram comes over affectionately and takes Hope's two hands.

"Only yesterday, it seems," he says, "that I held you on my knees, little gal, and now to be married."

All the audience waits in a luxury of expectation. They know that the farmer is going to get an awful jolt.

Then he gets it.

"He's the son of a rich Boston lawyer, Father, who—has a mortgage on a farm—"

The farmer has dropped Hope's hands, his face is darkening.

"And Ned is to have the farm—Ned Ellwood is his name, Father, see it here."

Hope timidly takes out a paper from her dress.

"Here on my marriage certificate."

But the farmer doesn't hear her. He stands a moment, his fists clenched, then bursts into wild rage.

"Ellwood, Lawyer Ellwood. My daughter marry a son of that man! By the living God, Hope, sooner than see you married to a son of his, I'd see you lying fathoms deep under the sea beside my son. God hears me say it, and may God so order it!"

And as Hiram Haycroft stands, with this fateful invocation on his lips, the freckled boy runs on the stage and says:

"Say, Hope, ain't you never coming to see that brindle cow?"

And with that the curtain slowly falls, and Act I is over.

No wonder that as the curtain falls there's a terrible feeling of sadness and apprehension all over the audience. No wonder that even before the curtain has reached the floor a great many of the men in that 1880 audience have risen and are walking up the aisles to get out of the theatre. They can't stand the strain of it,—the thought of the beautiful old New England homestead all brought to sorrow and tragedy like this. It's too much for them. They must have air. They've gone to look for it outside the theatre. Even though the playbill says that only ten hours elapse between Act I and II (pretty rapid work for 1880) they're taking a chance on it.

So the able-bodied men in the audience go out leaving behind only the young, the infirm, and the women (women never took anything to drink, anyway, before prohibition). There is a great sadness over the audience now because they know by experience that once the old homestead starts going to pieces like this things will go from bad to worse. Even the fact that the orchestra is now playing *In the Gloaming, Oh, My Darling* doesn't help things much.

So presently the men come back and the orchestra is stopped and the gas cut down and the curtain is hauled away up to the roof and it's—

ACT II—Same Evening. The Kitchen of the Haycroft Farm.

"You'll find us plain folk, sir, just plain folk. But if it'll please you to take what plain folk can offer you're heartily welcome. Now then, Phœbe girl, a chair here for the gentleman. Put another stick in the stove, Rube, it's a cold night in this November wind."

The stranger, in a strange voice, "Ay, it's a cold night."

The scene is in the farm kitchen, one of those big old farm kitchens of 1880 that filled the whole stage. There was a cooking stove,—about ten feet by six in the centre stage and a fireplace with a mantel off at one side, and doors and windows,—in fact all the things that will be needed in the act, not forgetting a shotgun hanging ominously on two hooks. At the back is a big table all laid out for about a dozen guests, with Phœbe all done up in her best things fussing round laying dishes. Martha Hay-croft, also in her best things (black satin with a sort of crispiness to it) is cooking at the stove. Putting the farm people with their best clothes was always supposed to imply a comic touch. Rube has on clothes like a congressman's, only lower in the coat tails and higher in the collar.

This, of course, was the supper that the farmer spoke of when he said they'd call in the neighbours.

Only for the moment all the eyes of the audience are turned on the stranger. He has a crop of straight white hair (a wig evidently) and a white beard—false, of course —and he walks partly bent with a stick, and he looks all about him, all round the room with such a queer look, as if he recognized it.

All the audience feel instinctively that that stranger is disguised. Indeed in this sort of play there always had to be somebody who turned out to be someone else.

"A raw night, sir," repeats the farmer, "there's an evil howl in the wind; I reckon there'll be stormy weather at sea, to-night, sir—"

The farmer is evidently right—for just as he says it somebody behind the scene turns on the wind with a wild and mournful howl. Luckily they don't leave it on long, just enough to let the audience know it's there.

"I just been down to the shore, sir," the farmer goes on, "I tend the light here at the foot of the farm. 'Twill be a bad night at sea to-night."

"A bad night for those at sea," repeats the stranger.

The wind howls again. Martha pauses in her cooking, looks a moment towards the window and murmurs, "The sea, the sea."

Martha, the farmer's wife had to play alternatively a pathetic character and a comic one. It was hard to do, but the audience understood it. So she mutters "The sea! the sea!" with the yearning of a mother for her lost son, and then goes back to blowing up pancakes on the cook-stove. If that violated unity of the drama we didn't know it in 1880, so it did no harm.

"But come, come," says the farmer, "this ain't no night for feeling down-hearted. I hear the neighbours outside. Come, Martha, we'll go out and bring them in."

This leaves Phœbe and Rube alone except for the stranger who has gone across the room and is standing with his back to them, lost in thought. So Rube and Phœbe do another love scene. Rube comes to her along side the table and has only just time to say "Phœbe!" with a slow grin and to try to take her by the waist when she lands him across the face with a pancake. The audience roar with delight and continue laughing till they suddenly come to a full stop when they see that there is something happening with the stranger.

He has been standing with his back turned, silent. Then without warning, he speaks, his back still turned, not in his counterfeited tone, but in a loud clear voice, the voice of youth:

"Rube!"

Rube and Phœbe start. "What voice is that?" says Rube, shaking with agitation.

The stranger turns, plucks away his white wig and his white beard and stands revealed.

"Jack! It's Mr. Jack, come back from the dead!" cries Phœbe.

"Ain't you drowned?" cries Rube.

They crowd close to him in eager recognition; and Jack, young and boyish now, laughs and greets them. "Let me run and call the boss and the missus," pleads Phœbe, but Jack restrains her.

"Not now," he says, "they mustn't know yet."

He goes on to reveal, all in whispers and in gestures which the audience are not intended to unravel, that his father and mother must not know yet. He takes from his pocket a bundle of something—is it paper or money or what? The audience can't see it decently but Rube and Phœbe seem to understand and he is just explaining about it when the noise is heard of the farmer and his wife and the farm guests all coming back.

The stranger motions Rube and Phœbe to secrecy and is disguised again in a minute.

In they all come, the farm people all dressed in the queer pathos of their Sunday things and there follows the great supper scene, without which no rural melodrama was complete. Hear how they chatter and laugh. "Well, for the land's sake, taste them doughnuts!" "Neighbour Jephson, try a slice of this pie." "Well, I don't mind if I do." "Farmer Haycroft here's your good health and Miss Hope's good health and of all present." "Hear! Hear!" and then someone chokes on a crumb and is beaten on the back.

The supper scene lasts ten minutes by the clock. The stranger has sat silent, beaming quiet approval and at the height of the merriment retired quietly to his room, a side room opening on the kitchen. Martha has lighted a candle for him and as he thanks her for it she says—"You're a stranger in these parts, sir? There's something in your voice I seem to know." All the audience want to shout "He's your son." It is a touch taken right out of Sophocles. Hope meantime busies herself among the guests. Hiram Haycroft drinks great flagons of cider. At intervals the wind is turned on against the window panes to remain the audience that it's a wild night outside.

Then for a moment the farmer leaves the room because he has to go and trim his light down on the shore.

While he is still out there is loud knocking at the door.

Rube goes to it and opens it—with a special biff of wind produced for his benefit—and then shows in two strangers.

A young man and an old. The young man is tall and bronzed and sailorlike and Hope runs to him at once, with a glad cry of "Ned! My Ned!" His arms are about her in a moment and the whole theatre knows that it is her husband.

"We've put in under the point," Ned explains, "and I come ashore. But it's only to say good-bye. The *Good Hope* can't lie there in this rising wind. We'll have to put off at once. This is my father, Hope. You'll be a daughter to him while I'm gone!"

Hope goes up to the old man and puts her two hands in his and says, oh, so sweetly, "I will indeed, sir, for Ned's sake."

But her mother has risen, shrinking, from her place.

"Ellwood," she says, "Lawyer Ellwood."

All the audience look at the old man. A fox certainly —oh, a sly old fox—just that look of mean cunning that stamped every rural lawyer in every melodrama for thirty years. But Hope sees nothing of it.

"No, Ned, you mustn't put to sea to-night. It's too wild a night. Hear how the rain is driving at the windows. You must stay here and your father, too. Mother, this is Ned, my husband, and this is his father, and these are our friends, Ned, and father's only gone to the light. He'll be back in just a minute—"

And at that moment the door swings open and Hiram Haycroft—shaking the wet from his black oilskins— strides back into the room. Hope comes to him pleadingly.

"Father, Father dear, this is my husband—"

But he doesn't see her. He is staring at Ellwood.

"You!" he shouts. "You that have sought to bring ruin upon me and mine!"

Ellwood comes toward him, raising a protesting hand. "Hiram!" he says.

"Out of my house!" shouts Haycroft. "Your accursed money is not due till to-morrow and to-morrow it shall be paid. Out! before I lay hands on you." He steps forward menacingly, his hand uplifted. Ned Ellwood steps in his way.

"Put down your hands," he says, "and listen to me."

Hiram refuses to listen. He reaches for the gun that hangs above the mantel. The affrighted guests crowd around him. There is noise and confusion, above which is Haycroft's voice, calling, "Out of my house! I say."

The father and son move to the door, but as they go Hope rushes to her husband.

"Father! he is my husband! Where he goes I go. Ned, take me with you, out into the night and the storm." (At these words the wind which has been quiet breaks out again.) "Out into the world, for better or for worse. Where you go I follow, my place is at your side!"

There is a burst of applause from the audience at this sentiment. That was the kind of girl they raised in 1880. There are none left now.

And so with her father's imprecations ringing in her ears Hope casts a little grey cloak over her head and shoulders and with arm clinging to her husband passes out into the storm.

The door closes after them.

There is a hush and silence.

Not even Rube and Phœbe can break it now. The farm guests, almost inarticulate, come and say good-night and pass out. Martha, lamp in hand, goes tearfully up the stairs. Rube and Phœbe fade away.

Hiram Haycroft sits alone. The lights are dimmed down. There is a flicker of light from the fire in the stove but little more. At times the rattle of the storm at the window makes him lift his head. Once he walks to the window and stands and gazes out into the darkness towards the sea.

And once he goes over to the dresser at the side of the room and takes from it the wallet that has in it his two thousand dollars, holds it a moment in his hand and then replaces it.

At intervals the storm is heard outside. The audience by instinct know that the act is not over. There is more tragedy to come.

The farmer rises slowly from his chair. He lays aside his oilskins. Then, still slowly, he takes off his boots—with a boot jack—a stage effect much valued in melodrama.

He moves about the room, a candle in his hand, bolts and chains the door, and so, step by step slowly and with much creaking, ascends the stairs to bed.

The audience follow in a breathless stillness. They know that something is going to happen.

Deep silence and waiting. You can hear the audience breathing. No one speaks.

Then a side door in the room is opened, slowly, cautiously. You can see a dark figure stealing across the stage —nearer and nearer to the drawer where the wallet of money is lying. Look! What is he doing? Is he taking it, or is he moving it? Is it a thief or what?

Then suddenly the farmer's voice from above.

"Who's that down there?"

You can half see the farmer as he stands on the upper landing, a candle in his hand.

"Who's that, I say?" he calls again.

The crouching figure crawls away, making for the door. What happens after that follows with a rush. The farmer comes hurrying down the stairs, tears open the drawer and with a loud cry of "Thief! A thief!" rouses the sleeping house. You hear the people moving above. You see the lights on the stairs as the crouching figure rushes for the door. The farmer has seized his shotgun. There is a cry of "Stand there, or I'll shoot," then the flash of fire and the roar of the gun and the crouching figure falls to the floor, the farmer shouting, "Lights here. Bring a light! A thief!"

It is Rube who enters first, the others crowding after. It is Rube who lifts the fallen body, Rube who holds the light on the pale face so that the audience may see who it is—but something has long since told them that. It is Rube who pulls aside the white wig and the white beard that had disguised the youthful features. There is a loud cry from the farmer's wife as she sinks down beside the body.

"Jack, Jack, it's my boy come back to me."

And the farmer, the gun still clenched and smoking in his hand cries:

"My son! I have killed my son."

And with that down sinks the sombre curtain on a silent audience.

That's the way, you see that the drama was put over in 1880. We weren't afraid of real effects—terror, agony, murder—anything and the more of it the better. In a modern drawing-room play the characters get no nearer to murder than to have *Pup No. 1*, dressed in grey tweeds, discuss the theory of homicide with *Pup No. 2*, dressed in a brown golf costume. That's all the excitement there is. But in this good old farm melodrama they weren't afraid of mixing the thing up.

So the farmer is ruined, he's driven his daughter from the door and has shot his son—and there you are.

When the play reaches this point, at the end of Act Two, there is nothing for it but a two years' wait. So the play bill at this point bears the legend *Two Years Elapse between Acts Two and Three*. The audience are glad of it. Without that they couldn't have stood the tragedy of it. But as it is there are two years; the men rise and file out up the aisle; very slowly—there was no need to hurry with two years ahead of them.

The gas is turned up now and the audience are gradually recovering; a boy comes down the aisle and shouts "Peanuts!" That helps a lot. And presently when the orchestra begins to play *My Mother Said That I Never Should* they begin to get reconciled to life again. Anyway, being used to this type of play they know that things aren't so bad as they seem. Jack can't really be dead. He'll be brought to life somehow. He was shot, but he can't have been killed. Every audience knows its own line of play; in fact in all the drama the audience has to be taken for granted or the play wouldn't be intelligible. Anybody who has seen a moving picture audience snap up the symbols and legends and conventions of a photoplay and get the required meaning out of it will know just what I mean. So it was in 1880. The audience got cheered up because they realized that Jack couldn't really be dead.

So they look at their programs with a revived interest to see what happens next.

Here it is:

ACT III—Two Years Later. The Fore Shore After Sunset. A Gathering Storm.

Ah! Look at the scene as the curtain goes up now. Isn't it grand! The rocks and the breaking water and the white foam in the twilight! How ever do they do it? And the lighthouse there at the right hand side, how it towers into the dark sky! Look at the fishermen all in black oilskins and sou'-westers, glistening in the wet, moving about on the shore and pointing to the sea.

Notice that short flash of yellow lightning and the rumble of thunder away behind the scene. And look at the long beams of the light from the lighthouse far out on the water.

Don't talk to me of a problem play, played in a modern drawing room as between a man in tweed and a woman in sequins. When I attend the theatre let there be a lighthouse and a gathering of huddled fishermen and danger lowering over the sea. As drama it is worth all the sex stuff that was ever slopped over the footlights.

"A wild night!"

It's a fisherman speaking—or no, it's Rube, only you would hardly know him—all in oilskins. In the New England play all the farmers turn into fishermen as the plot thickens. So it is Zeke, as another fisherman, who answers:

"It's all that! God help all poor souls out at sea to-night."

The lightning and thunder make good again, the fishermen and the women on the shore move to and fro, talking, and excited, and pointing at the sea. Rube and Zeke come together in the foreground, talking. Their function is to let the audience know all that has happened in two years.

"A wild night," Zeke repeats, "such a night as it was two years ago, you mind, the night that Mr. Jack was shot."

They both shake their heads. " 'Twould have been a sight better," says Rube, "if the farmer's bullet had killed him that night. A sad sight it is to see him as he is, witless and speechless. It's cruel hard on them all. Is he here to-night?"

"Ay, he's here to-night—he's always here on the shore when a storm is on. Look, see him there, always looking to the sea!"

The audience look at once and see in the little group standing in the gathering storm, Jack—holding to his mother hard and looking out to sea.

"She's leading him away. She'll be wanting him to go home. . . ."

So Jack isn't dead! But what is that queer, strange look on his face? Something blank, unhuman, witless. His mother leads him down the stage.

"Jack, come home, Jack. It's no place for you here in the storm."

The thunder and lightning break in again sharp and vivid and the wind roars behind the scenes.

Jack turns a vacant countenance upon his mother. His face is pale and thin. His eyes are bright.

The audience get it. Since he was shot down he has been there two years speechless and demented.

His mother keeps begging him to come home. He tries to drag her towards the sea. Demented as he is, there is a wild and growing excitement in his manner. He is pointing at the waves, gesticulating.

"What does he see?" Rube is asking. "What is it? He has a sailor's eyes. What does he see out there?"

And at that minute there comes a shout from the clustered fishermen on the Fore Shore.

"A ship! A ship! There's a vessel out on the reef. See! look!"

They run up and down, pointing and shouting. And far out on the waves lit for a moment by a flash of lightning, the audience sees a dismasted schooner—she's made of cardboard—out beside the breakers on the reef.

At this moment the freckled boy, all in oilskins, rushes breathless on to the stage. He hasn't grown an inch in two years but nobody cares about that.

"Mother, Rube," he gasps. "I've been down to the Long Point—I ran all the way—there is a schooner going on the reef. Look, you can see, and Mother, Mother—"

The boy is almost frenzied into excitement. The crowd gathers about him.

"Mother it's the *Good Hope,* her ship!"

"The *Good Hope?*" exclaims everybody.

The boy gasps on.

"They were lowering the boats—I could see them—but nothing can live in that sea—one boat went down—I saw it—and I could see her, Hope, standing by the mast. I could see her face when the lightning came. Then I ran here. We must go out; we must get the life boats; we've got to go. You men, who'll come?"

Come! they'll all come! Listen to the shout of them. See! they are dragging forth the life boat from its wooden house on the left of the stage. There are swinging lanterns and loud calls and the roaring of the wind. The stage is darkening and the lightning glares on the sea. But even as they are trying to launch the life boat, there's a new cry—

"Look—a boat! a boat! out there on the reef, right among the breakers."

The fishermen rush up and down in great excitement. "There's a woman in the boat! God help her! She's lost!"

"Mother, Mother, it's Hope! See she's alone in the boat, she's kneeling up; she's praying."

There are new cries:

"Man the life boat! Man the life boat!"

The great boat is dragged out and ready. The men are climbing in over the side.

Then a fisherman shouts out and is heard, clear and single, for a moment in the lull of the storm.

"There's only one man can pilot this boat across that reef, only Hiram Haycroft."

There are cries of "Hiram! Hiram!" They point out at the lighthouse from which the long beams still revolve on the water. "He can't leave the light."

Noise and commotion.

"He must leave the light."

"It's life or death on this one chance. Lads, stand ready there with the life boat and come, some of you, with me and bring him down." They rush towards the lighthouse. There is noise and thunder; a flash of light shows the boat, clearly in sight now, right out among the breakers and Hope seen for a moment kneeling in the bow praying, her face illuminated in the lightning. Then in a swirl of white water, the boat vanishes in the foam of the reef.

ACT IV

Then the scene changes—all done in a minute—from the shore to the *Lighthouse Tower*. It was what used to be called a "transformation scene." It involved an eclipse of darkness punctured by little gas jets, and a terrible thumping and bumping with an undertone of curses. You could hear a voice in the darkness say quite distinctly, "Get that blank blank drop over there," and you could see black figures running round in the transformation. Then there came an awful crash and a vision of a back curtain sliding down amongst the dark men. The lights flicked up again and all the audience broke into applause at the final wonder of it.

Look! It's the lighthouse tower with the big lights

burning and the storm howling outside. How bright and clear it is here inside the tower with its great windows looking out over the storm sixty feet above the sea.

He stands beside the lights, trimming the lamps, calm and steady at his task. The storm is all about him, but inside the lighthouse tower all is bright and still.

Hiram peers a moment from the lighthouse window. He opens the little door and steps out on the iron platform high above the sea. The wind roars about him and the crest of the driven water leaps to his very feet. He comes in, closing the door quietly and firmly behind him and turns again to his light.

"God help all poor souls at sea to-night," he says.

And then with a rush and clatter of feet they burst in upon him, the group of fishermen, Martha, and his demented son, crowding into the lighthouse tower and standing on the stairs. Jack is at the rear of all, but there is a strange look on his face, a light of new intelligence.

"Quick, Hiram, you must come. There's been a wreck. Look, there's a boat going on the reef. The men are ready in the life boat. You must steer her through. It's life or death. There's not a moment to lose."

Hiram looks for a moment at the excited crowd and then turns quietly to his task.

"My place is here," he says.

There is a moment's hush. Martha rushes to him and clutches him by the coat.

"Hiram, they haven't told you. The schooner that was wrecked to-night is the *Good Hope*."

Hiram staggers back against the wall.

"And the boat that's drifting on the reef, it's Hope, it's our daughter."

Hiram stands grasping the rail along the wall. He speaks panting with agitation, but firm:

"Martha—I'm sworn to tend the light. If the light fails God knows what it means to the ships at sea. If my child is lost it is God's will—but—my place is here."

And he turns back to the light.

The fishermen who have been crowding close to the window cry:

"Look down below. The boat—she's driving in here right on the rocks—the woman's still clinging to her."

Martha rushes to the window and calls, "My child, save my child! save her!" And at exactly this minute Jack steps out into the centre of the floor. His face is clear and plain beneath the light. There is no dementia left in it now.

"Father," he says, "Mother."

They all turn to look at him. But no one speaks.

"The rope," he says, "give me the rope."

He points to a long coil of rope that hangs against the wall. With a sailor's quickness of hand he takes the rope and runs a bowline knot in the end of it. In a moment, with the end of the line about his body, he throws open the door and rushes on the iron platform. "Hold fast to the line," he calls, and then the audience see him mount the iron rail, pause a moment, and then dive head first into the sea beneath.

There is shouting and clamor from the fishermen.

"There he is! Look, he's swimming to her! Hold fast there! . . . He's got her. . . . Now then, in with the line."

And with one glorious haul, up comes the line from the roaring sea with Jack at the end of it, and, tight held in his encircling arms, the fainting form of Hope, his sister.

Couldn't be done? Nonsense! That was nothing to what we used to see done in the old-time plays. If need be, Jack could have fished out a whole shipload.

There is a cry of "Saved, saved!" and Hiram Haycroft clasping the senseless form of his daughter to his heart, cries:

"My little gal! Cast up by the sea!"

And the curtain comes down in a roar of applause.

ACT V—Six Months Later. Scene. The Kitchen of the Haycroft Farm.

This last act in the melodrama is all to the good. There is no more tragedy, no strain, no trouble. The play is really over but this part is always put in as a sort of wind-up to make everybody happy. The audience are now sitting in a swim of luxurious sentimentality. How fine everything has turned out—Jack has got his mind back, and Hope is saved and her husband, too, and the old farm isn't mortgaged or sold and the Haycrofts are not ruined after all. Yes, and more than that; there are all kinds of little items of happiness to be thrown in.

So here we are back in the old farm kitchen, and here, of course, are Rube and Phœbe again. And Rube tries to grab Phœbe round the waist, but she says, "Oh, you Rube, you go along," and lands a dish towel in his face. But this time Rube *won't* go along. He manages to catch Phœbe and tell her that he wants her to be his wife and throw dishcloths at him all his life, and Phœbe calls him a "big thing," and gives him a kiss like a smack (worse than a dishcloth or a pancake). So there they are, all set for marriage, as they might have been in the first act if Rube had had the nerve.

Well, they are no sooner straightened out than in come the farmer and his son Jack and Ned, Hope's husband. The farmer seems very old and infirm, though suffused with the same air of peace and happiness as all the others.

The two young men help him into an arm rocking chair.
"Easy now." Then Hiram sits down with that expression
of difficulty "ay-ee-ee," always used to symbolize stage
rheumatism. There is no need for the farmer to become
so suddenly old in the last act. But it was a favorite convention of 1880 to make all the old people very infirm and
very happy at the end of the play.

So they begin to talk, just to pile on the happiness.

"I'm getting old, lads, I'm not the man I was."

"Old, Father," laughs Jack, "why, you're the youngest
and spryest of all of us—"

"I'm getting past work, boys," says the farmer, shaking his head, "past work—"

"Work," says Jack, "why should you work?" And as
the talk goes on you get to understand that Jack will never
go to sea again but will stay and work the farm and they've
just received the "papers" that appoint him keeper of the
light in his father's place, with a pension for the old man.
And Ned, Hope's husband, is going to stay right there too.
His father has bought him the farm just adjoining with
house and stock and everything and he and Hope are all
ready to move into it just as soon as—

But wait a minute.

His father! Lawyer Ellwood! And the terrible enmity
and feud!

Oh, pshaw, just watch that feud vanish! In the fifth
act of an old time melodrama a feud could be blown to the
four winds like thistledown.

Like this:—

There's a knocking at the door and Ned goes to it and
comes back all smiling and he says:

"There's someone at the door to see you, Mr. Haycroft.
An old friend he says, shall he come in?"

"An old friend?" And in slips Ellwood—the farmer's

enemy, Hope's father-in-law—looking pretty hale and hearty, but with the same touch of the old age of the fourth act visible.

He comes over and says:

"Well, Hiram, have you a shake of the hand for an old friend?"

And the farmer, rising, unsteadily:

"Why, Ephraim, it's not your hand I should be taking; it's your forgiveness I ought to ask for my mad folly these two years past."

"Forgiveness," says the lawyer; how honest and cheery he looks now, not a bit like the scoundrel he seemed in the second act—"forgiveness!"

And off he goes with *his* explanation.

That's the whole purpose of the fifth act,—explanation.

And what do you think! He'd been Hiram's friend all along and was not in earnest about wanting the money back from Hiram—didn't want it at all! And he knew all about Hope's love affair and Jack's safe return with his son and was tickled to death over it—and that night two years ago when the farmer drove him out he had come over to tell the Haycrofts that the debt was cancelled, and he was going to buy a farm and start the young people, Ned and Hope, in life—and it was the cancelled mortgage that Jack was trying to sneak over and put in the drawer when his father shot him down!—and—why, dear me, how simple it all is in the fifth act. Why didn't he explain? Why didn't he shout out, "Hiram, I'm not a villain at all, I'm your old friend—" Oh, pshaw, who ever did *explain* things in the second act of a melodrama? And where would the drama be if they did?

So they are still explaining and counter-explaining and getting happier and happier when the last climax is staged.

The audience hear Martha's voice as she comes on to the stage, talking back into the wings, "Carry him carefully there, Phœbe, for the land's sake, if you drop that precious child—"

And in they come.

Martha and Hope! Looking as sweet and fresh as when she started out years ago in the first act. And bringing up the rear Phœbe—*carrying the Baby.*

Yes, believe it or not, a baby!—or the very semblance of one all bundled up in white.

Hope's baby!

No melodrama was ever brought to its righteous end without a baby.

How the women all cuddle round it and croon over it! They put it on the farmer's lap—and say, isn't he just clumsy when he tries to take it—and when Rube offers to help, and Phœbe slaps his face with a dish rag, the audience just go into paroxysms of laughter.

So there you are—and everybody saved. All happy, the baby installed on the farmer's knees and explanations flowing like autumn cider.

All that is needed now is the farmer to get off the *Final Religious Sentiment* which is the end and benediction of the good old melodrama. So he utters it with all due solemnity: "Ay, lads, pin your hope in Providence and in the end you land safe in port."

It sounds as convincing as a proposition in Euclid. Then the curtain slowly comes down and the matinée audience melts away, out into the murky November evening, with the flickering gas lamps in the street, and the clanging bells of the old horse-cars in their ears, but with their souls uplifted and illuminated with the moral glow of the melodrama.

How My Wife and I Built Our Home for $4.90

Related in the Manner of the Best Models in the Magazines

I WAS leaning up against the mantelpiece in a lounge suit which I had made out of old ice bags, and Beryl, my wife, was seated at my feet on a low Louis Quinze tabouret which she had made out of a Finnan Haddie fishbox, when the idea of a bungalow came to both of us at the same time.

"It would be just lovely if we could do it!" exclaimed Beryl, coiling herself around my knee.

"Why not!" I replied, lifting her up a little by the ear. "With your exquisite taste—"

"And with your knowledge of material," added Beryl, giving me a tiny pinch on the leg. Oh, I am sure we could do it! One reads so much in all the magazines about people making summer bungalows and furnishing them for next to nothing. Oh, do let us try, Dogyard!"

We talked over our project all night, and the next morning we sallied forth to try to find a site for our new home. As Beryl (who was brimming over with fun as the result of talking all night) put it, "The first thing is to get the ground."

Here fortune favored us. We had hardly got to the edge of the town when Beryl suddenly exclaimed, "Oh, look, Dogyard, look, there's exactly the site!" It was a piece of waste land on the edge of a gully with a brickyard on one side of it and a gravel pit on the other. It had no trees on it, and it was covered with ragged heaps of tin cans, old newspapers, and stones, and a litter of broken lumber.

Beryl's quick eye saw the possibilities of the situation at once. "Oh, Dogyard!" she exclaimed, "isn't it just sweet? We can clear away all this litter and plant a catalpa tree to hide the brickyard and a hedge of copernicus or nux vomica to hide the gravel pit, and some bright flowers to hide the hedge. I wish I had brought some catalpa seed. They grow so quickly."

"We'd better at least wait," I said, "till we have bought the ground."

And here a sudden piece of good fortune awaited us. It so happened that the owner of the lot was on the spot at the time—he was seated on a stone whittling a stick while we were talking, and presented himself to us. After a short discussion he agreed to sell us the ground for one dollar in cash and fifty cents on a three years' mortgage. The deed of sale was written out on the spot and stamped with a two-cent stamp, and the owner of the lot took his departure with every expression of good will. And the magic sense of being owners of our own ground rendered us both jubilant.

That evening Beryl, seated on her little stool at my feet, took a pencil and paper and set down triumphantly a statement of the cost of our bungalow up to date. I introduce it here as a help to readers who may hope to follow in our footsteps:

Ground site	$1.50
Stamp for mortgage	.02
Car fare	.10
Total	$1.62

I checked over Beryl's arithmetic twice and found it strictly correct.

Next morning we commenced work in earnest. While Beryl cleared away the cans and litter, I set to work with spade and shovel excavating our cellar and digging out the foundations. And here I must admit that I had no light task. I can only warn those who wish to follow in our footsteps that they must be prepared to face hard work.

Owing perhaps to my inexperience, it took me the whole of the morning to dig out a cellar forty feet long and twenty feet wide. Beryl, who had meantime cleaned up the lot, stacked the lumber, lifted away the stones and planted fifty yards of hedge, was inclined to be a little impatient. But I reminded her that a contractor working with a gang of men and two or three teams of horses would have taken a whole week to do what I did in one morning.

I admitted that my work was not equal to the best records as related in the weekly home journals, where I have often computed that they move 100,000 cubic feet of earth in one paragraph, but at least I was doing my best. Beryl, whose disappointment never lasts, was all smiles again in a moment, and rewarded me by throwing herself around my neck and giving me a hug.

That afternoon I gathered up all the big stones and built them into walls around the cellar with partition walls across it, dividing it into rooms and compartments. I leveled the floor and packed it tight with sand and gravel and dug a drain ten feet deep from the cellar to the gully about thirty feet away.

There being still a good hour or so of daylight left, I dug a cistern four feet wide and twenty feet deep. I was looking round for something more to dig by moonlight, but Beryl put her foot down (on my head while I was in the drain) and forbade me to work any more for fear I might be fatigued.

Next morning we were able to begin our building in good earnest. On our way we stopped at the fifteen cent store for necessary supplies, and bought one hammer, fifteen cents; a saw, fifteen cents; half a gallon of nails, fifteen cents; a crane, fifteen cents; a derrick for hoisting, fifteen cents, and a needle and thread, for sewing on the roof, fifteen cents.

As an advice to young builders, I may say that I doubt if we were quite wise in all our purchases. The fifteen cent derrick is too light for the work, and the extra expenditure for the heavier kind (the twenty-five cent crane) would have been justified. The difference in cost is only (approximately) ten cents, and the efficiency of the big crane is far greater.

On arriving at our ground we were delighted to find that our masonry was well set and the walls firm and solid, while the catalapa trees were well above the ground and growing rapidly. We set to work at once to build in earnest.

We had already decided to utilize for our bungalow the waste material which lay on our lot. I drew Beryl's attention to the fact that if a proper use were made of the material wasted in building there would be no need to buy any material at all. "The elimination of waste," I explained, "by the utilization of all by-products before they have time to go by, is the central principle of modern industrial organization."

But observing that Beryl had ceased to listen to me, I drew on my carpenter's apron which I had made out of a piece of tar-paper, and set to work. My first care was to gather up all the loose lumber that lay upon and around our ground site, and saw it up into neatly squared pieces about twenty feet long. Out of these I made the joists, the studding, the partitions, rafters, and so on, which formed the frame of the house.

Putting up the house took practically the whole morning. Beryl, who had slipped on a potato bag over her dress, assisted me by holding up the side of the house while I nailed on the top.

By the end of the afternoon we had completed the sides of our house, which we made out of old newspapers soaked in glue and rolled flat. The next day we put on the roof, which was made of tin cans cut open and pounded flat.

For our hardwood floors, mantels, etc., we were fortunate in finding a pile of hardwood on a neighboring lot which had apparently been overlooked, and which we carried over proudly to our bungalow after dark. That same night we carried over jubilantly some rustic furniture which we had found, quite neglected, lying in a nearby cottage, the lock of which oddly enough, was opened quite easily with the key of Beryl's suitcase.

The rest of our furniture—plain tables, dressers, etc.—I was able to make from ordinary pine lumber which I obtained by knocking down a board fence upon an adjacent lot. In short, the reader is able to picture our bungalow after a week of labor, complete in every respect and only awaiting our occupation on the next day.

Seated that evening in our boarding house, with Beryl coiled around me, I calculated the entire cost of our enterprise—including ground site, lumber, derricks, cranes, glue, string, tin-tacks and other materials—as four dollars and ninety cents.

In return for it we had a pretty seven-roomed house, artistic in every respect, with living-room, bed-rooms, a boudoir, a den, a snuggery, a doggery—in short, the bungalow of which so many young people have dreamed.

Seated together that evening, Beryl and I were full of plans for the future. We both have a passionate love of animals and, like all country-bred people, a longing for the life of a farm. So we had long since decided to keep poultry. We planned to begin in a small way, and had brought home that evening from the fifteen-cent store a day-old chicken, such as are now so widely sold.

We put him in a basket beside the radiator in a little flannel coat that Beryl had made for him, and we fed him with a warm mash made of breakfast food and gravel. Our printed directions that we got with him told us that a fowl eats two ounces of grain per day and on that should lay five eggs in a week. I was easily able to prove to Beryl by a little plain arithmetic that if we fed this fellow 4 ounces a day he would lay 10 eggs in a week, or at 8 ounces per day he would lay 20 eggs in a week.

Beryl, who was seized at once with a characteristic fit of enthusiasm, suggested that we stick 16 ounces a day into him and begin right now. I had to remind her laughingly that at 8 ounces a day the fellow would probably be working up to a capacity, and carrying what we call in business his peak load. "The essential factor in modern business," I told her, "is to load yourself up to the peak and stay there."

In short, there was no end to our rosy dreams. In our fancy we saw ourselves in our bungalow, surrounded by hens, bees, cows and dogs, with hogs and goats nestling against our feet. Unfortunately our dreams were destined to be shattered. Up to this point our experience with building our bungalow had followed along after all the best models, and had even eclipsed them. But from now on we met a series of disasters of which we had had no warning. It is a pity that I cannot leave our story at this point.

On arriving at our bungalow next day we found notices posted up forbidding all trespassers, and two sour-looking men in possession. We learned that our title to the ground site was worthless, as the man from whom we had bought it had been apparently a mere passer-by. It appeared also that a neighboring contractor was making serious difficulties about our use of his material. It was divulged further that we had been mistaken in thinking that we had taken our rustic furniture from an empty cottage. There were people living in it, but they happened to be asleep when Beryl moved the furniture.

As for our hen—there is no doubt that keeping fowls is enormously profitable. It must be so, when one considers the millions of eggs consumed every day. But it demands an unremitting attention and above all—memory. If you own a hen you must never forget it—you must keep on saying to yourself—"How is my hen?" This was our trouble. Beryl and I were so preoccupied with our accumulated disaster, that we left our one-day-old chick behind the radiator and never thought of him for three weeks. He was then gone. We prefer to think that he flew away.

Softening the Stories for the Children

But Don't Do It: They Prefer Them Rough

"What is the story that you are reading, Peggy?" I asked of a wide-eyed child of eight, who sat buried in a story book.

"Little Red Riding Hood," she answered.

"Have you come to the part," I asked, "where the grandmother gets eaten?"

"She didn't get eaten!" the child protested in surprise.

"Yes,—the wolf comes to her cottage and knocks at the door and she thinks that it is Little Red Riding Hood and opens the door and the wolf eats her."

She shook her head.

"That's not it at all in this book," she said.

So I took a look at the page before her and I read:

"Then the wolf pushed open the door of the cottage and rushed in but the grandmother was not there as she happened not to be at home."

Exactly! The grandmother, being a truly up-to-date grandmother, was probably out on the golf links, or playing bridge with a few other grandmothers like herself.

At any rate she was not there and so she escaped getting eaten by the wolf. In other words, Little Red Riding Hood, like all the good old stories that have come down from the bad old times, is having to give way to the tendencies of a human age. It is supposed to be too horrible for the children to read. The awful fate of the grandmother, chawed up by the wolf,—or, no, swallowed *whole* like a Malpecque oyster, is too terrible for them to hear.

So the story, like a hundred other stories and pictures, has got to be censored, reëdited, and incidentally,—spoiled.

All of which rests on a fundamental error as to literature and as to children. There is no need to soften down a story for them. They like it rough.

"In the real story," I said to the little girl, "the grandmother was at home, and the wolf rushed in and ate her in one mouthful!"

"Oh! that's *much* better!" she exclaimed.

"And then, afterwards, when the hunters came in, they killed the wolf and cut his stomach open and the grandmother jumped out and was saved!"

"Oh, isn't that splendid!" cried the child.

In other words, all the terror that grown-up people see in this sort of story is there for grown-up people only. The children look clean over it, or past it, or under it. In reality, the vision of the grandmother feebly defending herself against the savage beast, or perhaps leaping round the room to get away from him, and jumping up on top of the grandfather's clock—is either horrible, or weird, or pathetic, or even comic, as we may happen to see it. But to the children it is just a story,—and a good one,—that's all.

And all the old stories are the same! Consider Jack the Giant-Killer. What a conglomeration of weeping and wailing, of people shut into low dungeons, of murder, of sudden death, of blood, and of horror! Jack, having inveigled an enormous giant into eating an enormous quantity of porridge, then rips him up the stomach with a huge sword! What a mess!

But it doesn't disturb Jack or his young readers one iota. In fact, Jack is off again at once with his young readers trailing eagerly after him, in order to cut off at one blow the three huge heads of a three-headed giant and make a worse mess still.

From the fairy stories and the giant stories the children presently pass on,—quite unscathed as I see it,—to the higher range of the blood-and-thunder stories of the pirates and the battles. Here again the reality, for the grown-up mind that can see it, is terrible and gruesome; but never so for the boys and girls who see in it only the pleasant adventure and bright diversity.

Take, for instance, this familiar scene as it appears and reappears in the history of Jack Dare-devil, or Ned Fear-nothing, or any of those noble boys who go to sea, in books, at the age of fourteen and retire, as admirals, at twenty-two.

"The fire from both ships was now becoming warm. A round shot tearing across the deck swept off four of our fellows. 'Ha! ha!' said Jack, as he turned towards Ned on the quarterdeck, 'this bids fair to become lively.' "

It certainly did. In fact, it would be lively already if one stopped to think of the literal and anatomical mean-ing of a round shot,—twenty-five pounds of red-hot iron, —tearing through the vitals of four men. But the boy reader never gets it this way. What is said is, that four of our fellows were "swept off,"—just that; merely "swept off" and that's the way the child reader takes it. And when the pirates "leap on deck," Jack himself "cuts down" four of them and Ned "cuts down" three. That's all they do,—"they cut them down," they just "shorten them" so to speak.

Very similar in scope and method was the good old "half-dime novel," written of the days of the "Prairie," and the mountain trail, the Feathered Indian and the Leathered Scout. In these, unsuspecting strangers got scalped in what is now the main street of Denver,—where they get skinned.

These stories used to open with a rush and kept in rapid oscillation all the time. In fact they began with the concussion of firearms.

"'Bang! Bang! Bang!' Three shots rang out over the prairie and three feathered Indians bit the dust."

It seemed always to be a favorite pastime of the Indians —"biting dust."

In grim reality,—to the grown-up mind,—these were stories of terror,—of midnight attack, of stealthy murder with a knife from without the folds of the tent, of sudden death in dark caverns, of pitiless enemies, and of cruel torture.

But not so to the youthful mind. He followed it all through quite gayly, sharing the high courage of his hero, —Dick Danger the Dauntless. "I must say," whispered Dick to Ned (this was when the Indians had them tied to a tree and were piling grass and sticks round it so as to burn them alive), "I must say, old man, things begin to look critical. Unless we can think of some way out of this fix, we are lost."

Notice, please, this word "lost": in reality they would be worse than lost. They'd be *cooked*. But in this class of literature the word "lost" is used to cover up a multitude of things. And, of course, Dick does think of a way out. It occurs to him that by moving his hands he can slip off the thongs that bind him, set Ned free, leap from the tree to the back of a horse, of two horses, and then by jumping over the edge of a chasm into the forest a thousand feet below, they can find themselves in what is called "comparative safety." After which the story goes calmly on, oblivious of the horrible scene that nearly brought it to an end.

But as the modern parent and the modern teacher have grown alarmed, the art of story-telling for children has got to be softened down. There must be no more horror and blood and violent death. Away with the giants and the ogres! Let us have instead the stories of the animal kingdom in which Wee-Wee the Mouse has tea on a broad leaf with Goo-Goo the Caterpillar, and in which Fuzzy the Skunk gives talks on animal life that would do for Zoölogy Class I at Harvard.

But do we,—do they,—can we escape after all from the cruel environment that makes up the life in which we live? Are the animals after all so much softer than the ogres, so much kinder than the pirates? When Slick the Cat crackles up the bones of Wee-Wee the Mouse, how does that stand! And when Old Mr. Hawk hovers in the air watching for Cheep-Cheep the chicken who tries in vain to hide under the grass, and calls for its lost mother,—how is that for terror! To my thinking the timorous and imaginative child can get more real terror from the pictured anguish of a hunted animal than from the deaths of all the Welsh giants that ever lived on Plynlimmon.

The tears of childhood fall fast and easily, and evil be to him who makes them flow.

How easily a child will cry over the story of a little boy lost, how easily at the tale of poverty and want, how inconsolably at death. Touch but ever so lightly these real springs of anguish and the ready tears will come. But at Red Riding Hood's grandmother! Never! She didn't *die!* She was merely *eaten.* And the sailors, and the pirates, and the Apache Indians! They don't *die,* not in any real sense to the child. They are merely "swept off," and "mowed down,"—in fact, scattered like the pieces on an upset chessboard.

The moral of all which is, don't worry about the apparent terror and bloodshed in the children's books, the real children's books. There is none there. It only represents the way in which little children, from generation to generation, learn in ways as painless as can be followed, the stern environment of life and death.

The Everlasting Angler

THE fishing season is now well under way. Will soon be with us. For lovers of fishing this remark is true all the year round. It has seemed to me that it might be of use to set down a few of the more familiar fish stories that are needed by any one wanting to qualify as an angler. There is no copyright on these stories, since Methuselah first told them, and anybody who wishes may learn them by heart and make free use of them.

I will begin with the simplest and best known. Everybody who goes fishing has heard it, and told it a thousand times. It is called:—

I

THE STORY OF THE FISH THAT WAS LOST

The circumstances under which the story is best told are these. The fisherman returns after his day's outing with his two friends whom he has taken out for the day, to his summer cottage. They carry with them their rods, their landing net and the paraphernalia of their profession. The fisherman carries also on a string a dirty looking collection of little fish, called by courtesy the "Catch." None of these little fish really measures more than about seven and a half inches long and four inches round the chest. The fisherman's wife and his wife's sister and the young lady who is staying with them come running to meet the fishing party, giving cries of admiration as they get a sight of the catch. In reality they would refuse to buy those fish from a butcher at a cent and a half a pound. But they fall into ecstasies and they cry, "Oh, aren't they beauties! Look at this big one!" The "big one" is about eight inches long. It looked good when they caught it but it has been shrinking ever since and it looks now as if it had died of consumption. Then it is that the fisherman says, in a voice in which regret is mingled with animation:

"Yes, but say, you ought to have seen the one that we lost. We had hardly let down our lines—"

It may be interjected here that all fishermen ought to realize that the moment of danger is just when you let down your line. That is the moment when the fish will put up all kinds of games on you, such as rushing at you in a compact mass so fast that you can't take them in, or selecting the largest of their number to snatch away one of your rods.

"We had hardly let down our lines," says the fishermen, "when Tom got a perfect monster. That fish would have weighed five pounds, wouldn't it, Tom?"

"Easily," says Tom.

"Well, Tom started to haul him in and he yelled to Ted and me to get the landing net ready and we had him right up to the boat, right up to the very boat," "Right up to the very boat," repeat Tom and Edward sadly. "When the damn line broke and biff! away he went. Say! he must have been two feet long, easily two feet!"

"Did you see him?" asks the young lady who is staying with them. This of course she has no right to ask. It's not a fair question. Among people who go fishing it is ruled out. You may ask if a fish pulled hard, and how much it weighed but you must not ask whether anybody *saw* the fish.

"We could see where he was," says Tom.

Then they go on up to the house carrying the "string"

or "catch" and all three saying at intervals, "Say, if we had only landed that big fellow!"

By the time this anecdote has ripened for winter use, the fish will have been drawn actually into the boat (thus settling all question of seeing it) and will there have knocked Edward senseless, and then leaped over the gunwale.

II

STORY OF THE EXTRAORDINARY BAIT

This is a more advanced form of fishing story. It is told by fishermen for fishermen. It is the sort of thing they relate to one another when fishing out of a motor boat on a lake, when there has been a slight pause in their activity and when the fish for a little while,—say for two hours, have stopped biting. So the fishermen talk and discuss the ways and means of their craft. Somebody says that grasshoppers make good bait: and somebody else asks whether any of them have ever tried Lake Erie soft shell crabs as bait, and then one,—whoever is lucky enough to get in first,—tells the good old bait story.

"The queerest bait I ever saw used," he says, shifting his pipe to the other side of his mouth, "was one day when I was fishing up in one of the lakes back in Maine. We'd got to the spot and got all ready when we suddenly discovered that we'd forgotten the bait—"

At this point any one of the listeners is entitled by custom to put in the old joke about not forgetting the whiskey.

"Well, there was no use going ashore. We couldn't have got any worms. It was too early for frogs, and it was ten miles to row back home. We tried chunks of meat from our lunch, but nothing doing! Well, then, just for fun I cut a white bone button off my pants and put it on the hook. Say! you ought to have seen those fish go for it. We caught, oh, easily twenty, yes, thirty, in about half an hour. We only quit after we'd cut off all our buttons and our pants were falling off us! Say, hold on, boys, I believe I've got a nibble! Sit steady!"

Getting a nibble of course will set up an excitement in any fishing party that puts an end to all story telling. After they have got straight again and the nibble has turned out to be "the bottom" as all nibbles are,—the moment would be fitting for anyone of them to tell the famous story called:

III

BEGINNER'S LUCK, OR THE WONDERFUL CATCH MADE BY THE NARRATOR'S WIFE'S LADY FRIEND

"Talking of that big catch that you made with the pants button," says another of the anglers, who really means that he is going to talk of something else, "reminds me of a queer thing I saw myself. We'd gone out fishing for pickerel, 'dorés,' they call them up there in the lake of Two Mountains. We had a couple of big row boats and we'd taken my wife and the ladies along,—I think there were eight of us, or nine perhaps. Anyway it doesn't matter. Well, there was a young lady there from Dayton, Ohio, and she'd never fished before. In fact she'd never been in a boat before. I don't believe she'd ever been near the water before."

All experienced listeners know now what is coming. They realize the geographical position of Dayton, Ohio, far from the water and shut in everywhere by land. Any prudent fish would make a sneak for shelter if he knew that a young lady from Dayton, Ohio, was after him.

"Well, this girl got an idea that she'd like to fish and we'd rigged up a line for her, just tied on to a cedar pole that we'd cut in the bush. Do you know you'd hardly believe that that girl had hardly got her line into the water when she got a monster. We yelled to her to play it or she'd lose it, but she just heaved it up into the air and right into the boat. She caught seventeen, or twenty-seven, I forget which, one after the other, while the rest of us got nothing. And the fun of it was she didn't know anything about fishing; she just threw the fish up into the air and into the boat. Next day we got her a decent rod with a reel and gave her a lesson or two and then she didn't catch any."

I may say with truth that I have heard this particular story told not only about a girl from Dayton, Ohio, but about a girl from Kansas, a young lady just out from England, about a girl fresh from Paris, and about another girl, not fresh,—the daughter of a minister. In fact if I wished to make sure of a real catch, I would select a girl fresh from Paris or New York and cut off some of my buttons, or hers, and start to fish.

IV

THE STORY OF WHAT WAS FOUND IN THE FISH

The stories, however, do not end with the mere catching of the fish. There is another familiar line of anecdote that comes in when the fish are to be cleaned and cooked. The fishermen have landed on the rocky shore beside the rushing waterfall and are cleaning their fish to cook them for the midday meal. There is an obstinate superstition that fish cooked thus taste better than first class kippered herring put up in a tin in Aberdeen where they know how. They don't, but it is an honourable fiction and reflects credit on humanity. What is more, all the fishing party compete eagerly for the job of cutting the inside out of the dead fish. In a restaurant they are content to leave that to anybody sunk low enough and unhappy enough to have to do it. But in the woods they fight for the job.

So it happens that presently one of the workers holds up some filthy specimen of something in his hand and says, "Look at that! See what I took out of the trout! Unless I mistake it is part of a deer's ear. The deer must have stooped over the stream to drink and the trout bit his ear off."

At which somebody says,—whoever gets it in first,—says:

"It's amazing what you find in fish. I remember once trolling for trout, the big trout, up in Lake Simcoe and just off Eight Mile Point we caught a regular whopper. We had no scales but he weighed easily twenty pounds. We cut him open on the shore afterwards, and say, would you believe it, that fish had inside him a brass buckle,—the whole of it,—and part of a tennis shoe, and a rain check from a baseball game, and seventy-five cents in change. It seems hard to account for it, unless perhaps he'd been swimming round some summer hotel."

These stories, I repeat, may now be properly narrated in the summer fishing season. But of course, as all fishermen know, the true time to tell them is round the winter fire, with a glass of something warm within easy reach, at a time when statements cannot be checked, when weights and measures must not be challenged and when fish grow to their full size and their true beauty. It is to such stories as these, whether told in summer or in winter, that the immemorial craft of the angler owes something of its continued charm.

Love Me, Love My Letters

The Use of Ink for the First Inklings of Love

THERE is a proverb which says a man is known by the company he keeps. There is a saying also that a man is best known by the song he sings. It is claimed, too, that people can always be distinguished by the books that they read, and by the pictures that they admire, and by the clothes that they wear.

All this may be true. But to my thinking, the truest test of character is found in the love letters that people write. Each different type of man or woman—including girls—has his, or her, or perhaps their, own particular way of writing love letters.

As witness to which, let me submit to the reader's judgment a carefully selected set of love letters present and past. I need hardly say that the letters are not imaginary, but that each of them is an actual sample taken right out of the post office—no, I don't think I need say it.

I

THE OLD-FASHIONED STYLE

Love letter of the year 1828 sent by messenger from Mr. Ardent Heartful, The Hall, Notts, England, to Miss Angela Blushanburn, The Shrubberies, Hops, Potts, Shrops, England, begging her acceptance of a fish:

"RESPECTED MISS ANGELA:

"With the consent of your honored father and your esteemed mother, I venture to send to you by the messenger who bears you this, a fish. It has, my respected Miss Angela, for some time been my most ardent desire that I might have the good fortune to present to you as the fruit of my own endeavors, a fish. It was this morning my good fortune to land while angling in the stream that traverses your property, with the consent of your father, a fish.

"In presenting for your consumption, with your parents' consent, respected Miss Angela, this fish, may I say that the fate of this fish which will thus have the inestimable privilege of languishing upon your table conveys nothing but envy to one who, while what he feels cannot be spoken, still feels as deeply as should feel, if it does feel, this fish.

"With the expression of a perfect esteem for your father and mother, believe me,

"Your devoted,
"ARDENT HEARTFUL."

II

THE NEWER STYLE OF TO-DAY

Love letter composed by Professor Albertus Dignus, senior professor of English rhetoric and diction at the University, and famous as the most brilliant essayist outside of the staff of the *London Times,* to Miss Maisie Beatit of the chorus of the Follies-in-Transit company at Memphis, Tenn.:

"Cuckoo! my little peacherino, and how is she to-night? I wish she was right here, yum, yum! I got her tootsie weenie letter this morning. I hustled to the post office so fast to get it I nearly broke my slats. And so it really longs for me, does she? and did you really mean it? Well, you certainly look like a piece of chocolate to me! In fact, you're some bird! You're my baby all right,"—and so forth for three pages. After which, the professor turns back to work on his essay—"The Deterioration of the English Language Among the Colored Races of Africa."

III

TRULY RURAL

Passionate Love Letter from Mr. Ephraim Cloverseed, Arcadia Post Office, Vermont, to Miss Nettie Singer, also of Arcadia, but at present on the cash in the Home Restaurant, 7860 Sixth Avenue, New York:

"DEAR NETTIE:

"There was a sharp frost last night which may do considerable harm to the fall wheat. Till last Tuesday there had not been no frost that you wouldn't have noticed any. Some think we are in for a hard winter. Some think if it clears off a bit between this and New Year's it may not be but some don't. I seen a couple of crows in the pasture yesterday but you can't always bank on that. I've been troubled again with my toe. But my rheumatism seems a whole lot better from that last stuff. My left leg has been pretty stiff again but the liniment has done my right arms good. Well, I will now close,

"EPHRAIM."

IV

HYDRAULIC LOVE

Letter from Mr. Harry P. Smith, hydraulic engineer and surveyor, writing to Miss Georgia Sims, from Red Gulch Creek in the wilds of New Ontario. Everybody knows that Harry has been just crazy over Georgia for three years.

"DEAR GEORGIA:

"We got in here through the bush yesterday and it certainly is a heck of a place to try to run a sight line in. The rock is mostly basaltic trap, but there are faults in it here and there that have been filled with alluvial deposit.

It would be pretty hard to give you an estimate of the probable mineral content. But I should say you would have a fair chance of striking gas here if you went deep enough. But your overhead would be a whopper. Well, Georgia, I must now close.

"HARRY."

THE ANSWERS THEY GOT

The answer received by Mr. Ardent Heartful, Anno Domini, 1828:

"Sir Joshua and Lady Blushanburn present their compliments to Mr. Ardent Heartful and desire to thank him for the fish which Mr. Heartful has had the kindness to forward to their daughter and which they have greatly enjoyed. Sir Joshua and Lady Blushanburn will be pleased if Mr. Heartful will present himself in person for such further conversation in regard to this fish as connects it with his future intentions."

WHAT THE PROFESSOR GOT

The answer from Miss Maisie Beatit of the Follies-in-Transit Company, Memphis, Tenn.:

"MY DEAR PROFESSOR:
"It was with the most agreeable feelings of gratification that I received your letter this morning.
"The sentiments which you express and the very evident manifestation thus conveyed of your affection towards myself fill me, sir, with the most lively satisfaction. . . ."
[After which Maisie got tired of copying word after word of the Complete Letter-Writer and so she just added in her own style,]
"Ain't you the Kidder? Our next jump is Kansas City.
"MAISIE."

WOMANLY EPISTLE SENT FROM POSTAL STATION B-28, NEW YORK, TO ARCADIA P. O., VERMONT

"DEAR EPHRAIM:

"I was glad to get your letter. I was sorry to hear there had been so much frost. I was glad to hear there are still crows in the bush. I was sorry to hear your toe is no better. I was glad to hear your rheumatism is some better. I am glad your leg is nicely. I must now close.

"NETTIE."

THE ANSWER FROM MISS GEORGIA SIMS, BLOOR STREET, TORONTO

She didn't answer.

.   .   .   .

Little query for the reader just at the end. Which of these various couples will get married first and stay married longest? Quite right. You guessed it immediately. There's no doubt about it, to persons of judgment in such things.

The Golfomaniac

WE ride in and out pretty often together, he and I, on a suburban train.

That's how I came to talk to him. "Fine morning," I said as I sat down beside him yesterday and opened a newspaper.

"Great!" he answered, "the grass is drying out fast now and the greens will soon be all right to play."

"Yes," I said, "the sun is getting higher and the days are decidedly lengthening."

"For the matter of that," said my friend, "a man could begin to play at six in the morning easily. In fact, I've often wondered that there's so little golf played before breakfast. We happened to be talking about golf, a few of us last night—I don't know how it came up—and we were saying that it seems a pity that some of the best part of the day, say, from five o'clock to seven-thirty, is never used."

"That's true," I answered, and then, to shift the subject, I said, looking out of the window:

"It's a pretty bit of country just here, isn't it?"

"It is," he replied, "but it seems a shame they make no use of it—just a few market gardens and things like that. Why, I noticed along here acres and acres of just glass—some kind of houses for plants or something—and whole fields full of lettuce and things like that. It's a pity they don't make something of it. I was remarking only the other day as I came along in the train with a friend of mine, that you could easily lay out an eighteen-hole course anywhere here."

"Could you?" I said.

"Oh, yes. This ground, you know, is an excellent light soil to shovel up into bunkers. You could drive some big ditches through it and make one or two deep holes—the kind they have on some of the French links. In fact, improve it to any extent."

I glanced at my morning paper. "I see," I said, "that it is again rumored that Lloyd George is at last definitely to retire."

"Funny thing about Lloyd George," answered my friend. "He never played, you know; most extraordinary thing—don't you think?—for a man in his position. Balfour, of course, was very different: I remember when I was over in Scotland last summer I had the honor of going around the course at Dumfries just after Lord Balfour. Pretty interesting experience, don't you think?"

"Were you over on business?" I asked.

"No, not exactly. I went to get a golf ball, a particular golf ball. Of course, I didn't go merely for that. I wanted to get a mashie as well. The only way, you know, to get just what you want is to go to Scotland for it."

"Did you see much of Scotland?"

"I saw it all. I was on the links at St. Andrews and I visited the Loch Lomond course and the course at Inverness. In fact, I saw everything."

"It's an interesting country, isn't it, historically?"

"It certainly is. Do you know they have played there for over five hundred years! Think of it! They showed me at Loch Lomond the place where they said Robert the Bruce played the Red Douglas (I think that was the other party—at any rate, Bruce was one of them), and I saw where Bonnie Prince Charlie disguised himself as a caddie when the Duke of Cumberland's soldiers were looking for him. Oh, it's a wonderful country historically."

.   .   .   .

After that I let a silence intervene so as to get a new start. Then I looked up again from my newspaper.

"Look at this," I said, pointing to a headline, *United States Navy Ordered Again to Nicaragua.* "Looks like more trouble, doesn't it?"

"Did you see in the paper a while back," said my companion, "that the United States Navy Department is now making golf compulsory at the training school at Annapolis? That's progressive, isn't it? I suppose it will have to mean shorter cruises at sea; in fact, probably lessen the use of the navy for sea purposes. But it will raise the standard."

"I suppose so," I answered. "Did you read about this extraordinary murder case on Long Island?"

"No," he said. "I never read murder cases. They don't interest me. In fact, I think this whole continent is getting over-preoccupied with them—"

"Yes, but this case had such odd features—"

"Oh, they all have," he replied, with an air of weariness. "Each one is just boomed by the papers to make a sensation—"

"I know, but in this case it seems that the man was killed with a blow from a golf club."

"What's that? Eh, what's that? Killed him with a blow from a golf club!!"

"Yes, some kind of club—"

"I wonder if it was an iron—let me see the paper—though, for the matter of that, I imagine that a blow with even a wooden driver, let alone one of the steel-handled drivers—where does it say it?—pshaw, it only just says 'a blow with golf club.' It's a pity the papers don't write these things up with more detail, isn't it? But perhaps it will be better in the afternoon paper. . . ."

"Have you played golf much?" I inquired. I saw it was no use to talk of anything else.

"No," answered my companion, "I am sorry to say I haven't. You see, I began late. I've only played twenty years, twenty-one if you count the year that's beginning in May. I don't know what I was doing. I wasted about half my life. In fact, it wasn't till I was well over thirty that I caught on to the game. I suppose a lot of us look back over our lives that way and realize what we have lost.

"And even as it is," he continued, "I don't get much chance to play. At the best I can only manage about four afternoons a week, though of course I get most of Saturday and all Sunday. I get my holiday in the summer, but it's only a month, and that's nothing. In the winter I manage to take a run South for a game once or twice and perhaps a little swack at it around Easter, but only a week at a time. I'm too busy—that's the plain truth of it." He sighed. "It's hard to leave the office before two," he said. "Something always turns up."

And after that he went on to tell me something of the technique of the game, illustrate it with a golf ball on the seat of the car, and the peculiar mental poise needed for driving, and the neat, quick action of the wrist (he showed me how it worked) that is needed to undercut a ball so that it flies straight up in the air. He explained to me how you can do practically anything with a golf ball, provided that you keep your mind absolutely poised and your eye in shape, and your body a trained machine. It appears that even Bobby Jones of Atlanta and people like that fall short very often from the high standard set up by my golfing friend in the suburban car.

.   .   .   .

So, later in the day, meeting someone in my club who was a person of authority on such things, I made inquiry about my friend. "I rode into town with Llewellyn Smith," I said. "I think he belongs to your golf club. He's a great player, isn't he?"

"A great player!" laughed the expert. "Llewellyn Smith? Why, he can hardly hit a ball! And anyway, he's only played about twenty years!"

Gertrude the Governess: or, Simple Seventeen

Synopsis of Previous Chapters:
There are no Previous Chapters.

IT was a wild and stormy night on the West Coast of Scotland. This, however, is immaterial to the present story, as the scene is not laid in the West of Scotland. For the matter of that the weather was just as bad on the East Coast of Ireland.

But the scene of this narrative is laid in the South of England and takes place in and around Knotacentinum Towers (pronounced as if written Nosham Taws), the seat of Lord Knotacent (pronounced as if written Nosh).

But it is not necessary to pronounce either of these names in reading them.

Nosham Taws was a typical English home. The main part of the house was an Elizabethan structure of warm red brick, while the elder portion, of which the Earl was inordinately proud, still showed the outlines of a Norman Keep, to which had been added a Lancastrian Jail and a Plantagenet Orphan Asylum. From the house in all directions stretched magnificent woodland and park with oaks and elms of immemorial antiquity, while nearer the house stood raspberry bushes and geranium plants which had been set out by the Crusaders.

About the grand old mansion the air was loud with the chirping of thrushes, the cawing of partridges and the clear sweet note of the rook, while deer, antelope and other quadrupeds strutted about the lawn so tame as to eat off the sun-dial. In fact, the place was a regular menagerie.

From the house downwards through the park stretched a beautiful broad avenue laid out by Henry VII.

Lord Nosh stood upon the hearthrug of the library. Trained diplomat and statesman as he was, his stern aristocratic face was upside down with fury.

"Boy," he said, "you shall marry this girl or I disinherit you. You are no son of mine."

Young Lord Ronald, erect before him, flung back a glance as defiant as his own.

"I defy you," he said. "Henceforth you are no father of mine. I will get another. I will marry none but a woman I can love. This girl that we have never seen—"

"Fool," said the Earl, "would you throw aside our estate and name of a thousand years? The girl, I am told, is beautiful; her aunt is willing; they are French; pah! they understand such things in France."

"But your reason—"

"I give no reason," said the Earl. "Listen, Ronald, I give one month. For that time you remain here. If at the end of it you refuse me, I cut you off with a shilling."

Lord Ronald said nothing; he flung himself from the room, flung himself upon his horse and rode madly off in all directions.

As the door of the library closed upon Ronald the Earl sank into a chair. His face changed. It was no longer that of the haughty nobleman, but of the hunted criminal. "He must marry the girl," he muttered. "Soon she will know all. Tutchemoff has escaped from Siberia. He knows and will tell. The whole of the mines pass to her, this property with it, and I—but enough." He rose, walked to the sideboard, drained a dipper full of gin and bitters, and became again a high-bred English gentleman.

It was at this moment that a high dogcart, driven by a groom in the livery of Earl Nosh, might have been seen entering the avenue of Nosham Taws. Beside him sat a young girl, scarce more than a child, in fact, not nearly so big as the groom.

The apple-pie hat which she wore, surmounted with black willow plumes, concealed from view a face so face-like in its appearance as to be positively facial.

It was—need we say it—Gertrude the Governess, who was this day to enter upon her duties at Nosham Taws.

At the same time that the dogcart entered the avenue at one end there might have been seen riding down it from the other a tall young man, whose long, aristocratic face proclaimed his birth and who was mounted upon a horse with a face even longer than his own.

And who is this tall young man who draws nearer to Gertrude with every revolution of the horse? Ah, who, indeed? Ah, who, who? I wonder if any of my readers could guess that this was none other than Lord Ronald.

The two were destined to meet. Nearer and nearer they came. And then still nearer. Then for one brief moment they met. As they passed Gertrude raised her head and directed towards the young nobleman two eyes so eye-like in their expression as to be absolutely circular, while Lord Ronald directed towards the occupant of the dogcart a gaze so gazelike that nothing but a gazelle, or a gas-pipe, could have emulated its intensity.

Was this the dawn of love? Wait and see. Do not spoil the story.

Let us speak of Gertrude, Gertrude De Mongmorenci McFiggin had known neither father nor mother. They had both died years before she was born. Of her mother she knew nothing, save that she was French, was extremely beautiful, and that all her ancestors and even her business acquaintances had perished in the Revolution.

Yet Gertrude cherished the memory of her parents. On her breast the girl wore a locket in which was enshrined a miniature of her mother, while down her neck inside at the back hung a daguerreotype of her father. She carried a portrait of her grandmother up her sleeve and had pictures of her cousins tucked inside her boot, while beneath her—but enough, quite enough.

Of her father Gertrude knew even less. That he was a high-born English gentleman who had lived as a wanderer in many lands, this was all she knew. His only legacy to Gertrude had been a Russian grammar, a Roumanian phrase-book, a theodolite, and a work on mining engineering.

From her earliest infancy Gertrude had been brought up by her aunt. Her aunt had carefully instructed her in Christian principles. She had also taught her Mohammedanism to make sure.

When Gertrude was seventeen her aunt had died of hydrophobia.

The circumstances were mysterious. There had called upon her that day a strange bearded man in the costume of the Russians. After he had left, Gertrude had found her aunt in a syncope from which she passed into an apostrophe and never recovered.

To avoid scandal it was called hydrophobia. Gertrude was thus thrown upon the world. What to do? That was the problem that confronted her.

It was while musing one day upon her fate that Gertrude's eye was struck with an advertisement.

"Wanted a governess; must possess a knowledge of French, Italian, Russian, and Roumanian, Music, and

Mining Engineering. Salary £1, 4 shillings and 4 pence halfpenny per annum. Apply between half-past eleven and twenty-five minutes to twelve at No. 41 A Decimal Six, Belgravia Terrace. The Countess of Nosh."

Gertrude was a girl of great natural quickness of apprehension, and she had not pondered over this announcement more than half an hour before she was struck with the extraordinary coincidence between the list of items desired and the things that she herself knew.

She duly presented herself at Belgravia Terrace before the Countess, who advanced to meet her with a charm which at once placed the girl at her ease.

"You are proficient in French?" she asked.

"*Oh, oui,*" said Gertrude modestly.

"And Italian?" continued the Countess.

"*Oh, si,*" said Gertrude.

"And German?" said the Countess in delight.

"*Ah, ja,*" said Gertrude.

"And Russian?"

"*Yaw.*"

"And Roumanian?"

"*Jep.*"

Amazed at the girl's extraordinary proficiency in modern languages, the Countess looked at her narrowly. Where had she seen those lineaments before? She passed her hand over her brow in thought, and spit upon the floor, but no, the face baffled her.

"Enough," she said, "I engage you on the spot; tomorrow you go down to Nosham Taws and begin teaching the children. I must add that in addition you will be expected to aid the Earl with his Russian correspondence. He has large mining interests at Tschminsk."

Tschminsk! why did the simple word reverberate upon Gertrude's ears? Why? Because it was the name written in her father's hand on the title page of his book on mining. What mystery was here?

It was on the following day that Gertrude had driven up the avenue.

She descended from the dogcart, passed through a phalanx of liveried servants drawn up seven-deep, to each of whom she gave a sovereign as she passed and entered Nosham Taws.

"Welcome," said the Countess, as she aided Gertrude to carry her trunk upstairs.

The girl presently descended and was ushered into the library, where she was presented to the Earl. As soon as the Earl's eye fell upon the face of the new governess he started visibly. Where had he seen those lineaments? Where was it? At the races, or the theatre—on a bus—no. Some subtler thread of memory was stirring in his mind. He strode hastily to the sideboard, drained a dipper and a half of brandy, and became again the perfect English gentleman.

While Gertrude has gone to the nursery to make the acquaintance of the two tiny golden-haired children who are to be her charges, let us say something here of the Earl and his son.

Lord Nosh was the perfect type of the English nobleman and statesman. The years that he had spent in the diplomatic service at Constantinople, St. Petersburg, and Salt Lake City had given to him a peculiar finesse and noblesse, while his long residence at St. Helena, Pitcairn Island, and Hamilton, Ontario, had rendered him impervious to external impressions. As deputy-paymaster of the militia of the county he had seen something of the sterner side of military life, while his hereditary office of Groom of the Sunday Breeches had brought him into direct contact with Royalty itself.

His passion for outdoor sports endeared him to his tenants. A keen sportsman, he excelled in fox-hunting, dog-hunting, pig-killing, bat-catching and the pastimes of his class.

In this latter respect Lord Ronald took after his father. From the start the lad had shown the greatest promise. At Eton he had made a splendid showing at battledore and shuttlecock, and at Cambridge had been first in his class at needlework. Already his name was whispered in connection with the All England ping-pong championship, a triumph which would undoubtedly carry with it a seat in Parliament.

Thus was Gertrude the Governess installed at Nosham Taws.

The days and the weeks sped past.

The simple charm of the beautiful orphan girl attracted all hearts. Her two little pupils became her slaves. "Me loves oo," the little Rasehellfrida would say, leaning her golden head in Gertrude's lap. Even the servants loved her. The head gardener would bring a bouquet of beautiful roses to her room before she was up, the second gardener a bunch of early cauliflowers, the third a spray of late asparagus, and even the tenth and eleventh a sprig of mangel-wurzel or an armful of hay. Her room was full of gardeners all the time, while at evening the aged butler, touched at the friendless girl's loneliness, would tap softly at her door to bring her a rye whisky and seltzer or a box of Pittsburg Stogies. Even the dumb creatures seemed to admire her in their own dumb way. The dumb rooks settled on her shoulder and every dumb dog around the place followed her.

And Ronald! ah, Ronald! Yes, indeed! They had met. They had spoken.

"What a dull morning," Gertrude had said. *"Quel triste matin! Was fur ein allerverdamnter Tag!"*

"Beastly," Ronald had answered.

"Beastly!!" The word rang in Gertrude's ears all day.

After that they were constantly together. They played tennis and ping-pong in the day, and in the evening, in accordance with the stiff routine of the place, they sat down with the Earl and Countess to twenty-five-cent poker, and later still they sat together on the verandah and watched the moon sweeping in great circles around the horizon.

It was not long before Gertrude realised that Lord Ronald felt towards her a warmer feeling than that of mere ping-pong. At times in her presence he would fall, especially after dinner, into a fit of profound subtraction.

Once at night, when Gertrude withdrew to her chamber and before seeking her pillow, prepared to retire as a preliminary to disrobing—in other words, before going to bed, she flung wide the casement (opened the window) and perceived (saw) the face of Lord Ronald. He was sitting on a thorn bush beneath her, and his upturned face wore an expression of agonised pallor.

Meantime the days passed. Life at the Taws moved in the ordinary routine of a great English household. At 7 a gong sounded for rising, at 8 a horn blew for breakfast, at 8.30 a whistle sounded for prayers, at 1 a flag was run up at half-mast for lunch, at 4 a gun was fired for afternoon tea, at 9 a first bell sounded for dressing, at 9.15 a second bell for going on dressing, while at 9.30 a rocket was sent up to indicate that dinner was ready. At midnight dinner was over, and at 1 a.m. the tolling of a bell summoned the domestics to evening prayers.

Meanwhile the month allotted by the Earl to Lord

Ronald was passing away. It was already July 15, then within a day or two it was July 17, and, almost immediately afterwards, July 18.

At times the Earl, in passing Ronald in the hall, would say sternly, "Remember, boy, your consent, or I disinherit you."

And what were the Earl's thoughts of Gertrude? Here was the one drop of bitterness in the girl's cup of happiness. For some reason that she could not devine the Earl showed signs of marked antipathy.

Once as she passed the door of the library he threw a bootjack at her. On another occasion at lunch alone with her he struck her savagely across the face with a sausage.

It was her duty to translate to the Earl his Russian correspondence. She sought in it in vain for the mystery. One day a Russian telegram was handed to the Earl. Gertrude translated it to him aloud.

"Tutchemoff went to the woman. She is dead."

On hearing this the Earl became livid with fury, in fact this was the day that he struck her with the sausage.

Then one day while the Earl was absent on a bat hunt, Gertrude, who was turning over his correspondence, with that sweet feminine instinct of interest that rose superior to ill-treatment, suddenly found the key to the mystery.

Lord Nosh was not the rightful owner of the Taws. His distant cousin of the older line, the true heir, had died in a Russian prison to which the machinations of the Earl, while Ambassador at Tschminsk, had consigned him. The daughter of this cousin was the true owner of Nosham Taws.

The family story, save only that the documents before her withheld the name of the rightful heir, lay bare to Gertrude's eye.

Strange is the heart of woman. Did Gertrude turn

from the Earl with spurning? No. Her own sad fate had taught her sympathy.

Yet still the mystery remained! Why did the Earl start perceptibly each time that he looked into her face? Sometimes he started as much as four centimetres, so that one could distinctly see him do it. On such occasions he would hastily drain a dipper of rum and vichy water and become again the correct English gentleman.

The denouement came swiftly. Gertrude never forgot it.

It was the night of the great ball at Nosham Taws. The whole neighbourhood was invited. How Gertrude's heart had beat with anticipation, and with what trepidation she had overhauled her scant wardrobe in order to appear not unworthy in Lord Ronald's eyes. Her resources were poor indeed, yet the inborn genius for dress that she inherited from her French mother stood her in good stead. She twined a single rose in her hair and contrived herself a dress out of a few old newspapers and the inside of an umbrella that would have graced a court. Round her waist she bound a single braid of bag-string, while a piece of old lace that had been her mother's was suspended to her ear by a thread.

Gertrude was the cynosure of all eyes. Floating to the strains of the music she presented a picture of bright girlish innocence that no one could see undisenraptured.

The ball was at its height. It was away up!

Ronald stood with Gertrude in the shrubbery. They looked into one another's eyes.

"Gertrude," he said, "I love you."

Simple words, and yet they thrilled every fibre in the girl's costume.

"Ronald!" she said, and cast herself about his neck.

At this moment the Earl appeared standing beside them

in the moonlight. His stern face was distorted with indignation.

"So!" he said, turning to Ronald, "it appears that you have chosen!"

"I have," said Ronald with hauteur.

"You prefer to marry this penniless girl rather than the heiress I have selected for you?"

Gertrude looked from father to son in amazement.

"Yes," said Ronald.

"Be it so," said the Earl, draining a dipper of gin which he carried, and resuming his calm. "Then I disinherit you. Leave this place, and never return to it."

"Come, Gertrude," said Ronald tenderly, "let us flee together."

Gertrude stood before them. The rose had fallen from her head. The lace had fallen from her ear and the bag-string had come undone from her waist. Her newspapers were crumpled beyond recognition. But dishevelled and illegible as she was, she was still mistress of herself.

"Never," she said firmly. "Ronald, you shall never make this sacrifice for me." Then to the Earl, in tones of ice, "There is a pride, sir, as great even as yours. The daughter of Metschnikoff McFiggin need crave a boon from no one."

With that she hauled from her bosom the daguerreotype of her father and pressed it to her lips.

The Earl started as if shot. "That name!" he cried, "that face! that photograph! stop!"

There! There is no need to finish; my readers have long since divined it. Gertrude was the heiress.

The lovers fell into one another's arms. The Earl's proud face relaxed. "God bless you," he said. The Countess and the guests came pouring out upon the lawn.

The breaking day illuminated a scene of gay congratulations.

Gertrude and Ronald were wed. Their happiness was complete. Need we say more? Yes, only this. The Earl was killed in the hunting-field a few days later. The Countess was struck by lightning. The two children fell down a well. Thus the happiness of Gertrude and Ronald was complete.

Letters to the New Rulers of the World

No. I. To the Secretary of the League of Nations.

RESPECTED SIR,

I have learned, as has everybody here in my home town, with unconcealed delight, of this new convention, that you have just concluded in regard to the Kalmuk Hinterland of the Oxus district. As we understand it here in our town, this convention will establish a distinct *modus vivendi* as between Mongolian Kalmuks and the Tartarian Honeysuckles. It will set up a new sphere of influence, the boundaries of which we are as yet unable to trace on the railway and steamship map of the world in our new Union Depot, but which we feel assured will extend at least fifty miles in either direction, and will stop only when it has to. As citizens of a great country it fills us with a new pride in this nation to reflect that the whole of this hinterland, both back and front, will now be thrown open to be proselytized, Christianized, and internationalized, penetrated and fumigated under the mandate of this country.

What you have done, sir, is a big thing, and when we realize that it has taken only six years for you to do it, we are filled with enthusiasm as to what you are destined to do. Nor has this been the sole result of your years of labour. The citizens of our town have followed with a fascinated interest each stage of your achievements. Your handling of the claims of Formosa to a share in the control of the Ho-han Canal was masterly. On the news that you had succeeded in submitting to arbitration the claims of the Dutch bondholders of the Peking-Hankow railway, our citizens turned out and held a torchlight procession on the Main Street. When the word came that you had successfully arranged a *status quo* on the backwaters of the Upper Congo, there was an enthusiasm and excitement upon our streets such as we have not seen since the silver election in 1896.

Under the circumstances, therefore, respected sir, I am certain that you will not mind a few words—I will not say of protest—but of friendly criticism. We readily admit in our town all that you have done for us. You have lifted us, as we fully recognize, into what is a larger atmosphere. When we look back to the narrow horizon of politics as they were in this town (you will recall our sending Alderman McGinnis and the Johnson boys to the penitentiary) we stand appalled. It is a splendid thing to think that our politics now turn upon the larger and bigger issues of the world, such as the Kalmuks, the Kolchucks and the internationalization of the Gulf of Kamchatka. It would have done you good, sir, could you have listened to the masterly debate at our Mechanics' Institute last week on the establishment of a six-nation control over the trolley line from Jerusalem and Jericho.

But, sir, to be very frank—there is a certain apprehension in our town that this thing is being pushed just a little too far. We are willing to be as international as anybody. Our citizens can breathe as large an atmosphere as the Kalmuks or the Cambodians or any of them. But what begins to worry us is whether these other people are going to be international too. We feel somehow that your League ought, if we may use a metaphor, to play a little bit nearer home, not all the games but at least some of them. There are a lot of things in this town that we think might properly claim your attention. I don't know whether you are aware of the state of our sewers and the need for practically ripping up the Main Street and relaying them. Here is a thing in which we think the Kalmuks might care to help us out. Also if you would discuss with the Cambodians of the Sumatra Hinterland the question of their taking a hand in the irrigation of Murphy's flats (just the other side, you remember, of where the old Murphy homestead was) it might make for good feeling all around.

Put very briefly, sir, our one criticism of your achievements—and it is only said in the kindest possible way—is that your League is all right, but somehow the gate receipts of it seem to go in the wrong direction.

No. II—To a Disconsolate King

MY DEAR CHARLES MARY AUGUSTUS FELIX SIGISMUND:

You will pardon me, I hope, this brief method of address. For the moment, I cannot recall the rest of your names.

I need hardly say how delighted and honoured I was to receive a letter from you written all in your own hand and spelt, as I saw at once, without help. It was perhaps wrong of you to pay insufficient postage on it. But I do not forget that you were once a king and cannot at once get over it. You write in what are evidently wretchedly low spirits. You say that you are living in Schlitzen-Bad-unter-Wein (if I get you right) in the simplest conceivable way. You have laid aside your royal title and are living incognito as the Hereditary Count in and of Salzensplitz. You have only a single valet and no retinue. You lunch, you tell me, very plainly each day upon a pint of Rheinwein and an egg, and at dinner you have merely a chop or a cutlet and a couple of quarts of Rudesberger. You retire to bed, it seems, after a plain supper—a forkful of macaroni, I think you said, with about half a tumbler of old Schnapps. Of all the thousands who fed at your table in the days of your kingship, none, you say, care now to share your simple fare. This is too bad. If they had you and your little table in New York, they could give you the choice of a line-up of friends that would reach from the Winter Garden to the Battery. But that is by the way.

The point is that you are singularly disconsolate. You tell me that at times you have thought of suicide. At other times you have almost made up your mind to work. Both of these things are bad, and I beg of you, my dear Sigismund, that before adopting either of these alternatives you will listen to a little quiet advice and will sit tight in Schlitzen-Bad-unter-Wein till things brighten up a bit. Unless I much mistake, my dear Charles Mary Felix, the world has not finished with you yet, nor won't have for a long time to come. It turns out, I am sorry to say, that the world is still an infinitely sillier place than we had imagined. You remember that morning when you ran away from your hereditary principality, concealed in a packing case and covered up with a load of hay. All the world roared with laughter at the ignominy and cowardice of your flight. You seemed all of a sudden changed into a comic figure. Your silly little dignity, the uniforms that you wore and that you changed twenty times a day, the medals which you bestowed upon yourself, the Insignia of the Duck's Feather which you yourself instituted—all these things became suddenly laughable. We thought that Europe had become sensible and rational, and was done with the absurdity of autocratic kings.

I tell you frankly, Charles Mary Felix, you and your silly baubles had been no sooner swept into the little heap, than a thousand new kinds of folly sprang up to replace you. The merry Checkoslovak and the Unredeemed

Italian ran up a bill of taxes for peaceful citizens like myself to pay. I have contributed my share to expeditions to Kieff, to Baku, and to Teheran and to Timbuctoo. General Choodenstich is conducting huge operations against General Gorfinski in Esthonia, and I can't even remember which is my general and where Esthonia is. I have occupied Anatolia, and I don't want it. I have got an international gendarmerie in Albania that I think are a pack of bums, eating their heads off at my expense. As to Bulgaria, Bukovina, and Bessarabia, I believe I voice the sentiments of millions of free-born income-tax payers when I say, take them, Charles Felix; they are all yours.

The time is coming, I am certain, when a new pack of fools will come and hunt you up in your exile at Schlitzen-Bad-unter-Wein, clap a Field Marshal's uniform on you, put you in a bomb-proof motor car and rush you back to your hereditary palace. They will announce that you have performed prodigies of personal bravery. You will wear again your twenty uniforms a day. You will give twenty-five cents to a blind beggar and be called the father of your people.

I give you notice, Mary Augustus, that when this happens, I shall not lift a finger to stop it. For it appears that our poor humanity, its head still singing with the cruel buffeting of the war, is incapable of moving forward, and can only stagger round in a circle.

No. III—To a Plumber

MY VERY DEAR SIR,

It is now four hours since you have been sitting under the sink in my kitchen, smoking. You have turned off the water in the basement of my house and you have made the space under the sink dry and comfortable and you are sit-

ting there. I understand that you are waiting for the
return of your fellow plumber who has gone away to bring
back a bigger wrench than the one that you have with you.

The moment is therefore opportune for me to write
these few lines which I shall presently place in an envelope
and deliver to you on your departure.

I do not wish in any way to seem to reflect upon the
apparent dilatoriness with which your work has been done.
I am certain that is only apparent and not real. I pass
over the fact that my house has now for two weeks been
without an adequate water-supply. I do not resent it
that you have spent each morning for a fortnight in my
kitchen. I am not insensible, sir, to the charm of your
presence there under the sink and I recognize the stimulus
which it affords to the intellectual life of my cook. I am
quite aware, sir, that all of these things are outside of the
legitimate scope of complaint. For I understand that they
are imposed upon you by your order. It is the command,
I believe, of your local union that you must not use a
wrench without sending for an assistant: it is an order of
your federated brotherhood that you must not handle a
screwdriver except in the presence of a carpenter and before witnesses: and it is the positive command of the international order to which you belong that you must not
finish any job until it has been declared finishable by a
majority vote of the qualified plumbers of your district.
These things, no doubt, make for the gayety and variety of
industry but interpose, I fear, a check upon the rapidity of
your operations.

But what I have wanted to say to you, good sir, is this.
You find yourself in possession of what used to be called
in the middle ages a Mystery,—something which you can
do and which other people can't. And you are working
your mystery for all it is worth. Indeed I am inclined

to think that you are working it for rather more than it is worth.

I think it only fair to tell you that a movement is now on foot which may jeopardize your existence. A number of our national universities have already opened departments of Plumbing which threaten to bring your mysterious knowledge within reach even of the most educated. Some of the brightest scientific minds of the country are applying themselves to find out just how you do it. I have myself already listened to a course of six speculative lectures on the theory of the kitchen tap, in which the lecturer was bold enough to say that the time is soon coming when it will be known, absolutely and positively, to the scientific world how to put on a washer. Already, sir, pamphlets are being freely circulated dealing with the origin and nature of the hot water furnace. It has been already discovered that the water moves to and fro in the pipes of the furnace with sufficient regularity and continuity of movement to render it capable of reduction to a scientific law. We shall know before long just what it is you do to the thing to stop it from sizzling.

You perceive then, my dear sir, that the moment is one which ought to give you room for anxious thought. You are perhaps not aware that a book has already been published under the ominous title *Every Man His Own Plumber*. It has been suppressed, very rightly, by the United States Government as tending to subvert society and reduce it to a pulp. But it at least foreshadows, sir, the grim possibilities of the future.

May I in conclusion make a personal request. If you have any friends who are in the bell-hanging business, or the electrical repair industry, or the broken window monopoly, or the loose-chair-leg combine, will you kindly show them this letter.

No. IV—To a Hotel Manager

NOBLE AND EXALTED SIR,

I am well aware as I stand before you at the desk of your rotunda, of what a worm I am. There is, as far as I can see it, no reasonable excuse for my existence. I have so it appears, "no reservation," and yet I have had the impertinence to come here and to sue for a room. The contempt with which you gaze upon me is only too well justified. It is of no use for me to plead that I did not know that I was coming and that my journey to your city was entirely unpremeditated. All this only indicates, as you justly express by the look upon your face, an ill-regulated life unfit for your consideration.

I am well aware, sir, that I ought to have written to you four months ago and entered myself upon your waiting list for accommodation: and I know that even in that case my chance of obtaining a room would have had to depend upon my continued merit of good conduct.

You inform me that if I lean up against this desk until one o'clock there is a possibility that a gentleman may vacate room 4601. This is glad news indeed. I shall stand here with pleasure and I am sure that you will not consider me disqualified if I stand first upon one leg and then upon the other. It is a habit that I have acquired in such hotels as yours.

Meantime, my dear sir, I should like, while I lean against the desk, to set down upon paper in a few words just what I think of you. I cannot help but contrast you, sir, with the old-time "Proprietor" whom you have replaced. The change, I do not doubt, is altogether salutary: and yet in certain aspects I cannot but regret it. The old-time "hotel man" was accustomed to meet me with an out-stretched hand and a genial smile. He greeted me by my

name and though I knew that he had read it on my valise
my gratification was none the less. A room? Why, that
man could find me a room if I turned up at midnight in
the middle of a Grand Army Convention. A room!
Why, the mere suggestion of my not getting a room filled
him with distress. Sooner than see me sleepless he would
put me in with two commercial men from the west (perfect gentlemen, as he himself informed me); he would put
me, along with four others, on the billiard table; establish
me behind a screen in a quiet corner of a corridor; or
stop, rather than see me suffer, he would offer (it was a
safe thing) to turn out of his own room. As to a bath
neither he nor I ever thought of it.

Observe that this man's hotel was very different from
yours. In it was no palm room filled with rubber trees
and resonant with the music of a Hungarian Orchestra: no
Peacock corridor in which the Dangerous Debutante in the
drooping hat shoots languorous glances at the passer-by.
In point of pleasure and relaxation in his hotel there was
nothing, other than the bar. That was the sole resort,—
a quiet place below the stairs with a sanded floor and a long
counter. And here it was that we stood in friendly converse, drinking whiskey and water while the chief clerk
was "fixing me up" for a room. In those brave days we
drank whiskey and water right after breakfast. We were
supposed to need it.

Now, sir, I admit that you and your kind have made
wonderful changes in our hotels. You have filled them
with music and palm trees and debutantes. You have
taught our people to drink English tea at five o'clock in
the afternoon; you have borrowed the Café Chantant of
the French and combined it with the grill room of the
British. You have introduced afternoon dances and midnight suppers and you have gathered about you,—I admit

it and I thank you for it,—all the prettiest women in New York to decorate your corridors.

You have become, and in a certain sense you are entitled to be, one of the New Rulers of the World. But this I ask. Do not push your sovereignty too far. If you do, there will be the inevitable reaction and revolution. A movement will be put on foot to build in your city a few hotels of the by-gone type of the old days when the guests were guests indeed and the kindly publican their host: a hotel with only one bath for every twenty-five guests: with dinner served only in the main dining room when the bell rings: without a single rubber tree in the whole extent of it, but,—and this is the essential point,—with something of the old-fashioned courtesy and kindliness and quiet which you are banishing from your palatial doors.

What! The gentleman has vacated room 4601? Ah! a gentleman indeed! Quick, give me the pen and let me sign. I take back all that I have written. And by the way, which is the way to the lunch room where the Syrian dancing girls are? I shall want to eat there.

No. V—To a Prohibitionist

MY DEAR SIR:

Before I begin this letter let me explain that, of course, I am myself a believer in prohibition. I think that water, especially clear, cold water—I don't care for muddy water —is a beautiful drink. I had a glass of it the other day, and it seemed wonderfully limpid and transparent—almost like gin.

Moreover, in the town in which I live, my friends and I have seen prohibition in actual operation, and we are all enthusiastic over it. Crime is lessening every day. Murder is becoming almost unknown. Not a single one of my friends was murdered all last summer. The sale of boys' boots had increased a hundred per cent. Some of the boys here have no less than eight or ten pairs. Bank deposits are rising. Credit is expanding, and work is almost ceasing.

These are very gratifying things, and when we look back upon the old days, my friends and I wonder how we could have led the life that we did. I remember that very often in the middle of the morning we used deliberately to go out from our business and drink a glass of lager beer. Why we did this I cannot now conceive. Beer, sir, as you yourself are aware, contains neither proteids nor albumen. It has less nitrogen in it than common starch, and is not nearly so rich in effervescent hydrogen as ordinary baking soda: in short, its food value is not to be compared with tan bark or with common mucilage. Nowadays, if I find that I flag at all in morning work, I take a little nip of baking soda and a couple of licks of mucilage and in a moment I am willing and anxious to work again.

I remember, too, that in the old times in the winter evenings we used to sit around the fire in one another's houses smoking and drinking hot toddy. No doubt you remember the awful stuff. We generally used to make ours with Bourbon whiskey and hot water, with just a dash of rum, with half a dozen lumps of white sugar in it, and with nutmeg powdered over the top. I think we used to put a curled slice of lemon peel into the rotten stuff and then served it in a tall tumbler with a long spoon in it. We used to sit and sup this beastly mixture all evening and carry on a perfectly aimless conversation with no selected subject of discussion, and with absolutely no attempt to improve our minds at all.

As things are now I have entirely cut all such idle acquaintanceship and such waste of time. I like to come home after my work and, after drinking four or five glasses of water, spend the evening with some good book of statistics, improving myself. I am then ready to converse, should an occasion arise, in such a way as to put conversation where it ought to be.

You will, therefore, readily understand that all my friends and I are enthusiastic over prohibition. If you were to ask us to go back to things as they were (but please do not do so), we should vote against it by a majority of easily two hundred per cent. It is on this account, with all the more confidence, that I am able to draw your attention to one or two points, in themselves very small things, in which we think that the present régime might be amended.

The first of these is the mere percentage, as it is commonly called, of the beer that is permitted to be sold. This is evidently a matter of very secondary concern and one on which no one would wish to dogmatize. But my friends and I feel that this percentage might profitably be placed at about, say, in rough numbers—twenty per cent. We should feel that at twenty per cent. we were getting a more adequate return upon the money expended. At the same time we lay no great stress on the particular figure itself. Twenty, thirty, or possibly still better, forty per cent. would prove quite acceptable to us.

Another point is the abolition of the bar. Here we are all agreed. The bar is done with forever. We never want to see it back. But we do feel that if we could have some quiet place where one could purchase beverages of the kind I have described, some plain room with tables and a seat or two and possibly a free lunch counter and a weighing machine, we should feel better to carry out the general purport of the prohibition idea. There are several of my friends who have not been weighed since the first of

July of 1919, and are suffering grave inconvenience thereby.

I do not suggest that such a place should be allowed to operate after the old unrestrained fashion of the bars that kept open practically all night. It should be placed under sharp regulation. My friends and I feel that any such place should be rigidly closed at two o'clock A.M. with perhaps special facilities for access at a later hour to the weighing machine and the lunch counter. These, however, are mere details of organization which, as we see it, do not in the least impair the general principle.

As to whiskey and the stronger spirits, we feel that there is not a single word to be said for them. My friends and I are convinced that the use of these things as a beverage is deleterious to the last degree. We unite in declaring that they should be regarded as medicine and as medicine only. Two or three small incidents have occurred among us lately which have corroborated our opinions upon this point. Not very long ago one of my friends was taken, just outside of my door, with a very sharp pain, or stitch, in his side. For the moment I was at a loss what to do when it occurred to me that possibly a medicinal application of whiskey might prove effective. I took him into my house and administered it at once and was delighted to observe the color come back into his cheeks. It was some hours before I was enabled to remove him: but I finally ventured to put him into a hack, crosswise on the two seats, and the poor fellow was, I believe, safely placed against his own door by the hackman without further mishap.

Such incidents as this have convinced us that the sale of whiskey should be rigidly restricted to those who need it at the time when they need it, and in the quantity that they happen to need.

These suggestions, my dear sir, are intended merely as suggestions, as mere adumbrations of possible modifications of the present system. We understand that there is some talk of reconsidering and redrafting the eighteenth amendment to the constitution. If this is so, I think it would be well to embody these suggestions in the new amendment. I am certain that upon these terms the Supreme Court of the United States would have no trouble with its interpretation.

No. VI—To a Spiritualist

DEAR FRIEND AND BROTHER IN THE DARKNESS,

I sent you last week a thought wave or movement of the ether. But it has apparently not reached you. I willed it in your direction and it seemed at the time to be moving toward you with gratifying rapidity. But I fear that it has gone clean past you. I am not, however, surprised or discouraged at this. In the little Spiritualistic circle in which I belong we have already learned to take the failures with the successes. We directed last week a thought wave at Senator Lodge but we have no reason to think that it hit him. The week before we had sent one, with special force, at Mr. Mackenzie King and there is no sign that it struck him. Our medium, Miss Mutt, tells us that very often a thought wave becomes supercharged and loses touch with the etherical vibrations and we all think this very likely. So I am not discouraged that my little message of congratulation and suggestion has gone astray. If I only had you near me I could get the message into you in a moment by putting the tips of my fingers on your cranium and willing it into you. But as I cannot do that I hope you will not mind if I have recourse to pen and ink.

What I want to say to you first of all is to congratulate

you upon the splendid work that you have been doing in the world during the last few years. Until your recent activities began things were getting into a dreadful condition. Belief in everything seemed to be dying out. All idea of a material hell had had to be abandoned and there seemed nothing left. But now all that has been completely changed and I am sure that the little circle to which I belong is only one among thousands that are bringing hope and light to a world that was growing dark.

I am sure that you will be glad to learn that in our little circle our experiments have been singularly successful. We began in the very simplest way because Miss Mutt, our medium, said that it was better to begin with simple things so as to find out whether our members offered an easy mark to the ether waves sent from the Other Side, and they did. As our first experiment we all sat around a table with our fingers just barely touching it. We all had our eyes bandaged except Miss Mutt and we put the light out in the room to avoid the cross vibrations.

We were all delighted to find that the table at once began lifting its legs in the air and making raps on the floor and presently it ran right around the room and then climbed up the wall. Miss Mutt had to coax it down again. This of course is only a very simple thing and Miss Mutt, our medium, explained it all very clearly by telling us that the table had moved out of the subliminal plane and had got into a plane of its own. But at first it seemed quite surprising.

After that we went on to quite a lot of other experiments and sent telepathic messages clear out into space beyond the stars, and produced actual bodies and raised the dead and things like that. These are only little things, of course, and to you I am sure they sound nothing. But I can't tell you how these simple little experiments pleased and delighted us.

Our séances in our little circle have now taken a more or less regular form. We meet on Tuesday evenings at 8 and first we have coffee and then Miss Mutt goes into a trance and calls up for us the spirits of any of the great people in history. The members generally vote as to who is to be called up but if there is any dispute the hostess of the evening decides what spirit is to come. We have had Machiavelli and Queen Elizabeth and a Roman Emperor who was awfully good though I forget his name for the minute. Machiavelli gave us a most interesting talk on the tariff and made it as clear as anything. He said that where he is they understand all about it. At nine o'clock Miss Mutt comes out of the trance and we have cake and ice cream and arrange where the next meeting is to be.

So I need hardly tell you that in our little circle we appreciate very much indeed the sort of work that you and other leaders are doing. Miss Mutt our medium says that it will be splendid when you yourself are on the Other Side. We shall send a wave at you right away.

I am sure then that you will not take amiss the very few words of criticism that I feel inclined to add to my letter. Perhaps I should not exactly call it criticism so much as suggestion as to how things might be made better still. As things are now we have all felt a certain amount of disappointment at what seems to be the low mental standard of the spirits that talk to us. Machiavelli for instance seemed to get all mixed up about what *ad valorem* duties meant and when McSmiley, one of our members who is in the wool trade, asked him about schedule K, he seemed to get quite angry and he said that where he was there was no schedule K. Miss Mutt, our medium, reminded us afterward that Machiavelli had died of softening of the brain so I suppose that accounts for it. But I never knew that George Washington's brain had softened too before he died and that poor Longfellow had had it very badly,—indeed apparently for years.

I think, Sir, that it will help along séances like ours immensely if you could manage to do something to keep up the education of the spirits. Miss Mutt says that they have books on the other side just as we do here. But one wonders if they read them. I suppose that in a sense they must get fearfully restless rushing round in the void, and it must be hard for them to sit down quietly and pick up a book. But I do believe that if they could be persuaded to do so, it would be a splendid thing for them. Perhaps too they could be taught to play bridge, or to knit. But I think that something really ought to be done to brighten up their minds a little. McSmiley left our little group after the Machiavelli evening because he said the spirits were just a pack of dubs. We all felt that this was wrong but we decided at once to send out a thought wave at you and ask about it. I am so sorry that nothing seems to have hit you.

The Marine Excursion of the Knights of Pythias

HALF-PAST six on a July morning! The *Mariposa Belle* is at the wharf, decked in flags, with steam up ready to start.

Excursion day!

Half-past six on a July morning, and Lake Wissanotti lying in the sun as calm as glass. The opal colours of the morning light are shot from the surface of the water.

Out on the lake the last thin threads of the mist are clearing away like flecks of cotton wool.

The long call of the loon echoes over the lake. The air is cool and fresh. There is in it all the new life of the land of the silent pine and the moving waters. Lake Wissanotti in the morning sunlight! Don't talk to me of the Italian lakes, or the Tyrol or the Swiss Alps. Take them away. Move them somewhere else. I don't want them.

Excursion Day, at half-past six of a summer morning! With the boat all decked in flags and all the people in Mariposa on the wharf, and the band in peaked caps with big cornets tied to their bodies ready to play at any minute! I say! Don't tell me about the Carnival of Venice and the Delhi Durbar. Don't! I wouldn't look at them. I'd shut my eyes! For light and colour give me every time an excursion out of Mariposa down the lake to the Indian's Island out of sight in the morning mist. Talk of your Papal Zouaves and your Buckingham Palace Guard! I want to see the Mariposa band in uniform and the Mariposa Knights of Pythias with their aprons and their insignia and their picnic baskets and their five-cent cigars!

Half-past six in the morning, and all the crowd on the wharf and the boat due to leave in half an hour. Notice it!—in half an hour. Already she's whistled twice (at six, and at six fifteen), and at any minute now, Christie Johnson will step into the pilot house and pull the string for the warning whistle that the boat will leave in half an hour. So keep ready. Don't think of running back to Smith's Hotel for the sandwiches. Don't be fool enough to try to go up to the Greek Store, next to Netley's, and buy fruit. You'll be left behind for sure if you do. Never mind the sandwiches and the fruit! Anyway, here comes Mr. Smith himself with a huge basket of provender that would feed a factory. There must be sandwiches in that. I think I can hear them clinking. And behind Mr. Smith is the German waiter from the caff with another basket— indubitably lager beer; and behind him, the bar-tender of the hotel, carrying nothing, as far as one can see. But of course if you know Mariposa you will understand that why he looks so nonchalant and empty-handed is because he has two bottles of rye whiskey under his linen duster. You know, I think, the peculiar walk of a man with two bottles of whiskey in the inside pockets of a linen coat. In Mariposa, you see, to bring beer to an excursion is quite in keeping with public opinion. But, whiskey,—well, one has to be a little careful.

Do I say that Mr. Smith is here? Why, everybody's here. There's Hussell the editor of the *Newspacket,* wearing a blue ribbon on his coat, for the Mariposa Knights of Pythias are, by their constitution, dedicated to temperance and there's Henry Mullins, the manager of the Exchange Bank, also a Knight of Pythias, with a small flask of Pogram's Special in his hip pocket as a sort of amendment to the constitution. And there's Dean Drone, the

Chaplain of the Order, with a fishing-rod (you never saw such green bass as lie among the rocks at Indian's Island), and with a trolling line in case of maskinonge, and a landing net in case of pickerel, and with his eldest daughter, Lilian Drone, in case of young men. There never was such a fisherman as the Rev. Rupert Drone.

.   .   .   .

Perhaps I ought to explain that when I speak of the excursion as being of the Knights of Pythias, the thing must not be understood in any narrow sense. In Mariposa practically everybody belongs to the Knights of Pythias just as they do to everything else. That's the great thing about the town and that's what makes it so different from the city. Everybody is in everything.

You should see them on the seventeenth of March, for example, when everybody wears a green ribbon and they're all laughing and glad,—you know what the Celtic nature is,—and talking about Home Rule.

On St. Andrew's Day every man in town wears a thistle and shakes hands with everybody else, and you see the fine old Scotch honesty beaming out of their eyes.

And on St. George's Day!—well, there's no heartiness like the good old English spirit, after all; why shouldn't a man feel glad that he's an Englishman?

Then on the Fourth of July there are stars and stripes flying over half the stores in town, and suddenly all the men are seen to smoke cigars, and to know all about Roosevelt and Bryan and the Philippine Islands. Then you learn for the first time that Jeff Thorpe's people came from Massachusetts and that his uncle fought at Bunker Hill (it must have been Bunker Hill,—anyway Jefferson will swear it was in Dakota all right enough); and you find that George Duff has a married sister in Rochester and that her husband is all right; in fact, George was down there as recently as eight years ago. Oh, it's the most American town imaginable is Mariposa,—on the Fourth of July.

But wait, just wait, if you feel anxious about the solidity of the British connection, till the twelfth of the month, when everybody is wearing an orange streamer in his coat and the Orangemen (every man in town) walk in the big procession. Allegiance! Well, perhaps you remember the address they gave to the Prince of Wales on the platform of the Mariposa station as he went through on his tour to the west. I think that pretty well settled that question.

So you will easily understand that of course everybody belongs to the Knights of Pythias and the Masons and Odd Fellows, just as they all belong to the Snow Shoe Club and the Girls' Friendly Society.

And meanwhile the whistle of the steamer has blown again for a quarter to seven:—loud and long this time, for anyone not here now is late for certain, unless he should happen to come down in the last fifteen minutes.

What a crowd upon the wharf and how they pile on to the steamer! It's a wonder that the boat can hold them all. But that's just the marvellous thing about the *Mariposa Belle*.

I don't know,—I have never known,—where the steamers like the *Mariposa Belle* come from. Whether they are built by Harland and Wolff of Belfast, or whether, on the other hand, they are not built by Harland and Wolff of Belfast, is more than one would like to say offhand.

The *Mariposa Belle* always seems to me to have some of those strange properties that distinguish Mariposa itself. I mean, her size seems to vary so. If you see her there in the winter, frozen in the ice beside the wharf with a snow-drift against the windows of the pilot house, she looks a pathetic little thing the size of a butternut. But in the summer time, especially after you've been in Mariposa for a month or two, and have paddled alongside of her in a canoe, she gets larger and taller, and with a great sweep of black sides, till you see no difference between the *Mariposa Belle* and the *Lusitania*. Each one is a big steamer and that's all you can say.

Nor do her measurements help you much. She draws about eighteen inches forward, and more than that,—at least half an inch more, astern, and when she's loaded down with an excursion crowd she draws a good two inches more. And above the water,—why, look at all the decks on her! There's the deck you walk on to, from the wharf, all shut in, with windows along it, and the after cabin with the long table, and above that the deck with all the chairs piled upon it, and the deck in front where the band stand round in a circle, and the pilot house is higher than that, and above the pilot house is the board with the gold name and the flag pole and the steel ropes and the flags; and fixed in somewhere on the different levels is the lunch counter where they sell the sandwiches, and the engine room, and down below the deck level, beneath the water line, is the place where the crew sleep. What with steps and stairs and passages and piles of cordwood for the engine,—oh, no, I guess Harland and Wolff didn't build her. They couldn't have.

Yet even with a huge boat like the *Mariposa Belle*, it would be impossible for her to carry all of the crowd that you see in the boat and on the wharf. In reality, the crowd is made up of two classes,—all of the people in Mariposa who are going on the excursion and all those who are not. Some come for the one reason and some for the other.

The two tellers of the Exchange Bank are both there standing side by side. But one of them,—the one with the cameo pin and the long face like a horse,—is going, and the other,—with the other cameo pin and the face like another horse,—is not. In the same way, Hussell of the *Newspacket* is going, but his brother, beside him, isn't. Lilian Drone is going, but her sister can't; and so on all through the crowd.

. . . . . .

And to think that things should look like that on the morning of a steamboat accident.

How strange life is!

To think of all these people so eager and anxious to catch the steamer, and some of them running to catch it, and so fearful that they might miss it,—the morning of a steamboat accident. And the captain blowing his whistle, and warning them so severely that he would leave them behind, —leave them out of the accident! And everybody crowding so eagerly to be in the accident.

Perhaps life is like that all through.

Strangest of all to think, in a case like this, of the people who were left behind, or in some way or other prevented from going, and always afterwards told of how they had escaped being on board the *Mariposa Belle* that day!

Some of the instances were certainly extraordinary.

Nivens, the lawyer, escaped from being there merely by the fact that he was away in the city.

Towers, the tailor, only escaped owing to the fact that, not intending to go on the excursion he had stayed in bed till eight o'clock and so had not gone. He narrated afterwards that waking up that morning at half-past five, he had thought of the excursion and for some unaccountable reason had felt glad that he was not going.

. . . . . .

The case of Yodel, the auctioneer, was even more inscrutable. He had been to the Odd Fellows' excursion on the train the week before and to the Conservative picnic the week before that, and had decided not to go on this trip. In fact, he had not the least intention of going. He narrated afterwards how the night before someone had stopped him on the corner of Nippewa and Tecumseh Streets (he indicated the very spot) and asked: "Are you going to take in the excursion to-morrow?" and he had said, just as simply as he was talking when narrating it: "No." And ten minutes after that, at the corner of Dalhousie and Brock Streets (he offered to lead a party of verification to the precise place) somebody else had stopped him and asked: "Well, are you going on the steamer trip to-morrow?" Again he had answered: "No," apparently almost in the same tone as before.

He said afterwards that when he heard the rumour of the accident it seemed like the finger of Providence, and he fell on his knees in thankfulness.

There was the similar case of Morison (I mean the one in Glover's hardware store that married one of the Thompsons). He said afterwards that he had read so much in the papers about accidents lately,—mining accidents, and aeroplanes and gasoline,—that he had grown nervous. The night before his wife had asked him at supper: "Are you going on the excursion?" He had answered: "No, I don't think I feel like it," and had added: "Perhaps your mother might like to go." And the next evening just at dusk, when the news ran through the town, he said the first thought that flashed through his head was: "Mrs. Thompson's on that boat."

He told this right as I say it—without the least doubt or confusion. He never for a moment imagined she was on the *Lusitania* or the *Olympic* or any other boat. He knew she was on this one. He said you could have knocked him down where he stood. But no one had. Not even when he got half-way down,—on his knees, and it would have been easier still to knock him down or kick him. People do miss a lot of chances.

Still, as I say, neither Yodel nor Morison nor anyone thought about there being an accident until just after sundown when they—

Well, have you ever heard the long booming whistle of a steamboat two miles out on the lake in the dusk, and while you listen and count and wonder, seen the crimson rockets going up against the sky and then heard the fire bell ringing right there beside you in the town, and seen the people running to the town wharf?

That's what the people of Mariposa saw and felt that summer evening as they watched the Mackinaw life-boat go plunging out into the lake with seven sweeps to a side and the foam clear to the gunwale with the lifting stroke of fourteen men!

But, dear me, I am afraid that this is no way to tell a story. I suppose the true art would have been to have said nothing about the accident till it happened. But when you write about Mariposa, or hear of it, if you know the place, it's all so vivid and real that a thing like the contrast between the excursion crowd in the morning and the scene at night leaps into your mind and you must think of it.

. . . . . .

But never mind about the accident,—let us turn back again to the morning.

The boat was due to leave at seven. There was no doubt about the hour,—not only seven, but seven sharp. The notice in the *Newspacket* said: "The boat will leave sharp at seven;" and the advertising posters on the telegraph poles on Missinaba Street that began, "Ho, for Indian's Island!" ended up with the words: "Boat leaves at seven sharp." There was a big notice on the wharf that said: "Boat leaves sharp on time."

So at seven, right on the hour, the whistle blew loud and long, and then at seven fifteen three short peremptory blasts, and at seven thirty one quick angry call,—just one, —and very soon after that they cast off the last of the ropes and the *Mariposa Belle* sailed off in her cloud of flags, and the band of the Knights of Pythias, timing it to a nicety, broke into the "Maple Leaf Forever!"

I suppose that all excursions when they start are much the same. Anyway, on the Mariposa Belle everybody went running up and down all over the boat with deck chairs and camp stools and baskets, and found places, splendid places to sit, and then got scared that there might be better ones and chased off again. People hunted for places out of the sun and when they got them swore that they weren't going to freeze to please anybody; and the people in the sun said that they hadn't paid fifty cents to be roasted. Others said that they hadn't paid fifty cents to get covered with cinders, and there were still other who hadn't paid fifty cents to get shaken to death with the propeller.

Still, it was all right presently. The people seemed to get sorted out into the places on the boat where they belonged. The women, the older ones, all gravitated into the cabin on the lower deck and by getting round the table with needlework, and with all the windows shut, they soon had it, as they said themselves, just like being at home.

All the young boys and the toughs and the men in the band got down on the lower deck forward, where the boat was dirtiest and where the anchor was and the coils of rope.

And upstairs on the after deck there were Lilian Drone and Miss Lawson, the high school teacher, with a book of German poetry,—Gothey I think it was,—and the bank teller and the younger men.

In the centre, standing beside the rail, were Dean Drone

and Dr. Gallagher, looking through binocular glasses at the shore.

Up in front on the little deck forward of the pilot house was a group of the older men, Mullins and Duff and Mr. Smith in a deck chair, and beside him Mr. Golgotha Gingham, the undertaker of Mariposa, on a stool. It was part of Mr. Gingham's principles to take in an outing of this sort, a business matter, more or less,—for you never know what may happen at these water parties. At any rate, he was there in a neat suit of black, not, of course, his heavier or professional suit, but a soft clinging effect as of burnt paper that combined gaiety and decorum to a nicety.

. . . .

"Yes," said Mr. Gingham, waving his black glove in a general way towards the shore, "I know the lake well, very well. I've been pretty much all over it in my time."

"Canoeing?" asked somebody.

"No," said Mr. Gingham, "not in a canoe." There seemed a peculiar and quiet meaning in his tone.

"Sailing, I suppose," said somebody else.

"No," said Mr. Gingham. "I don't understand it."

"I never knowed that you went on to the water at all, Gol," said Mr. Smith, breaking in.

"Ah, not now," explained Mr. Gingham; "it was years ago, the first summer I came to Mariposa. I was on the water practically all day. Nothing like it to give a man an appetite and keep him in shape."

"Was you camping?" asked Mr. Smith.

"We camped at night," assented the undertaker, "but we put in practically the whole day on the water. You see we were after a party that had gone up here from the city on his vacation and gone out in a sailing canoe. We were dragging. We were up every morning at sunrise, lit a fire on the beach and cooked breakfast, and then we'd light our pipes and be off with the net for a whole day. It's a great life," concluded Mr. Gingham wistfully.

"Did you get him?" asked two or three together.

There was a pause before Mr. Gingham answered.

"We did," he said, "down in the reeds past Horseshoe Point. But it was no use. He turned blue on me right away."

After which Mr. Gingham fell into such a deep reverie that the boat had steamed another half-mile down the lake before anybody broke the silence again.

Talk of this sort,—and after all what more suitable for a day on the water?—beguiled the way.

. . . .

Down the lake, mile by mile over the calm water, steamed the *Mariposa Belle*. They passed Poplar Point where the high sand-banks are with all the swallows' nests in them, and Dean Drone and Dr. Gallagher looked at them alternately through the binocular glasses, and it was wonderful how plainly one could see the swallows and the banks and the shrubs,—just as plainly as with the naked eye.

And a little further down they passed the Shingle Beach, and Dr. Gallagher, who knew Canadian history, said to Dean Drone that it was strange to think that Champlain had landed there with his French explorers three hundred years ago; and Dean Drone, who didn't know Canadian history, said it was stranger still to think that the hand of the Almighty had piled up the hills and rocks long before that; and Dr. Gallagher said it was wonderful how the French had found their way through such a pathless wilderness; and Dean Drone said that it was wonderful also to think that the Almighty had placed even the smallest shrub in its appointed place. Dr. Gallagher said it filled him with admiration. Dean Drone said it filled him with awe.

Dr. Gallagher said he'd been full of it ever since he was a boy; and Dean Drone said so had he.

Then a little further, as the *Mariposa Belle* steamed on down the lake, they passed the Old Indian Portage where the great grey rocks are; and Dr. Gallagher drew Dean Drone's attention to the place where the narrow canoe track wound up from the shore to the woods, and Dean Drone said he could see it perfectly well without the glasses.

Dr. Gallagher said that it was just here that a party of five hundred French had made their way with all their baggage and accoutrements across the rocks of the divide and down to the Great Bay. And Dean Drone said that it reminded him of Xenophon leading his ten thousand Greeks over the hill passes of Armenia down to the sea. Dr. Gallagher said that he had often wished he could have seen and spoken to Champlain, and Dean Drone said how much he regretted to have never known Xenophon.

And then after that they fell to talking of relics and traces of the past, and Dr. Gallagher said that if Dean Drone would come round to his house some night he would show him some Indian arrow heads that he had dug up in his garden. And Dean Drone said that if Dr. Gallagher would come round to the rectory any afternoon he would show him a map of Xerxes' invasion of Greece. Only he must come some time between the Infant Class and the Mothers' Auxiliary.

So presently they both knew that they were blocked out of one another's houses for some time to come, and Dr. Gallagher walked forward and told Mr. Smith, who had never studied Greek, about Champlain crossing the rock divide.

Mr. Smith turned his head and looked at the divide for half a second and then said he had crossed a worse one up north back of the Wahnipitae and that the flies were Hades,

—and then went on playing freeze out poker with the two juniors in Duff's bank.

So Dr. Gallagher realized that that's always the way when you try to tell people things, and that as far as gratitude and appreciation goes one might as well never read books or travel anywhere or do anything.

In fact, it was at this very moment that he made up his mind to give the arrows to the Mariposa Mechanics' Institute,—they afterwards became, as you know, the Gallagher Collection. But, for the time being, the doctor was sick of them and wandered off round the boat and watched Henry Mullins showing George Duff how to make a John Collins without lemons, and finally went and sat down among the Mariposa band and wished that he hadn't come.

So the boat steamed on and the sun rose higher and higher, and the freshness of the morning changed into the full glare of noon, and they went on to where the lake began to narrow in at its foot, just where the Indian's Island is,—all grass and trees and with a log wharf running into the water. Below it the Lower Ossawippi runs out of the lake, and quite near are the rapids, and you can see down among the trees the red brick of the power house and hear the roar of the leaping water.

The Indian's Island itself is all covered with trees and tangled vines, and the water about it is so still that it's all reflected double and looks the same either way up. Then when the steamer's whistle blows as it comes into the wharf, you hear it echo among the trees of the island, and reverberate back from the shores of the lake.

The scene is all so quiet and still and unbroken, that Miss Cleghorn—the sallow girl in the telephone exchange, that I spoke of—said she'd like to be buried there. But all the people were so busy getting their baskets and gathering up their things that no one had time to attend to it.

I mustn't even try to describe the landing and the boat crunching against the wooden wharf and all the people running to the same side of the deck and Christie Johnson calling out to the crowd to keep to the starboard and nobody being able to find it. Everyone who has been on a Mariposa excursion knows all about that.

Nor can I describe the day itself and the picnic under the trees. There were speeches afterwards, and Judge Pepperleigh gave such offence by bringing in Conservative politics that a man called Patriotus Canadiensis wrote and asked for some of the invaluable space of the Mariposa *Times-Herald* and exposed it.

I should say that there were races too, on the grass on the open side of the island, graded mostly according to ages, —races for boys under thirteen and girls over nineteen and all that sort of thing. Sports are generally conducted on that plan in Mariposa. It is realized that a woman of sixty has an unfair advantage over a mere child.

Dean Drone managed the races and decided the ages and gave out the prizes; the Wesleyan minister helped, and he and the young student, who was relieving in the Presbyterian Church, held the string at the winning point.

They had to get mostly clergymen for the races because all the men had wandered off, somehow, to where they were drinking lager beer out of two kegs stuck on pine logs among the trees.

But if you've ever been on a Mariposa excursion you know all about these details anyway.

So the day wore on and presently the sun came through the trees on a slant and the steamer whistle blew with a great puff of white steam and all the people came straggling down to the wharf and pretty soon the *Mariposa Belle* had floated out on to the lake again and headed for the town, twenty miles away.

    .   .   .   .

I suppose you have often noticed the contrast there is between an excursion on its way out in the morning and what it looks like on the way home.

In the morning everybody is so restless and animated and moves to and fro all over the boat and asks questions. But coming home, as the afternoon gets later and later and the sun sinks beyond the hills, all the people seem to get so still and quiet and drowsy.

So it was with the people on the *Mariposa Belle*. They sat there on the benches and the deck chairs in little clusters, and listened to the regular beat of the propeller and almost dozed off asleep as they sat. Then when the sun set and the dusk drew on, it grew almost dark on the deck and so still that you could hardly tell there was anyone on board.

And if you had looked at the steamer from the shore or from one of the islands, you'd have seen the row of lights from the cabin windows shining on the water and the red glare of the burning hemlock from the funnel, and you'd have heard the soft thud of the propeller miles away over the lake.

Now and then, too, you could have heard them singing on the steamer,—the voices of the girls and the men blended into unison by the distance, rising and falling in long-drawn melody: "O—Can-a-da—O—Can-a-da."

You may talk as you will about the intoning choirs of your European cathedrals, but the sound of "O Can-a-da," borne across the waters of a silent lake at evening is good enough for those of us who know Mariposa.

I think that it was just as they were singing like this: "O—Can-a-da," that word went round that the boat was sinking.

If you have ever been in any sudden emergency on the water, you will understand the strange psychology of it,— the way in which what is happening seems to become known all in a moment without a word being said. The news is transmitted from one to the other by some mysterious process.

At any rate, on the *Mariposa Belle* first one and then the other heard that the steamer was sinking. As far as I could ever learn the first of it was that George Duff, the bank manager, came very quietly to Dr. Gallagher and asked him if he thought that the boat was sinking. The doctor said no, that he had thought so earlier in the day but that he didn't now think that she was.

After that Duff, according to his own account, had said to Macartney, the lawyer, that the boat was sinking, and Macartney said that he doubted it very much.

Then somebody came to Judge Pepperleigh and woke him up and said that there was six inches of water in the steamer and that she was sinking. And Pepperleigh said it was perfect scandal and passed the news on to his wife and she said that they had no business to allow it and that if the steamer sank that was the last excursion she'd go on.

So the news went all round the boat and everywhere the people gathered in groups and talked about it in the angry and excited way that people have when a steamer is sinking on one of the lakes like Lake Wissanotti.

Dean Drone, of course, and some others were quieter about it, and said that one must make allowances and that naturally there were two sides to everything. But most of them wouldn't listen to reason at all. I think, perhaps, that some of them were frightened. You see the last time but one that the steamer had sunk, there had been a man drowned and it made them nervous.

What? Hadn't I explained about the depth of Lake Wissanotti? I had taken it for granted that you knew; and in any case parts of it are deep enough, though I don't suppose in this stretch of it from the big reed beds up to within a mile of the town wharf, you could find six feet of water in it if you tried. Oh, pshaw! I was not talking about a steamer sinking in the ocean and carrying down its screaming crowds of people into the hideous depths of green water. Oh, dear me, no! That kind of thing never happens on Lake Wissanotti.

But what does happen is that the *Mariposa Belle* sinks every now and then, and sticks there on the bottom till they get things straightened up.

On the lakes round Mariposa, if a person arrives late anywhere and explains that the steamer sank everybody understands the situation.

You see when Harland and Wolff built the *Mariposa Belle*, they left some cracks in between the timbers that you fill up with cotton waste every Sunday. If this is not attended to, the boat sinks. In fact, it is part of the law of the province that all the steamers like the *Mariposa Belle* must be properly corked,—I think that is the word,— every season. There are inspectors who visit all the hotels in the province to see that it is done.

So you can imagine now that I've explained it a little straighter, the indignation of the people when they knew that the boat had come uncorked and that they might be stuck out there on a shoal or a mud-bank half the night.

I don't say either that there wasn't any danger; anyway, it doesn't feel very safe when you realize that the boat is settling down with every hundred yards that she goes, and you look over the side and see only the black water in the gathering night.

Safe! I'm not sure now that I come to think of it that it isn't worse than sinking in the Atlantic. After all, in the Atlantic there is wireless telegraphy, and a lot of trained sailors and stewards. But out on Lake Wissanotti, —far out, so that you can only just see the lights of the town away off to the south,—when the propeller comes to a stop,—and you can hear the hiss of steam as they start to rake out the engine fires to prevent an explosion,—and when you turn from the red glare that comes from the furnace doors as they open them, to the black dark that is gathering over the lake,—and there's a night wind beginning to run among the rushes,—and you see the men going forward to the roof of the pilot house to send up the rockets to rouse the town,—safe? Safe yourself, if you like; as for me, let me once get back into Mariposa again, under the night shadow of the maple trees, and this shall be the last, last time I'll go on Lake Wissanotti.

Safe! Oh, yes! Isn't it strange how safe other people's adventures seem after they happen? But you'd have been scared, too, if you'd been there just before the steamer sank, and seen them bringing up all the women on to the top deck.

I don't see how some of the people took it so calmly; how Mr. Smith, for instance, could have gone on smoking and telling how he'd had a steamer "sink on him" on Lake Nipissing and a still bigger one, a side-wheeler, sink on him in Lake Abbitibbi.

Then, quite suddenly, with a quiver, down she went. You could feel the boat sink, sink,—down, down,—would it never get to the bottom? The water came flush up to the lower deck, and then—thank heaven—the sinking stopped and there was the *Mariposa Belle* safe and tight on a reed bank.

Really, it made one positively laugh! It seemed so queer and, anyway, if a man has a sort of natural courage, danger makes him laugh. Danger? pshaw! fiddlesticks! everybody scouted the idea. Why, it is just the little things like this that give zest to a day on the water.

Within half a minute they were all running round looking for sandwiches and cracking jokes and talking of making coffee over the remains of the engine fires.

. . . .

I don't need to tell at length how it all happened after that.

I suppose the people on the *Mariposa Belle* would have had to settle down there all night or till help came from the town, but some of the men who had gone forward and were peering out into the dark said that it couldn't be more than a mile across the water to Miller's Point. You could almost see it over there to the left,—some of them, I think, said "off on the port bow," because you know when you get mixed up in these marine disasters, you soon catch the atmosphere of the thing.

So pretty soon they had the davits swung out over the side and were lowering the old lifeboat from the top deck into the water.

"There were men leaning out over the rail of the *Mariposa Belle* with lanterns that threw the light as they let her down, and the glare fell on the water and the reeds. But when they got the boat lowered, it looked such a frail, clumsy thing as one saw it from the rail above, that the cry was raised: "Women and children first!" For what was the sense, if it should turn out that the boat wouldn't even hold women and children, of trying to jam a lot of heavy men into it?

So they put in mostly women and children and the boat pushed out into the darkness so freighted down it would hardly float.

In the bow of it was the Presbyterian student who was relieving the minister, and he called out that they were in the hands of Providence. But he was crouched and ready to spring out of them at the first moment.

So the boat went and was lost in the darkness except for the lantern in the bow that you could see bobbing on the water. Then presently it came back and they sent another load, till pretty soon the decks began to thin out and everybody got impatient to be gone.

It was about the time that the third boatload put off that Mr. Smith took a bet with Mullins for twenty-five dollars, that he'd be home in Mariposa before the people in the boats had walked round the shore.

No one knew just what he meant, but pretty soon they saw Mr. Smith disappear down below into the lowest part of the steamer with a mallet in one hand and a big bundle of marline in the other.

They might have wondered more about it, but it was just at this time that they heard the shouts from the rescue boat—the big Mackinaw lifeboat—that had put out from the town with fourteen men at the sweeps when they saw the first rockets go up.

I suppose there is always something inspiring about a rescue at sea, or on the water.

After all, the bravery of the lifeboat man is the true bravery,—expended to save life, not to destroy it.

Certainly they told for months after of how the rescue boat came out to the *Mariposa Belle*.

I suppose that when they put her in the water the lifeboat touched it for the first time since the old Macdonald Government placed her on Lake Wissanotti.

Anyway, the water poured in at every seam. But not for a moment,—even with two miles of water between them and the steamer,—did the rowers pause for that.

By the time they were half-way there the water was almost up to the thwarts, but they drove her on. Panting and exhausted (for mind you, if you haven't been in a fool boat like that for years, rowing takes it out of you), the rowers stuck to their task. They threw the ballast over and chucked into the water the heavy cork jackets and life-belts that encumbered their movements. There was no thought of turning back. They were nearer to the steamer than the shore.

"Hang to it, boys," called the crowd from the steamer's deck, and hang they did.

They were almost exhausted when they got them; men leaning from the steamer threw them ropes and one by one every man was hauled aboard just as the lifeboat sank under their feet.

Saved! by Heaven, saved by one of the smartest pieces of rescue work ever seen on the lake.

There's no use describing it; you need to see rescue work of this kind by lifeboats to understand it.

Nor were the lifeboat crew the only ones that distinguished themselves.

Boat after boat and canoe after canoe had put out from Mariposa to the help of the steamer. They got them all.

Pupkin, the other bank teller, with a face like a horse, who hadn't gone on the excursion,—as soon as he knew that the boat was signalling for help and that Miss Lawson was sending up rockets,—rushed for a row boat, grabbed an oar (two would have hampered him), and paddled madly out into the lake. He struck right out into the dark with the crazy skiff almost sinking beneath his feet. But they got him. They rescued him. They watched

him, almost dead with exhaustion, make his way to the
steamer, where he was hauled up with ropes. Saved!
Saved!

.   .   .   .

They might have gone on that way half the night, picking up the rescuers, only, at the very moment when the
tenth load of people left for the shore,—just as suddenly
and saucily as you please, up came the *Mariposa Belle* from
the mud bottom and floated.

FLOATED?

Why, of course she did. If you take a hundred and
fifty people off a steamer that has sunk, and if you get a
man as shrewd as Mr. Smith to plug the timber seams with
mallet and marline, and if you turn ten bandsmen of the
Mariposa band on to your hand pump on the bow of the
lower decks—float? why, what else can she do?

Then, if you stuff in hemlock into the embers of the fire
that you were raking out, till it hums and crackles under
the boiler, it won't be long before you hear the propeller
thud—thudding at the stern again, and before the long
roar of the steam whistle echoes over to the town.

And so the *Mariposa Belle,* with all steam up again and
with the long train of sparks careering from the funnel,
is heading for the town.

But no Christie Johnson at the wheel in the pilot house
this time.

"Smith! Get Smith!" is the cry.

Can he take her in? Well, now! Ask a man who has
had steamers sink on him in half the lakes from Temiscam-
ing to the Bay, if he can take her in? Ask a man who
has run a York boat down the rapids of the Moose when
the ice is moving, if he can grip the steering wheel of the
Mariposa Belle? So there she steams safe and sound to
the town wharf!

Look at the lights and the crowd! If only the federal census taker could count us now! Hear them calling and shouting back and forward from the deck to the shore! Listen! There is the rattle of the shore ropes as they get them ready, and there's the Mariposa band,—actually forming in a circle on the upper deck just as she docks, and the leader with his baton,—one—two—ready now,—

"O CAN-A-DA!"

My Lost Dollar

MY friend Todd owes me a dollar. He has owed it to me for twelve months, and I fear there is little prospect of his ever returning it. I can realize whenever I meet him that he has forgotten that he owes me a dollar. He meets me in the same frank friendly way as always. My dollar has clean gone out of his mind. I see that I shall never get it back.

On the other hand I know that I shall remember all my life that Todd owes me a dollar. It will make no difference, I trust, to our friendship, but I shall never be able to forget it. I don't know how it is with other people; but if any man borrows a dollar from me I carry the recollection of it to the grave.

Let me relate what happened. Todd borrowed this dollar last year on the 8th of April (I mention the date in case this should ever meet Todd's eye), just as he was about to leave for Bermuda. He needed a dollar in change to pay his taxi; and I lent it to him. It happened quite simply and naturally, I hardly realized it till it was all over. He merely said "Let me have a dollar, will you!" And I said, "Certainly. Is a dollar enough?" I believe, in fact I *know*, that when Todd took that dollar he meant to pay for it.

He sent me a note from Hamilton, Bermuda. I thought when I opened it that the dollar would be in it. But it wasn't. He merely said that the temperature was up to nearly 100. The figure misled me for a moment.

Todd came back in three weeks. I met him at the train, —not because of the dollar, but because I really esteem him. I felt it would be nice for him to see someone waiting for him on the platform after being away for three weeks. I said, "Let's take a taxi up to the Club." But he answered, "No, let's walk."

We spent the evening together, talking about Bermuda. I was thinking of the dollar but of course I didn't refer to it. One simply can't. I asked him what currency is used in Bermuda, and whether the American Dollar goes at par. (I put a slight emphasis on *the* American Dollar), but found again that I could not bring myself to make any reference to it.

It took me some time (I see Todd practically every day at my Club) to realize that he had completely forgotten the dollar. I asked him one day what his trip cost him and he said that he kept no accounts. A little later I asked him if he felt settled down after his trip, and he said that he had practically forgotten about it. So I knew it was all over.

In all this I bear Todd no grudge. I have simply added him to the list of men who owe me a dollar and who have forgotten it. There are quite a few of them now. I make no difference in my demeanour to them, but I only wish that I could forget.

I meet Todd very frequently. Only two nights ago I met him out at dinner and he was talking, apparently without self-consciousness, about Poland. He said that Poland would never pay her debts. You'd think a thing like that would have reminded him, wouldn't you? But it didn't seem to.

But meantime a thought,—a rather painful thought,—has begun to come in to my mind at intervals. It is this. If Todd owes me a dollar and has forgotten it, it is possible—indeed it is theoretically probable—that there must be men to whom I owe a dollar which I have forgotten.

There may be a list of them. The more I think of it the less I like it, because I am quite sure that if I had once forgotten a dollar, I should never pay it, on this side of the grave.

If there *are* such men I want them to speak out. Not all at once: but in reasonable numbers, and as far as may be in alphabetical order, and I will immediately, write their names down on paper. I don't count here men who may have lent me an odd dollar over a bridge table: and I am not thinking (indeed I am taking care not to think) of the man who lent me thirty cents to pay for a bottle of plain soda in the Detroit Athletic Club last month. I always find that there's nothing like plain soda after a tiring ride across the Canadian frontier, and that man who advanced that thirty cents knows exactly why I felt that I had done enough for him. But if any man ever lent me a dollar to pay for a taxi when I was starting for Bermuda, I want to pay it.

More than that: I want to start a general movement, a *Back to Honesty* movement, for paying all these odd dollars that are borrowed in moments of expansion. Let us remember that the greatest nations were built up on the rock basis of absolute honesty.

In conclusion may I say that I do particularly ask that no reader of this book will be careless enough to leave this copy round where it might be seen by Major Todd, of the University Club of Montreal.

Personal Experiments with the Black Bass

IT was my good fortune to spend a large part of the summer just past in fishing for bass. The season may be regarded as now definitely closed, and the time is appropriate for a scientific summarizing of the results achieved and the information gained.

My experiments are entitled to all the greater weight in as much as a large part of them were conducted in the immediate presence of so well known a man as Mr. John Counsell of Hamilton, Ontario, who acted as my assistant. Mr. Counsell very kindly permits me to say that all statements, measurements, and estimates of weight contained in the following discussion are personally vouched for by him. He has even offered to lend his oath, or any number of his oaths, to the accuracy of my statements. But it has been thought wiser not to use Mr. Counsell's oath in print.

I take this opportunity in turn to express my high appreciation of the hardihood, the endurance and the quiet courage manifested by my assistant throughout our experiments. If Mr. Counsell was ever afraid of a bass I never knew it. I have seen him immersed in mud on the banks of the river where we fished. I have observed him submerged under rapids; I have seen Mr. Counsell fall from the top of rocks into water so deep and remain under so long that I was just cranking up our car to go home, and yet I never knew him to hesitate for a moment to attack a black bass at sight and kill it.

I can guarantee to anybody who is hesitating whether or not to invite Mr. Counsell to go fishing, that he is a man who may safely be taken anywhere where the bass are, and is an adornment to any party of sportsmen.

I turn therefore with added confidence to the tabulated results drawn by myself and Mr. Counsell from our experiments.

In the first place, we are able to throw much light on the vexed question as to the circumstances under which the bass bite. There has been a persistent belief that during the glare of the middle part of the day the bass do not bite. This belief is correct. They do not. It is also true that in the sunnier part of the morning itself the black bass do not, or does not, bite. Nor do they, or rather does it, bite during the more drowsy part of the afternoon.

Let the angler, therefore, on a day when the sun is bright in a cloudless sky, lay aside his rod from eight in the morning till six in the afternoon. On such a day as this the fish do not bite. The experienced angler knows this. He selects a suitable tree, lies down beneath it and waits. Nor do the bass, oddly enough, bite, on a cloudy day. The bass dislike clouds. Very often the appearance of a single cloud on the horizon is a sign for the experienced angler to retire to a quiet spot upon the bank and wait till the cloud goes by. It has been said that the bass bite well in the rain. This is an error. They don't.

Another popular error that ought, in the interest of the young angler to be dispelled is that the bass bite in the evening; that is not so. The bass loves the day, and at the first sign of darkness it sinks to the bottom of the water from which it obstinately refuses to move.

I am well aware that the young angler might find himself seriously discouraged at what has just been said. "What then!" he might ask, "do the bass never bite at all? Is it never possible to get a bite from them?" To this I answer very positively that they both do and it is.

The results, in fine, of the experiments carried on by Mr. Counsell and myself lead us to the conclusion that the bass bites at midnight. We offer this only as a preliminary hypothesis, for which perhaps a more ample verification will be found in the ensuing season. We ourselves have never fished till midnight. And we observed that even the most persistent angler, as the darkness gathers around him, becomes discouraged, and at some time before midnight, quits. Here he is in error. Our advice to the angler in all such cases is to keep on until midnight. The black bass which is chary of biting in the glare of the day and which dislikes the cool of the evening, must, we argue, be just in the mood needed at midnight.

Nor let the young angler run away with the idea that the black bass *never* bits in the daytime. If he (the young angler) does this he must be hauled in again on the reel of actual experience. They do and they have. I recall in particular one case in point in the experiments of Mr. Counsell and myself. At the time of which I speak we were fishing from a rocky ledge at the edge of the river that was the scene of our operations. The circumstances were most propitious. The hour was just before daylight, so that there was still an agreeable sense of chilliness in the air. It was raining heavily as we took our places on the rock. Much of this rain, though not all of it, had gone down our shirts. There had been a certain amount of lightning, two cracks of which had hit Mr. Counsell in the neck. In short, the surroundings, were all that the most ardent fisherman could desire.

For a moment the rain cleared, a first beam of sunlight appeared through the woods on the bank, and at that very moment Mr. Counsell called to me that he had a bite. I immediately dropped my rod into the river, and urged Mr. Counsell to avoid all excitement; to keep as calm as possible, and to maintain his hold upon his line. Mr. Counsell in turn exhorted me to be cool, and assured me of his absolute readiness should the fish bite again to take whatever action the circumstances might seem to us to warrant. I asked him in the meantime whether he was prepared to give me an idea of the dimensions of the fish which had bitten him. He assured me that he could, and to my great delight informed me that the fish was at least three feet long. The reader may imagine, then, with what suppressed excitement Mr. Counsell and I waited for this monster to return and bite again. Nor had we long to wait. Not more than two or three minutes had elapsed when I suddenly saw my assistant's line in violent commotion, Mr. Counsell exerting his whole strength in a magnificent combat with the fish. I called to Mr. Counsell to be cautious and adjured him to the utmost calmness, running up and down on the bank and waving my arms to emphasize what I said. But there was no need for such an exhortation. Mr. Counsell had settled down to one of those steady fights with the black bass which are the proudest moments in the angler's life. The line was now drawn absolutely taut and motionless. Mr. Counsell was exerting his full strength at one end and the fish, apparently lying at a point of vantage at the very bottom of the river, was exerting its full strength at the other. But here intervened one of those disappointments which the angler must learn to bear as best he may. The bass is nothing if not cunning. And an older, larger fish of the extraordinary size and mass of the one in question shows often an almost incredible strategy in escaping from the hook. After a few minutes of hard strain my assistant suddenly became aware that the fish had left his hook, and at the very moment of escaping had contrived to fasten the hook deep into a log at the bottom of the river. Investigation with a pike pole showed this to be the case. This trick on the part of the bass is, of course, familiar to all experienced anglers. It was fortunate in this case that Mr. Counsell had contrived to get such an accurate estimate of the size of the fish before it escaped.

The young angler may well ask how it is that we are able to know the size of a fish as soon as it bites, without even the slightest glimpse of it. To this I can merely answer that we do know. It is, I suppose, an instinct. The young angler will get it himself if he goes on fishing long enough.

Nor need it be supposed that there is anything unusual or out of the way in the means of escape adopted by the particular bass in question. Indeed, I have on various occasions known the bass not merely to contrive to pass the hook into a log, but even, after it has been firmly hooked, to substitute a smaller fish than itself. I recall in particular one occasion when Mr. Counsell called to me that he had a fish. I ran to his side at once, encouraging and exhorting him as I did so. In this instance the fish came towards the top of the water with a rush: we were both able to distinguish it clearly as it moved below the surface. It was a magnificent black bass measuring seventeen inches from its face to its tail, and weighing four and a half pounds. The gleam of its scales as it shot through the foaming water is a sight that I shall not readily forget. The fish dived low. Meantime, Mr. Counsell had braced himself so as to exert his full strength and I placed myself behind him with my arms around his body to prevent the fish from dragging him into the stream. By this strategy the fish was thrown clear up on the rock, where Mr. Counsell attacked it at once and beat the breath out of it with a boat hook. But judge of our surprise when we found that the fish landed was not the fish originally caught on the hook. The bass had contrived in its downward plunge to free itself from the hook and to replace itself by a yellow perch six inches long.

From what has been said above, it is only too clear that the life of the black bass fisherman has its disappointments and its hardships. The black bass is wary and elusive, more crafty, for example, than the lobster, and a gamer fighter than the sardine. The angler must face danger and discomfort. He gets rained upon: he falls into the river: he gets struck by lightning. But, for myself, when the ice of the winter has cleared away and the new season opens up, I ask no better fate than to be out again at daybreak with Mr. Counsell sitting on a rock beside the river, with the rain soaking into our shirts, waiting for a bite.

The Restoration of Whiskers a Neglected Factor in the Decline of Knowledge

THERE comes a time in the life of western civilization when it is the duty of every well-wisher of the world to speak out what is in his mind. Such a time is now. The growth of the clean-shaving habit in this epoch is becoming everywhere a serious national menace. The loss of dignity and prestige, the decline of respect towards the aged, the notable change in the character and calibre of our legislators, college presidents and ministers of the gospel, is, and are, assuming proportions which urgently demand concerted national action.

The writer of this article stood recently upon the corner of Broadway and Forty-second Street in New York,—that is to say I stood there myself,—let there be no concealment in this thing,—stood there and counted the clean-shaven men who passed and the men with whiskers. Out of the first half million counted only 4.19 men per cent had whiskers.

(The man that I counted as .19 had just a little fringe of fluff, so to speak, on his cheeks. It was hard to class him. So I called him .19).

The same calculation may be made with the same results in any of the great eastern cities. It is not till one passes a line drawn through Fargo, Omaha, and Galveston that whiskers reach 15 per cent. And this 15 per cent line *is moving westwards!* Ten years ago it was at Decatur, Illinois. It is not there now! In another ten years the line will have reached the Rocky Mountains. In twenty years the entire nation will be clean-shaven.

The moment to act is now. It is time for the people to pause and realize what whiskers have meant to human civilization.

We turn to the records of history; Adam,—he had a dark brown beard slightly pointed; Noah,—he had a long white beard that reached his waist. Imagine Noah clean-shaven and with his eyebrows darkened with black dye, and with little beady eyes looking down under a straw hat! You can't? Of course not. And yet that man saved our whole race.

Nestor and Aristotle had white beards. Socrates' whiskers covered so much of his face that you could hardly see him through them. Cæsar had a rough red beard. The Vikings had long side moustaches. So had Buffalo Bill, and Charles the Second, and Bret Harte. Grant and Lee wore beards. But these great precedents are being disregarded. All the dignitaries and leaders of to-day are fashioning themselves into the likeness of schoolboys.

Take the typical case of the college presidents. A generation ago the college president had a flowing white beard. It was part of his equipment. I remember well the venerable gentleman who was the head of the University when I received my degree thirty something years ago. I shall always recall the profound respect that the students felt toward him. Yet it was not what the man *said*: it was the way in which he laid his snow white whiskers on his reading desk. This lent profundity to all his thought. It was, I think, in the year 1892 that the president of a western college shaved off his whiskers and threw them in the Mississippi. The fatal idea spread. President after president was tempted by it. Then at this very juncture the invention of the safety razor,—removing all danger to human life from the process of shaving,—brought a clean shave within the reach even of the most cautious. The president of the modern college and his senior professors are not to be distinguished from their first year students. Remove the whiskers and you remove the man. The whole stature and appearance of him shrink: his shoulders contract: his frame diminishes: his little bowler hat swallows and envelops his trivial skull.

The loss of scholarship is irreparable. Is it any wonder that Greek is dead, that Latin is dying and that the old time learning of the colleges gives place to a mere mechanical routine.

But most deploring of all is the damage that is being done to imaginative literature. Here, for example, are a few quotations selected, quite at random, from the great literature of the past to show the close interdependence of personality and whiskers:—

"The Duke remained seated in deep thought, passing his luxuriant beard slowly through his fingers."

(Ouida.)

Imagine what an impressive thing that must have been. The Duke could take his beard and let it trickle slowly through his fingers like rippling silk. No wonder that the Duke could *think*, when he could do that!

But all that can remain of that sort of passage in the books of to-day would run,

"The Duke remained seated in deep thought, passing his fingers aimlessly through the air a foot from his face, as if seeking, groping for something that he could not find."

Here again is a selection from the poet Gray's magnificent description of a Welsh bard.

"All loose his hoary hair, his beard
   Streamed like a meteor to the troubled wind."

(Gray, The Bard.)

The splendid picture,—the bard standing in the wind with the sparks flying from his whiskers in all directions, —is gone.

Or again, take Longfellow,—the opening lines of Evangeline.

"This is the forest primeval, the murmuring pines and the
     hemlocks
 Stand like Druids of old with beards that rest on their
     bosoms."

What a pity to have to change this to read:

"This is the forest primeval, the round smooth trunk of
     the gum tree
 Looks like a college professor divested entirely of
     whiskers."

In place of these noble pictures of the past we have nothing but the smooth-shaven hero of modern fiction, with his soopy-looking face, hardly to be distinguished from a girl's. He may be seen on the cover of any of our monthly magazines. What can he do? He can *press his clean-shaven face close, close to hers.* One admits, of course, that he has a certain advantage here. If he had whiskers he couldn't get nearly as close to her. But can he let his beard stream like a meteor to the wind with sparks of phosphorus flying off it in all directions? Can he "pass his beard through his hand?" No. Can he stand like a Druid of old? He can't.

As yet, happily, there are certain domains of our national life to which the prevailing degeneracy has not penetrated. The stage, the moving picture and the grand opera still hold their own. The stage villain still has his black beard. The Southern colonel still retains his mustachios. The scholar, the wise man and the magician of the moving picture keeps his black skull cap and his long white beard. The Wagnerian opera is as hirsute as ever. And those who have been privileged to see the pretty little operetta that Reginald de Koven left behind him, will have been pleased to note that Rip Van Winkle has a beard like an Ostermoor mattress reaching to his ears.

But can the stage stand alone? It can not. Something must be done. . . .

Fortunately for our civilization the best section of the public is already becoming alarmed. An effort is being made. A number of big, warm-hearted men, and a quantity of great big warm-blooded women are banding themselves together. This is a good sign. Whenever they do this,—and it is what they always do,—one feels that as soon as a sufficient number are all banded together something will be done.

As far as the United States is concerned to my mind there is only one possible remedy,—an amendment to the Constitution. Something, of course, might be done with magic lantern slides, or with moving pictures, or by taking up subscriptions. But these things demand money and time. Amending the Constitution does not. Experience is showing that it is a very, very simple thing, demanding only a little good will and forbearance as to which amendment gets through first. It is only fair that certain amendments now under discussion should have precedence. The proposal sent up from Kansas for amending the Constitution so as to improve the breed of steers in the West, and the Illinois amendment for shortening the distance between Chicago and the sea, are both admirable. But when these are carried an amendment in regard to the restoration of whiskers should be the earliest of our national cares. Individual freedom has its limits.

It is *not* true that a man's whiskers are his own. It is *not* true that he has the right to remove them. John Stuart Mill thought so. But Mill was wrong. Every individual is but a part of society; and if his station is such that a flowing white beard is demanded by it, his duty is obvious. No one would wish to carry too far the supremacy of the State. But a constitutional provision of a temperate character imposing compulsory white beards on college presidents, ministers, poets, ambassadors and grand opera singers would take rank at once as equal in common sense and general utility with some of the most notable amendments to the Constitution of this Country.

THEN AND NOW

THE COLLEGE NEWS OF FORTY YEARS AGO AND THE COLLEGE NEWS OF TO-DAY

Medicals Take a Night Off

(AS REPORTED FORTY YEARS AGO)

Last night the students of the Medical Faculty took a night off and held their annual parade of the town. Forming up on the campus outside the windows of the dissecting room, the "Meds" moved in a compact body down College Avenue. Policeman McKonicky, who tried to stop them at the corner of Main Street, was knocked senseless and was deposited by two of the boys down the coal chute of the First National Bank. After upsetting a horse-car, the driver of which sustained certain injuries by inadvertently falling under the horse, the boys proceeded to the corner of Main and First Streets where speeches were made exalting the progress of the Medical School, and where two more policemen were knocked senseless. The procession moved uptown again towards the president's residence carrying with it the front door of the First Baptist Church. After setting fire to the president's house the students adjourned to the campus where they started a bonfire in which, unfortunately, one or two bystanders were accidentally burned about the feet, hands, head and body. The arrival of a body of mounted police supported by a couple of squadrons of cavalry brought the evening to a close.

President Foible, on being interviewed this morning, stated that the damages to his house were quite insignificant, amounting to little more than the destruction of his furniture. The police who were unfortunately injured in their attempt to interfere with the students are reported as doing nicely. The driver of the street-car will be at work again in a week, and a cheerful tone pervades the whole college. The president further stated that the relations between the students and the town had never been better.

Medicals Take a Night Off

(AS REPORTED TO-DAY)

Last night the students at the Medical Faculty took a night off from their arduous labours and were the guests of the Ladies' Reception Committee at the Y.W.C.A. building on Third Street. After the singing of a few of the better-known medical hymns and after being treated to a harmonium solo in B flat by the organist of the Insane Asylum, the students listened with evident enjoyment to a talk by the Rev. Mr. Week of the First Baptist Church on the subject "Where is Hell? Is it Here?" After the pastor had said everything that could be said on this interesting topic, each student was given a dish of ice cream and a doughnut. The president of the college in thanking the ladies of the Y.W.C.A. for their cordial reception said that he was sure the students would now return to their studies with renewed eagerness. After singing "Rock me to Sleep, Mother," the gathering broke up at nine-thirty.

Philosophical Society Meets

(AS IT USED TO FORTY YEARS AGO)

Last night the Philosophical Society held the third of its bi-weekly beer parties in the supper room of the men's residence. After the reading of the minutes, coupled with the drinking of beer, followed by the usual routine of drinking the health of the outgoing officers of the week and the toast of welcome to the officers of the week following, the Chairman invited the members to fill their glasses and listen, if they cared to, to a paper by Mr. Easy on the Nicomachean Ethics of Aristotle. Mr. Easy, while expressing his regret that he had not had time to prepare a paper on the Nicomachean Ethics of Aristotle, delivered in place of it an excellent rendition of Bret Harte's "Heathen Chinee." At the close of the recitation the Chairman announced that the debate which had been announced on the topic *Are Mathematical Judgments Synthetically a Priori* had been abandoned owing to the fact that the topic involved more preparation than the members of the society were prepared to give to it. He suggested instead that the society, after filling its glasses, should invite Mr. Freak of the senior class to give his imitation of two cats quarreling on a roof. The invitation was followed by similar exercises and the meeting was sustained to a late hour, those of the members who went home leaving at about two a.m.

Philosophical Society Meets

(AS IT DOES TO-DAY)

Last night a very pleasing meeting of the Philosophical Society was held in the parlour of the Women's Residence in the Martha Washington Building. Professor Strong in opening the meeting, said that she was glad to see among the members of the society a very creditable number of men, if she might use the phrase. She said no professor could feel that her work was satisfactory unless she could attract a certain number of men students. The professor then read her paper on the *Sociological Elimination of the Delinquent*. As the paper only lasted an hour and a half it was listened to in a luxury of enjoyment. The professor then having thrown the meeting open to questions, and a question having been asked, she very kindly spoke for another hour. At the close of the address a vote was taken on the resolution *That the Humbler Classes of Society Ought to be Chloroformed*, and was carried unanimously.

Discipline Committee Reports

(AS IT REPORTED FORTY YEARS AGO)

The report is published this morning of the semi-annual meeting of the Discipline Committee of the Faculty of the College. This committee, consisting of the senior professors of the Faculty, was established, as readers will recall, about two years ago with the object of elevating the moral tone of the student body by expulsion, fines and the application of the criminal law. The chairman reported that the committee had every reason to be gratified with the progress made during the period of its existence. The number of cases of suspension of students from lectures had increased under the operation of the committee by forty per cent; students warned, by sixty per cent; students found guilty of drunkenness, by seventy per cent; and students expelled for unbecoming and insubordinate conduct, ninety-five per cent. The report enumerates a new schedule of fines calculating to raise still higher the discipline of the institution, and recommends hereafter that every student guilty of striking or kicking a professor be brought before the committee and warned. The committee adds a further recommendation to the effect that measures be taken to let the student body understand that their presence at the University can only be tolerated within reasonable limits.

Student Control Committee Reports

(AS IT REPORTS TO-DAY)

The report is published this morning of the semi-annual meeting of the Students' Control Committee at the University. This Committee, as readers will recall, was established about two years ago with a view to raising the academic standard of the college. It is empowered not only to institute inquiries as to the capacity of the professors, but to recommend the expulsion of those of them who seem to the students' committee to be lacking in personality, or deficient in pep. The opening pages of the report deal with the case of the president of the college. A sub-committee, appointed from among the fourth-year students in accountancy, have been sitting on the case of the president for six weeks. Their report is in the main favourable, and their decision is that he may stay. But the sub-committee pass severe strictures on his home life, and recommend that he has too many children for him to be able to give full attention to his college work, and suggests a change in the future.

The committee accepts and adopts the recommendation of the second year class in philosophy who report that the professor's lectures are over their heads, and ask for his dismissal. A similar request comes from the third year students in mathematics who report that the professor's lectures are below their standards.

The committee has received and laid upon the table the report of the fourth year class in commerce to the effect that they have thus far failed to understand any of the lectures that were ever given them, and ask that they be given their degrees and let go. The committee acknowledges in its report the gratifying statement made by the chairman of the Trustees in his annual report to the effect that student control marks another milestone on the arduous path that it is leading the college to its ultimate end.

Old Junk and New Money

A Little Study in the Latest Antiques

I WENT the other day into the beautiful home of my two good friends, the Hespeler-Hyphen-Joneses, and I paused a moment, as my eye fell on the tall clock that stood in the hall.

"Ah," said Hespeler-Hyphen-Jones, "I see you are looking at the clock—a beautiful thing, isn't it?—a genuine antique."

"Does it go?" I asked.

"Good gracious, no!" exclaimed my two friends. "But isn't it a beautiful thing!"

"Did it ever go?"

"I doubt it," said Hespeler-Hyphen-Jones. "The works, of course, are by Salvolatile—one of the really *great* clockmakers, you know. But I don't know whether the works ever went. That, I believe, is one way in which you can always tell a Salvolatile. If it's a genuine Salvolatile, it won't go."

"In any case," I said, "it has no hands."

"Oh, dear, no," said Mrs. Jones. "It never had, as far as we know. We picked it up in such a queer little shop in Amalfi and the man assured us that it never had had any hands. He guaranteed it. That's one of the things, you know, that you can tell by. Charles and I were terribly keen about clocks at that time and really studied them, and the books all agreed that no genuine Salvolatile has any hands."

"And was the side broken, too, when you got it?" I asked.

"Ah, no," said my friend. "We had that done by an expert in New York after we got back. Isn't it exquisitely done? You see, he has made the break to look exactly as if someone had rolled the clock over and stamped on it. Every genuine Salvolatile is said to have been stamped upon like that.

"Of course, our break is only imitation, but it's extremely well done, isn't it? We go to Ferrugi's, that little place on Fourth Avenue, you know, for everything that we want broken. They have a splendid man there. He can break anything."

"Really!" I said.

"Yes, and the day when we wanted the clock done, Charles and I went down to see him do it. It was really quite wonderful, wasn't it, Charles?"

"Yes, indeed. The man laid the clock on the floor and turned it on its side and then stood looking at it intently, and walking round and round it and murmuring in Italian as if he were swearing at it. Then he jumped in the air and came down on it with both feet."

"Did he?" I asked.

"Yes, and with such wonderful accuracy. Our friend Mr. Appin-Hyphen-Smith—the great expert, you know—was looking at our clock last week and he said it was marvelous, hardly to be distinguished from a genuine *fractura*."

"But he did say, didn't he, dear," said Mrs. Jones, "that the better way is to throw a clock out of a fourth-story window? You see, that was the height of the Italian houses in the Thirteenth Century—is it the Thirteenth Century I mean, Charles?"

"Yes," said Charles.

"Do you know, the other day I made the silliest mistake about a spoon. I thought it was a Twelfth Century spoon and said so and in reality it was only Eleven and a half. Wasn't it, Charles?"

"Yes," said Charles.

"But do come into the drawing-room and have some tea. And, by the way, since you are interested in antiques, do look please at my teapot."

"It looks an excellent teapot," I said, feeling it with my hand, "and it must have been very expensive, wasn't it?"

"Oh, not *that* one," interposed Mr. Hespeler-Hyphen-Jones. "That is nothing. We got that here in New York at Hoffany's—to make tea in. It *is* made of solid silver, of course, and all that, but even Hoffany's admitted that it was made in America and was probably not more than a year or so old and had never been used by anybody else. In fact, they couldn't guarantee it in any way."

"Oh, I see," I said.

"But let me pour you out tea from it and then do look at the perfect darling beside it. Oh, don't touch it, please, it won't stand up."

"Won't stand up?" I said.

"No," said Hespeler-Jones, "that's one of the tests. We know from that it is genuine Swaatsmaacher. None of them stand up."

"Where did you buy it," I asked, "here?"

"Oh, heavens, no, you couldn't buy a thing like that here! As a matter of fact, we picked it up in a little gin shop in Obehellandam in Holland. Do you know Obehellandam?"

"I don't," I said.

"It's just the dearest little place, nothing but little wee smelly shops filled with most delightful things—all antique, everything broken. They guarantee that there is nothing in the shop that wasn't smashed at least a hundred years ago."

"You don't use the teapot to make tea," I said.

"Oh, no," said Mrs. Hespeler-Jones as she handed me a cup of tea from the New York teapot. "I don't think you could. It leaks."

"That again is a thing," said her husband, "that the experts always look for in a Swaatsmaacher. If it doesn't leak, it's probably just a faked-up thing not twenty years old."

"Is it silver?" I asked.

"Ah, no. That's another test," said Mrs. Jones. "The real Swaatsmaachers were always made of pewter bound with barrel-iron off the gin barrels. They try to imitate it now by using silver, but they can't get it."

"No, the silver won't take the tarnish," interjected her husband. "You see, it's the same way with ever so many of the old things. They rust and rot in a way that you simply cannot imitate. I have an old drinking horn that I'll show you presently—Ninth Century, isn't it, dear?— that is all coated inside with the most beautiful green slime, absolutely impossible to reproduce."

"Is it?" I said.

"Yes, I took it to Squeeziou's, the Italian place in London. (They are the great experts on horns, you know; they can tell exactly the century and the breed of cow.) And they told me that they had tried in vain to reproduce that peculiar and beautiful rot. One of their head men said that he thought that this horn had probably been taken from a dead cow that had been buried for fifty years. That's what gives it its value, you know."

"You didn't buy it in London, did you?" I asked.

"Oh, no," answered Hespeler-Jones. "London is perfectly impossible—just as hopeless as New York. You can't buy anything real there at all."

"Then where do you get all your things?" I asked, as I looked round at the collection of junk in the room.

"Oh, we pick them up here and there," said Mrs. Jones. "Just in any out-of-the-way corners. That little stool we found at the back of a cow stable in Loch Aberlocherty. They were actually using it for milking. And the two others—aren't they beautiful? though really it's quite wrong to have two chairs alike in the same room—came from the back of a tiny little whiskey shop in Galway. Such a delight of an old Irishman sold them to us and he admitted that he himself had no idea how old they were. They might, he said, be Fifteenth Century, or they might not.

"But, oh, Charles," my hostess interrupted herself to say, "I've just had a letter from Jane (Jane is my sister, you know) that is terribly exciting. She's found a table at a tiny place in Brittany that she thinks would exactly do in our card room. She says that it is utterly unlike anything else in the room and has quite obviously no connection with cards. But let me read what she says—let me see, yes, here's where it begins:

"' . . . a perfectly sweet little table. It probably had four legs originally and even now has two which, I am told, is a great find, as most people have to be content with one. The man explained that it could either be leaned up against the wall or else suspended from the ceiling on a silver chain. One of the boards of the top is gone, but I am told that that is of no consequence, as all the best specimens of Brittany tables have at least one board out.'

"Doesn't that sound fascinating, Charles? Do send Jane a cable at once not to miss it."

. . . .

And when I took my leave a little later, I realized once and for all that the antique business is not for me.

Oxford as I See It

My private station being that of a university professor, I was naturally deeply interested in the system of education in England. I was therefore led to make a special visit to Oxford and to submit the place to a searching scrutiny. Arriving one afternoon at four o'clock, I stayed at the Mitre Hotel and did not leave until eleven o'clock next morning. The whole of this time, except for one hour spent in addressing the undergraduates, was devoted to a close and eager study of the great university. When I add to this that I had already visited Oxford in 1907 and spent a Sunday at All Souls with Colonel L. S. Amery, it will be seen at once that my views on Oxford are based upon observations extending over fourteen years.

At any rate I can at least claim that my acquaintance with the British university is just as good a basis for reflection and judgment as that of the numerous English critics who come to our side of the water. I have known a famous English author to arrive at Harvard University in the morning, have lunch with President Lowell, and then write a whole chapter on the Excellence of Higher Education in America. I have known another one come to Harvard, have lunch with President Lowell, and do an entire book on the Decline of Serious Study in America. Or take the case of my own university. I remember Mr. Rudyard Kipling coming to McGill and saying in his address to the undergraduates at 2.30 P.M., "You have here a great institution." But how could he have gathered this information? As far as I know he spent the entire morning with Sir Andrew Macphail in his house beside the campus, smoking cigarettes. When I add that he distinctly refused to visit the Palaeontologic Museum, that he saw nothing of our new hydraulic apparatus, or of our classes in Domestic Science, his judgment that we had here a great institution seems a little bit superficial. I can only put beside it, to redeem it in some measure, the hasty and ill-formed judgment expressed by Lord Milner, "McGill is a noble university": and the rash and indiscreet expression of the Prince of Wales, when we gave him an LL.D. degree, "McGill has a glorious future."

To my mind these unthinking judgments about our great college do harm, and I determined, therefore, that anything that I said about Oxford should be the result of the actual observation and real study based upon a bona fide residence in the Mitre Hotel.

On the strength of this basis of experience I am prepared to make the following positive and emphatic statements. Oxford is a noble university. It has a great past. It is at present the greatest university in the world: and it is quite possible that it has a great future. Oxford trains scholars of the real type better than any other place in the world. Its methods are antiquated. It despises science. Its lectures are rotten. It has professors who never teach and students who never learn. It has no order, no arrangement, no system. Its curriculum is unintelligible. It has no president. It has no state legislature to tell it how to teach, and yet—it gets there. Whether we like it or not, Oxford gives something to its students, a life and a mode of thought, which in America as yet we can emulate but not equal.

If anybody doubts this let him go and take a room at the Mitre Hotel (ten and six for a wainscotted bedroom, period of Charles I) and study the place for himself.

These singular results achieved at Oxford are all the

more surprising when one considers the distressing conditions under which the students work. The lack of an adequate building fund compels them to go on working in the same old buildings which they have had for centuries. The buildings at Brasenose College have not been renewed since the year 1525. In New College and Magdalen the students are still housed in the old buildings erected in the sixteenth century. At Christ Church I was shown a kitchen which had been built at the expense of Cardinal Wolsey in 1527. Incredible though it may seem, they have no other place to cook in than this and are compelled to use it to-day. On the day when I saw this kitchen, four cooks were busy roasting an ox whole for the students' lunch: this at least is what I presumed they were doing from the size of the fire-place used, but it may not have been an ox; perhaps it was a cow. On a huge table, twelve feet by six and made of slabs of wood five inches thick, two other cooks were rolling out a game pie. I estimated it as measuring three feet across. In this rude way, unchanged since the time of Henry VIII, the unhappy Oxford students are fed. I could not help contrasting it with the cosy little boarding houses on Cottage Grove Avenue where I used to eat when I was a student at Chicago, or the charming little basement dining-rooms of the students' boarding houses in Toronto. But then, of course, Henry VIII never lived in Toronto.

The same lack of a building-fund necessitates the Oxford students living in the identical old boarding houses they had in the sixteenth and seventeenth centuries. Technically they are called "quadrangles," "closes" and "rooms"; but I am so broken in to the usage of my student days that I can't help calling them boarding houses. In many of these the old stairway has been worn down by the feet of ten generations of students: the windows have little latticed panes: there are old names carved here and there upon the stone, and a thick growth of ivy covers the walls. The boarding house at St. John's College dates from 1509, the one at Christ Church from the same period. A few hundred thousand pounds would suffice to replace these old buildings with neat steel and brick structures like the normal school at Schenectady, N. Y., or the Peel Street High School at Montreal. But nothing is done. A movement was indeed attempted last autumn towards removing the ivy from the walls, but the result was unsatisfactory and they are putting it back. Anyone could have told them beforehand that the mere removal of the ivy would not brighten Oxford up, unless at the same time one cleared the stones of the old inscriptions, put in steel fire-escapes, and in fact brought the boarding houses up to date.

But Henry VIII being dead, nothing was done. Yet in spite of its dilapidated buildings and its lack of fire-escapes, ventilation, sanitation, and up-to-date kitchen facilities, I persist in my assertion that I believe that Oxford, in its way, is the greatest university in the world. I am aware that this is an extreme statement and needs explanation. Oxford is much smaller in numbers, for example, than the State University of Minnesota, and is much poorer. It has, or had till yesterday, fewer students than the University of Toronto. To mention Oxford beside the 26,000 students of Columbia University sounds ridiculous. In point of money, the $39,000,000 endowment of the University of Chicago, and the $35,000,000 one of Columbia, and the $43,000,000 of Harvard seem to leave Oxford nowhere. Yet the peculiar thing is that it is not nowhere. By some queer process of its own it seems to get there every time. It was therefore of the very greatest interest to me, as a profound scholar, to try to investigate just how this peculiar excellence of Oxford arises.

It can hardly be due to anything in the curriculum or programme of studies. Indeed, to anyone accustomed to the best models of a university curriculum as it flourishes in the United States and Canada, the programme of studies is frankly quite laughable. There is less Applied Science in the place than would be found with us in a theological college. Hardly a single professor at Oxford would recognize a dynamo if he met it in broad daylight. The Oxford student learns nothing of chemistry, physics, heat, plumbing, electric wiring, gas-fitting or the use of a blow-torch. Any American college student can run a motor car, take a gasoline engine to pieces, fix a washer on a kitchen tap, mend a broken electric bell, and give an expert opinion on what has gone wrong with the furnace. It is these things indeed which stamp him as a college man, and occasion a very pardonable pride in the minds of his parents. But in all these things the Oxford student is the merest amateur.

This is bad enough. But after all one might say this is only the mechanical side of education. True: but one searches in vain in the Oxford curriculum for any adequate recognition of the higher and more cultured studies. Strange though it seems to us on this side of the Atlantic, there are no courses at Oxford in Housekeeping, or in Salesmanship, or in Advertising, or on Comparative Religion, or on the influence of the Press. There are no lectures whatever on Human Behavior, on Altruism, on Egotism, or on the Play of Wild Animals. Apparently, the Oxford student does not learn these things. This cuts him off from a great deal of the larger culture of our side of the Atlantic. "What are you studying this year?" I once asked a fourth-year student at one of our great colleges. "I am electing Salesmanship and Religion," he answered. Here was a young man whose training was destined inevitably to turn him into a moral business man: either that or nothing. At Oxford Salesmanship is not taught and Religion takes the feeble form of the New Testament. The more one looks at these things the more amazing it becomes that Oxford can produce any results at all.

The effect of the comparison is heightened by the peculiar position occupied at Oxford by the professors' lectures. In the colleges of Canada and the United States the lectures are supposed to be a really necessary and useful part of the student's training. Again and again I have heard the graduates of my own college assert that they had got as much, or nearly as much, out of the lectures at college as out of athletics or the Greek letter society or the Banjo and Mandolin Club. In short, with us the lectures form a real part of the college life. At Oxford it is not so. The lectures, I understand, are given and may even be taken. But they are quite worthless and are not supposed to have anything much to do with the development of the student's mind. "The lectures here," said a Canadian student to me, "are punk." I appealed to another student to know if this was so. "I don't know whether I'd call them exactly punk," he answered, "but they're certainly rotten." Other judgments were that the lectures were of no importance: that nobody took them: that they don't matter: that you can take them if you like: that they do you no harm.

It appears further that the professors themselves are not keen on their lectures. If the lectures are called for they give them; if not, the professor's feelings are not hurt. He merely waits and rests his brain until in some later year the students call for his lectures. There are men at Oxford who have rested their brains this way for over thirty years: the accumulated brain power thus dammed up is said to be colossal.

I understand that the key to this mystery is found in the operations of the person called the tutor. It is from him, or rather with him, that the students learn all that they know: one and all are agreed on that. Yet it is a little odd to know just how he does it. "We go over to his rooms," said one student, "and he just lights a pipe and talks to us." "We sit round with him," said another, "and he simply smokes and goes over our exercises with us." From this and other evidence I gather that what an Oxford tutor does is to get a little group of students together and smoke at them. Men who have been systematically smoked at for four years turn into ripe scholars. If anybody doubts this, let him go to Oxford and he can see the thing actually in operation. A well-smoked man speaks and writes English with a grace that can be acquired in no other way.

In what was said above, I seem to have been directing criticism against the Oxford professors as such: but I have no intention of doing so. For the Oxford professor and his whole manner of being I have nothing but a profound respect. There is indeed the greatest difference between the modern up-to-date American idea of a professor and the English type. But even with us in older days, in the bygone time when such people as Henry Wadsworth Longfellow were professors, one found the English idea; a professor was supposed to be a venerable kind of person, with snow-white whiskers reaching to his stomach. He was expected to moon around the campus oblivious of the world around him. If you nodded to him he failed to see you. Of money he knew nothing; of business, far less.

He was, as his trustees were proud to say of him, "a child."

On the other hand he contained within him a reservoir of learning of such depth as to be practically bottomless. None of this learning was supposed to be of any material or commercial benefit to anybody. Its use was in saving the soul and enlarging the mind.

At the head of such a group of professors was one whose beard was even whiter and longer, whose absence of mind was even still greater, and whose knowledge of money, business, and practical affairs was below zero. Him they made the president.

All this is changed in America. A university professor is now a busy, hustling person, approximating as closely to a business man as he can do it. It is on the business man that he models himself. He has a little place that he calls his "office," with a typewriter machine and a stenographer. Here he sits and dictates letters, beginning after the best business models, "in re yours of the eighth ult., would say, etc., etc." He writes these letters to students, to his fellow professors, to the president, indeed to any people who will let him write to them. The number of letters that he writes each month is duly counted and set to his credit. If he writes enough he will get a reputation as an "executive," and big things may happen to him. He may even be asked to step out of the college and take a post as an "executive" in a soap company or an advertising firm. The man, in short, is a "hustler," an "advertiser" whose highest aim is to be a "live-wire." If he is not, he will presently be dismissed, or, to use the business term, be "let go," by a board of trustees who are themselves hustlers and live-wires. As to the professor's soul, he no longer needs to think of it as it has been handed over along with all the others to a Board of Censors.

The American professor deals with his students according to his lights. It is his business to chase them along over a prescribed ground at a prescribed pace like a flock of sheep. They all go humping together over the hurdles with the professor chasing them with a set of "tests" and "recitations," "marks" and "attendances," the whole apparatus obviously copied from the time-clock of the business man's factory. This process is what is called "showing results." The pace set is necessarily that of the slowest, and thus results in what I have heard Mr. Edward Beatty describe as the "convoy system of education."

In my own opinion, reached after fifty-two years of profound reflection, this system contains in itself the seeds of destruction. It puts a premium on dulness and a penalty on genius. It circumscribes that latitude of mind which is the real spirit of learning. If we persist in it we shall presently find that true learning will fly away from our universities and will take rest wherever some individual and enquiring mind can mark out its path for itself.

Now the principal reason why I am led to admire Oxford is that the place is little touched as yet by the measuring of "results," and by this passion for visible and provable "efficiency." The whole system at Oxford is such as to put a premium on genius and to let mediocrity and dulness go their way. On the dull student Oxford, after a proper lapse of time, confers a degree which means nothing more than that he lived and breathed at Oxford and kept out of jail. This for many students is as much as society can expect. But for the gifted students Oxford offers great opportunities. There is no question of his hanging back till the last sheep has jumped over the fence. He need wait for no one. He may move forward as fast as he likes, following the bent of his genius. If he has in him any ability beyond that of the common herd, his tutor, interested in his studies, will smoke at him until he kindles him into a flame. For the tutor's soul is not harassed by herding dull students, with dismissal hanging by a thread over his head in the class room. The American professor has no time to be interested in a clever student. He has time to be interested in his "deportment," his letter-writing, his executive work, and his organising ability and his hope of promotion to a soap factory. But with that his mind is exhausted. The student of genius merely means to him a student who gives no trouble, who passes all his "tests," and is present at all his "recitations." Such a student also, if he can be trained to be a hustler and an advertiser, will undoubtedly "make good." But beyond that the professor does not think of him. The everlasting principle of equality has inserted itself in a place where it has no right to be, and where inequality is the breath of life.

American or Canadian college trustees would be horrified at the notion of professors who apparently do no work, give few or no lectures and draw their pay merely for existing. Yet these are really the only kind of professors worth having,—I mean, men who can be trusted with a vague general mission in life, with a salary guaranteed at least till their death, and a sphere of duties entrusted solely to their own consciences and the promptings of their own desires. Such men are rare, but a single one of them, when found, is worth ten "executives" and a dozen "organisers."

The excellence of Oxford, then, as I see it, lies in the peculiar vagueness of the organisation of its work. It starts from the assumption that the professor is a really learned man whose sole interest lies in his own sphere: and that a student, or at least the only student with whom the university cares to reckon seriously, is a young man who desires to know. This is an ancient mediæval attitude long since buried in more up-to-date places under successive strata of compulsory education, state teaching, the democratisation of knowledge and the substitution of the shadow for the substance, and the casket for the gem. No doubt, in newer places the thing has got to be so. Higher education in America flourishes chiefly as a qualification for entrance into a money-making profession, and not as a thing in itself. But in Oxford one can still see the surviving outline of a nobler type of structure and a higher inspiration.

I do not mean to say, however, that my judgment of Oxford is one undiluted stream of praise. In one respect at least I think that Oxford has fallen away from the high ideals of the Middle Ages. I refer to the fact that it admits women students to its studies. In the Middle Ages women were regarded with a peculiar chivalry long since lost. It was taken for granted that their brains were too delicately poised to allow them to learn anything. It was presumed that their minds were so exquisitely hung that intellectual effort might disturb them. The present age has gone to the other extreme: and this is seen nowhere more than in the crowding of women into colleges originally designed for men. Oxford, I regret to find, has not stood out against this change.

To a profound scholar like myself, the presence of these young women, many of them most attractive, flittering up and down the streets of Oxford in their caps and gowns, is very distressing.

Who is to blame for this and how they first got in I do not know. But I understand that they first of all built a private college of their own close to Oxford, and then edged themselves in foot by foot. If this is so they only followed up the precedent of the recognised method in use in America. When an American college is established, the women go and build a college of their own overlooking the grounds. Then they put on becoming caps and gowns and stand and look over the fence at the college athletics. The male undergraduates, who were originally and by nature a hardy lot, were not easily disturbed. But inevitably some of the senior trustees fell in love with the first year girls and became convinced that coeducation was a noble cause. American statistics show that between 1880 and 1900 the number of trustees and senior professors who married girl undergraduates or who wanted to do so reached a percentage of,—I forget the exact percentage; it was either a hundred or a little over.

I don't know just what happened at Oxford but presumably something of the sort took place. In any case the women are now all over the place. They attend the college lectures, they row in a boat, and they preambulate the High Street. They are even offering a serious competition against the men. Last year they carried off the ping-pong championship and took the chancellor's prize for needlework, while in music, cooking and millinery the men are said to be nowhere.

There is no doubt that unless Oxford puts the women out while there is yet time, they will overrun the whole university. What this means to the progress of learning few can tell and those who know are afraid to say.

Cambridge University, I am glad to see, still sets its face sternly against this innovation. I am reluctant to count any superiority in the University of Cambridge. Having twice visited Oxford, having made the place a subject of profound study for many hours at a time, having twice addressed its undergraduates, and having stayed at the Mitre Hotel, I consider myself an Oxford man. But I must admit that Cambridge has chosen the wiser part.

Last autumn, while I was in London on my voyage of

discovery, a vote was taken at Cambridge to see if the women who have already a private college nearby, should be admitted to the university. They were triumphantly shut out; and as a fit and proper sign of enthusiasm the undergraduates went over in a body and knocked down the gates of the women's college. I know that it is a terrible thing to say that any one approved of this. All the London papers came out with headings that read,—ARE OUR UNDERGRADUATES TURNING INTO BABOONS? and so on. The *Manchester Guardian* draped its pages in black and even the London *Morning Post* was afraid to take bold ground in the matter. But I do know also that there was a great deal of secret chuckling and jubilation in the London clubs. Nothing was expressed openly. The men of England have been to terrorised by the women for that. But in safe corners of the club, out of earshot of the waiters and away from casual strangers, little groups of elderly men chuckled quietly together. "Knocked down their gates, eh?" said the wicked old men to one another, and then whispered guiltily behind an uplifted hand, "Serve 'em right." Nobody dared to say anything outside. If they had someone would have got up and asked a question in the House of Commons. When this is done all England falls flat upon its face.

But for my part when I heard of the Cambridge vote, I felt as Lord Chatham did when he said in parliament, "Sir, I rejoice that America has resisted." For I have long harboured views of my own upon the higher education of women. In these days, however, it requires no little hardihood to utter a single word of criticism against it. It is like throwing half a brick through the glass roof of a conservatory. It is bound to make trouble. Let me hasten, therefore, to say that I believe most heartily in the higher education of women; in fact, the higher the better. The only question to my mind is: What is "higher education" and how do you get it? With which goes the secondary enquiry, What is a woman and is she just the same as a man? I know that it sounds a terrible thing to say in these days, but I don't believe she is.

Let me say also that when I speak of coeducation I speak of what I know. I was coeducated myself some thirty-five years ago, at the very beginning of the thing. I learned my Greek alongside of a bevy of beauty on the opposite benches that mashed up the irregular verbs for us very badly. Incidentally, those girls are all married long since, and all the Greek they know now you could put under a thimble. But of that presently.

I have had further experience as well. I spent three years in the graduate school of Chicago, where coeducational girls were as thick as autumn leaves,—and some thicker. And as a college professor at McGill University in Montreal, I have taught mingled classes of men and women for twenty years.

On the basis of which experience I say with assurance that the thing is a mistake and has nothing to recommend it but its relative cheapness. Let me emphasise this last point and have done with it. Coeducation is of course a great economy. To teach ten men and ten women in a single class of twenty costs only half as much as to teach two classes. Where economy must rule, then, the thing has got to be. But where the discussion turns not on what is cheapest, but on what is best, then the case is entirely different.

The fundamental trouble is that men and women are different creatures, with different minds and different aptitudes and different paths in life. There is no need to raise here the question of which is superior and which is inferior (though I think, the Lord help me, I know the answer to that too). The point lies in the fact that they are different.

But the mad passion for equality has masked this obvious fact. When women began to demand, quite rightly, a share in higher education, they took for granted that they wanted the same curriculum as the men. They never stopped to ask whether their aptitudes were not in various directions higher and better than those of the men, and whether it might not be better for their sex to cultivate the things which were best suited to their minds. Let me be more explicit. In all that goes with physical and mathematical science, women, on the average, are far below the standard of men. There are, of course, exceptions. But they prove nothing. It is no use to quote to me the case of some brilliant girl who stood first in physics at Cornell. That's nothing. There is an elephant in the zoo that can count up to ten, yet I refuse to reckon myself his inferior.

Tabulated results spread over years, and the actual experience of those who teach show that in the whole domain of mathematics and physics women are outclassed. At McGill the girls of our first year have wept over their failures in elementary physics these twenty-five years. It is time that someone dried their tears and took away the subject.

But, in any case, examination tests are never the whole story. To those who know, a written examination is far from being a true criterion of capacity. It demands too much of mere memory, imitativeness, and the insidious willingness to absorb other people's ideas. Parrots and crows would do admirably in examinations. Indeed, the colleges are full of them.

But take, on the other hand, all that goes with the æsthetic side of education, with imaginative literature and the cult of beauty. Here women are, or at least ought to be, the superiors of men. Women were in primitive times the first story-tellers. They are still so at the cradle side. The original college woman was the witch, with her incantations and her prophecies and the glow of her bright imagination, and if brutal men of duller brains had not burned it out of her, she would be incanting still. To my thinking, we need more witches in the colleges and less physics.

I have seen such young witches myself,—if I may keep the word: I like it,—in colleges such as Wellesley in Massachusetts and Bryn Mawr in Pennsylvania, where there isn't a man allowed within the three mile limit. To my mind, they do infinitely better thus by themselves. They are freer, less restrained. They discuss things openly in their classes; they lift up their voices, and they speak, whereas a girl in such a place as McGill, with men all about her, sits for four years as silent as a frog full of shot.

But there is a deeper trouble still. The careers of the men and women who go to college together are necessarily different, and the preparation is all aimed at the man's career. The men are going to be lawyers, doctors, engineers, business men, and politicians. And the women are not.

There is no use pretending about it. It may sound an awful thing to say, but the women are going to be married. That is, and always has been, their career; and, what is more, they know it; and even at college, while they are studying algebra and political economy, they have their eye on it sideways all the time. The plain fact is that, after a girl has spent four years of her time and a great deal of her parents' money in equipping herself for a career that she is never going to have, the wretched creature goes and gets married, and in a few years she has forgotten which is the hypothenuse of a right-angled triangle, and she doesn't care. She has much better things to think of.

At this point someone will shriek: "But surely, even for marriage, isn't it right that a girl should have a college education?" To which I hasten to answer: most assuredly. I freely admit that a girl who knows algebra, or once knew it, is a far more charming companion and a nobler wife and mother than a girl who doesn't know x from y. But the point is that: Does the higher education that fits a man to be a lawyer also fit a person to be a wife and mother? Or, in other words, is a lawyer a wife and mother? I say he is not. Granted that a girl is to spend four years in time and four thousand dollars in money in going to college, why train her for a career that she is never going to adopt? Why not give her an education that will have a meaning and a harmony with the real life that she is to follow?

For example, suppose that during her four years every girl lucky enough to get a higher education spent at least six months of it in the training and discipline of a hospital as a nurse. There is more education and character-making in that than in a whole bucketful of algebra.

But no, the woman insists on snatching her share of an education designed by Erasmus or William of Wykeham or William of Occam for the creation of scholars and lawyers; and when later on in her home there is a sudden sickness or accident, and the life or death of those nearest to her hangs upon skill and knowledge and a trained fortitude in emergency, she must needs send in all haste for a hired woman to fill the place that she herself has never learned to occupy.

But I am not here trying to elaborate a whole curriculum. I am only trying to indicate that higher education for the man is one thing, for the woman another. Nor do

I deny the fact that women have got to earn their living. Their higher education must enable them to do that. They cannot all marry on their graduation day. But that is no great matter. No scheme of education that anyone is likely to devise will fail in this respect.

The positions that they hold as teachers or civil servants they would fill all the better if their education were fitted to their wants.

Some few, a small minority, really and truly "have a career,"—husbandless and childless,—in which the sacrifice is great and the honour to them, perhaps, all the higher. And others no doubt dream of a career in which a husband and a group of blossoming children are carried as an appendage to a busy life at the bar or on the platform. But all such are the mere minority, so small as to make no difference to the general argument.

But there—I have written quite enough to make plenty of trouble except perhaps at Cambridge University. So I return with relief to my general study of Oxford. Viewing the situation as a whole, I am led then to the conclusion that there must be something in the life of Oxford itself that makes for higher learning. Smoked at by his tutor, fed in Henry VIII's kitchen, and sleeping in a tangle of ivy, the student evidently gets something not easily obtained in America. And the more I reflect on the matter the more I am convinced that it is the sleeping in the ivy that does it. How different it is from student life as I remember it!

When I was a student at the University of Toronto thirty years ago, I lived,—from start to finish,—in seventeen different boarding houses. As far as I am aware these houses have not, or not yet, been marked with tablets. But they are still to be found in the vicinity of McCaul and Darcy, and St. Patrick Streets. Anyone who doubts the truth of what I have to say may go and look at them.

I was not alone in the nomadic life that I led. There were hundreds of us drifting about in this fashion from one melancholy habitation to another. We lived as a rule two or three in the house, sometimes alone. We dined in the basement. We always had beef, done up in some way after it was dead, and there were always soda biscuits on the table. They used to have a brand of soda biscuits in those days in the Toronto boarding houses that I have not seen since. They were better than dog biscuits but with not so much snap. My contemporaries will all remember them. A great many of the leading barristers and professional men of Toronto were fed on them.

In the life we led we had practically no opportunities for association on a large scale, no common rooms, no reading rooms, nothing. We never saw the magazines,—personally I didn't even know the names of them. The only interchange of ideas we ever got was by going over to the Cær Howell Hotel on University Avenue and interchanging them there.

I mention these melancholy details not for their own sake but merely to emphasize the point that when I speak of students' dormitories, and the larger life which they offer, I speak of what I know.

If we had had at Toronto, when I was a student, the kind of dormitories and dormitory life that they have at Oxford, I don't think I would ever have graduated. I'd have been there still. The trouble is that the universities on our Continent are only just waking up to the idea of what a university should mean. They were, very largely, instituted and organised with the idea that a university was a place where young men were sent to absorb the contents of books and to listen to lectures in the class rooms. The student was pictured as a pallid creature, burning what was called the "midnight oil," his wan face bent over his desk. If you wanted to do something for him you gave him a book: if you wanted to do something really large on his behalf you gave him a whole basketful of them. If you wanted to go still further and be a benefactor to the college at large, you endowed a competitive scholarship and set two or more pallid students working themselves to death to get it.

The real thing for the student is the life and environment that surrounds him. All that he really learns he learns, in a sense, by the active operation of his own intellect and not as the passive recipient of lectures. And for this active operation what he really needs most is the continued and intimate contact with his fellows. Students must live together and eat together, talk and smoke together. Experience shows that that is how their minds really grow. And they must live together in a rational and comfortable way. They must eat in a big dining room or hall, with oak beams across the ceiling, and the stained glass in the windows, and with a shield or tablet here or there upon the wall, to remind them between times of the men who went before them and left a name worthy of the memory of the college. If a student is to get from his college what it ought to give him, a college dormitory, with the life in common that it brings, is his absolute right. A university that fails to give it to him is cheating hm.

If I were founding a university—and I say it with all the seriousness of which I am capable—I would found first a smoking room; then when I had a little more money in hand I would found a dormitory; then after that, or more probably with it, a decent reading room and a library. After that, if I still had money over that I couldn't use, I would hire a professor and get some text books.

This chapter has sounded in the most part like a continuous eulogy of Oxford with but little in favour of our American colleges. I turn therefore with pleasure to the more congenial task of showing what is wrong with Oxford and with the English university system generally, and the aspect in which our American universities far excel the British.

The point is that Henry VIII is dead. The English are so proud of what Henry VIII and the benefactors of earlier centuries did for the universities that they forget the present. There is little or nothing in England to compare with the magnificent generosity of individuals, provinces and states, which is building up the colleges of the United States and Canada. There used to be. But by some strange confusion of thought the English people admire the noble gifts of Cardinal Wolsey and Henry VIII and Queen Margaret, and do not realise that the Carnegies and Rockefellers and the William Macdonalds are the Cardinal Wolseys of to-day. The University of Chicago was founded upon oil. McGill University rests largely on a basis of tobacco. In America the world of commerce and business levies on itself a noble tribute in favour of the higher learning. In England, with a few conspicuous exceptions, such as that at Bristol, there is little of the sort. The feudal families are content with what their remote ancestors have done: they do not try to emulate it in any great degree.

In the long run this must count. Of all the various reforms that are talked of at Oxford, and of all the imitations of American methods that are suggested, the only one worth while, to my thinking, is to capture a few millionaires, give them honorary degrees at a million pounds sterling apiece, and tell them to imagine that they are Henry VIII. I give Oxford warning that if this is not done the place will not last another two centuries.

The Snoopopaths or Fifty Stories in One

THIS particular study in the follies of literature is not so much a story as a sort of essay. The average reader will therefore turn from it with a shudder. The condition of the average reader's mind is such that he can take in nothing but fiction. And it must be thin fiction at that—thin as gruel. Nothing else will "sit on his stomach."

Everything must come to the present day reader in this form. If you wish to talk to him about religion, you must dress it up as a story and label it *Beth-sheba, or The Curse of David;* if you want to improve the reader's morals, you must write him a little thing in dialogue called *Mrs. Potiphar Dines Out.* If you wish to expostulate with him about drink you must do so through a narrative called *Red Rum*—short enough and easy enough for him to read it, without overstraining his mind, while he drinks cocktails.

But whatever the story is about it has got to deal—in order to be read by the average reader—with A MAN and A WOMAN. I put these words in capitals to indicate that they have got to stick out of the story with the crudity of a drawing done by a child with a burnt stick. In other words, the story has got to be snoopopathic. This is a word derived from the Greek—"snoopo"—or if there never was a Greek verb snoopo, at least there ought to have been one—and it means just what it seems to mean. Nine out of ten short stories written in America are snoopopathic.

In snoopopathic literature, in order to get its full effect, the writer generally introduces his characters simply as "the man" and "the woman." He hates to admit that they have names. He opens out with them something after this fashion:

"The Man lifted his head. He looked about him at the gaily-bedizzled crowd that besplotched the midnight cabaret with riotous patches of colour. He crushed his cigar against the brass of an Egyptian tray—'Bah!' he murmured, 'Is it worth it?' Then he let his head sink again."

You notice it? He lifted his head all the way up and let it sink all the way down, and you still don't know who he is.

For The Woman the beginning is done like this:

"The Woman clenched her white hands till the diamonds that glittered upon her fingers were buried in the soft flesh. 'The shame of it,' she murmured. Then she took from the table the telegram that lay crumpled upon it and tore it into a hundred pieces. 'He dare not!' she muttered through her closed teeth. She looked about the hotel room with its garish furniture. 'He has no right to follow me here,' she gasped."

All of which the reader has to take in without knowing who the woman is, or which hotel she is staying at, or who dare not follow her or why. But the modern reader loves to get this sort of shadowy incomplete effect. If he were told straight out that the woman's name was Mrs. Edward Dangerfield of Brick City, Montana, and that she had left her husband three days ago and that the telegram told her that he had discovered her address and was following her, the reader would refuse to go on.

This method of introducing the characters is bad enough. But the new snoopopathic way of describing them is still worse. The Man is always detailed as if he were a horse. He is said to be "tall, well set up, with straight legs."

Great stress is always laid on his straight legs. No magazine story is acceptable now unless The Man's legs are absolutely straight. Why this is, I don't know. All my friends have straight legs—and yet I never hear them make it a subject of comment or boasting. I don't believe I have, at present, a single friend with crooked legs.

But this is not the only requirement. Not only must The Man's legs be straight, but he must be "clean-limbed," whatever that is; and of course he must have a "well-tubbed look about him." How this look is acquired, and whether it can be got with an ordinary bath and water, are things on which I have no opinion.

The Man is of course "clean-shaven." This allows him to do such necessary things as "turning his clean-shaven face towards the speaker," "laying his clean-shaven cheek in his hand," and so on. But everyone is familiar with the face of the up-to-date clean-shaven snoopopathic man. There are pictures of him by the million on magazine covers and book jackets, looking into the eyes of The Woman—he does it from a distance of about six inches—with that snoopy earnest expression of brainlessness that he always wears. How one would enjoy seeing a man—a real one with Nevada whiskers and long boots—land him one solid kick from behind.

Then comes The Woman of the snoopopathic story. She is always "beautifully groomed" (Who these grooms are that do it, and where they can be hired, I don't know), and she is said to be "exquisitely gowned."

It is peculiar about The Woman that she never seems to wear a *dress*—always a "gown." Why this is, I cannot tell. In the good old stories that I used to read, when I could still read for the pleasure of it, the heroines—that was what they used to be called—always wore dresses. But now there is no heroine, only a woman in a gown.

I wear a gown myself—at night. It is made of flannel and reaches to my feet, and when I take my candle and go out to the balcony where I sleep, the effect of it on the whole is not bad. But as to its "revealing every line of my figure"—as The Woman's gown is always said to—and as to its "suggesting even more than it reveals"—well, it simply does *not*. So when I talk of "gowns" I speak of something that I know all about.

Yet whatever The Woman does, her "gown" is said to "cling" to her. Whether in the street or in a cabaret or in the drawing-room, it "clings." If by any happy chance she throws a lace wrap about her, then *it* clings; and if she lifts her gown—as she is apt to—it shows—not what I should have expected—but a *jupon*, and even that clings. What a *jupon* is I don't know. With my gown, I never wear one. These people I have described, The Man and The Woman—The Snoopopaths—are, of course, not husband and wife, or brother and sister, or anything so simple and old-fashioned as that. She is someone else's wife. She is *The Wife of the Other Man*. Just what there is, for the reader, about other men's wives, I don't understand. I know tons of them that I wouldn't walk round a block for. But the reading public goes wild over them. The old-fashioned heroine was unmarried. That spoiled the whole story. You could see the end from the beginning. But with Another Man's Wife, the way is blocked. Something has *got* to happen that would seem almost obvious to anyone.

The writer, therefore, at once puts the two snoopos—The Man and The Woman—into a frightfully indelicate position. The more indelicate it is, the better. Sometimes she gets into his motor by accident after the theatre, or they both engage the drawing-room of a Pullman car by mistake, or else, best of all, he is brought accidentally into her room at a hotel at night. There is something about a hotel room at night, apparently, which throws the modern reader into convulsions. It is always easy to arrange a scene of this sort. For example, taking the sample beginning that I gave above, The Man—whom I left sitting at the cabaret table, above, rises unsteadily—it is the recognised way of rising in a cabaret—and, settling the reckoning with the waiter, staggers into the street. For myself I never do a reckoning with the waiter. I just pay the bill as he adds it, and take a chance on it.

As The Man staggers into the "night air," the writer has time—just a little time, for the modern reader is impatient —to explain who he is and why he staggers. He is rich. That goes without saying. All clean-limbed men with straight legs are rich. He owns copper mines in Montana. All well-tubbed millionaires do. But he has left them, left everything, because of the Other Man's Wife. It was that or madness—or worse. He had told himself so a thousand times. (This little touch about "worse" is used in all the stories. I don't just understand what the "worse" means. But snoopopathic readers reach for it with great readiness.) So The Man had come to New York (the only place where stories are allowed to be laid) under an assumed name, to forget, to drive her from his mind. He had plunged into the mad round of—I never could find it myself, but it must be there, and as they all plunge into it, it must be as full of them as a sheet of Tanglefoot is of flies.

"As The Man walked home to his hotel, the cool, night air steadied him, but his brain is still filled with the fumes of the wine he had drunk." Notice these "fumes." It must be great to float round with them in one's brain, where they apparently lodge. I have often tried to find them, but I never can. Again and again I have said, "Waiter, bring me a Scotch whiskey and soda with fumes." But I can never get them.

Thus goes The Man to his hotel. Now it is in a room in this same hotel that The Woman is sitting, and in which she has crumpled up the telegram. It is to this hotel that she has come when she left her husband, a week ago. The readers know, without even being told, that she left him "to work out her own salvation"—driven, by his cold brutality, beyond the breaking point. And there is laid upon her soul, as she sits there with clenched hands, the dust and ashes of a broken marriage and a loveless life, and the knowledge, too late, of all that might have been.

And it is to this hotel that The Woman's Husband is following her.

But The Man does not know that she is in the hotel; nor that she has left her husband; it is only accident that brings them together. And it is only by accident that he has come into her room, at night, and stands there—rooted to the threshold.

Now as a matter of fact, in real life, there is nothing at all in the simple fact of walking into the wrong room of a hotel by accident. You merely apologise and go out. I had this experience myself only a few days ago. I walked right into a lady's room—next door to my own. But I simply said, "Oh, I beg your pardon, I thought this was No. 343."

"No," she said, "this is 341."

She did not rise and "confront" me, as they always do in the snoopopathic stories. Neither did her eyes flash, nor her gown cling to her as she rose. Nor was her gown made of "rich old stuff." No, she merely went on reading her newspaper.

"I must apologise," I said. "I am a little short-sighted, and very often a *one* and a *three* look so alike that I can't tell them apart. I'm afraid—"

"Not at all," said the lady. "Good evening."

"You see," I added, "this room and my own being so alike, and mine being 343 and this being 341, I walked in before I realised that instead of walking into 343 I was walking into 341."

She bowed in silence, without speaking, and I felt that it was now the part of exquisite tact to retire quietly without further explanation, or at least with only a few murmured words about the possibility of to-morrow being even colder than to-day. I did so, and the affair ended with complete *savoir faire* on both sides.

But the Snoopopaths, Man and Woman, can't do this sort of thing, or, at any rate, the snoopopathic writer won't let them. The opportunity is too good to miss. As soon as The Man comes into The Woman's room—before he knows who she is, for she has her back to him—he gets into a condition dear to all snoopopathic readers.

His veins simply "surged." His brain beat against his temples in mad pulsation. His breath "came and went in quick, short pants." (This last might perhaps be done by one of the hotel bellboys, but otherwise it is hard to imagine.)

And The Woman—"Noiseless as his step had been she seemed to *sense* his presence. A wave seemed to sweep over her—" She turned and rose "fronting him full." This doesn't mean that he was full when she fronted him. Her gown—but we know about that already. "It was a coward's trick," she panted.

Now if The Man had had the kind of *savoir faire* that I have, he would have said: "Oh, pardon me! I see this room is 341. My own room is 343, and to me a *one* and a *three* often look so alike that I seem to have walked into 341 while looking for 343." And he could have explained in two words that he had no idea that she was in New York, was not following her, and not proposing to interfere with her in any way. And she would have explained also in two sentences why and how she came to be there. But this wouldn't do. Instead of it, The Man and The Woman go through the grand snoopopathic scene which is so intense that it needs what is really a new kind of language to convey it.

"Helene," he croaked, reaching out his arms—his voice tensed with the infinity of his desire.

"Back," she iced. And then, "Why have you come here?" she hoarsed. "What business have you here?"

"Nope," he glooped, "none. I have no business." They stood sensing one another.

"I thought you were in Philadelphia," she said—her gown clinging to every fibre of her as she spoke.

"I was," he wheezed.

"And you left it?" she sharped, her voice tense.

"I left it," he said, his voice glumping as he spoke. "Need I tell you why?" He had come nearer to her. She could hear his pants as he moved.

"No, no," she gurgled. "You left it. It is enough. I can understand"—she looked bravely up at him—"I can understand any man leaving it." Then as he moved still nearer her, there was the sound of a sudden swift step in the corridor. The door opened and there stood before them—The Other Man, the Husband of The Woman— Edward Dangerfield.

This, of course, is the grand snoopopathic climax, when the author gets all three of them—The Man, The Woman, and The Woman's Husband—in a hotel room at night. But notice what happens.

He stood in the opening of the doorway looking at them, a slight smile upon his lips. "Well?" he said. Then he entered the room and stood for a moment quietly looking into The Man's face.

"So," he said, "it was you." He walked into the room and laid the light coat that he had been carrying over his arm upon the table. He drew a cigar case from his waist-coat pocket.

"Try one of these Havanas," he said.

Observe the *calm* of it. This is what the snoopopath loves—no rage, no blustering—calmness, cynicism. He walked over towards the mantel-piece and laid his hat upon it. He set his boot upon the fender.

"It was cold this evening," he said. He walked over to the window and gazed a moment into the dark.

"This is a nice hotel," he said. (This scene is what the author and the reader love; they hate to let it go. They'd willingly keep the man walking up and down for hours saying "Well!")

The Man raised his head! "Yes, it's a good hotel," he said. Then he let his head fall again.

This kind of thing goes on until, if possible, the reader is persuaded into thinking that there is nothing going to happen. Then:—

"He turned to The Woman. 'Go in there,' he said, pointing to the bedroom door. Mechanically she obeyed." This, by the way, is the first intimation that the reader has that the room in which they were sitting was not a bed-room. The two men were alone. Dangerfield walked over to the chair where he had thrown his coat.

"I bought this coat in St. Louis last fall," he said. His voice was quiet, even passionless. Then from the pocket of the coat he took a revolver and laid it on the table. Marsden watched him without a word.

"Do you see this pistol?" said Dangerfield.

Marsden raised his head a moment and let it sink.

Of course the ignorant reader keeps wondering why he doesn't explain. But how can he? What is there to say? He has been found out of his own room at night. The penalty for this in all the snoopopathic stories is death. It is understood that in all the New York hotels the night porters shoot a certain number of men in the corridors every night.

"When we married," said Dangerfield, glancing at the closed door as he spoke, "I bought this and the mate to it —for her—just the same, with the monogram on the butt —see! And I said to her, 'If things ever go wrong between you and me, there is always this way out.'"

He lifted the pistol from the table, examining its mechanism. He rose and walked across the room till he stood with his back against the door, the pistol in his hand, its barrel pointing straight at Marsden's heart. Marsden never moved. Then as the two men faced one another thus, looking into one another's eyes, their ears caught a sound from behind the closed door of the inner room—a sharp, hard, metallic sound as if someone in the room within had raised the hammer of a pistol—a jewelled pistol like the one in Dangerfield's hand.

And then—

A loud report, and with a cry, the cry of a woman, one shrill despairing cry—

Or no, hang it—I can't consent to end up a story in that fashion, with the dead woman prone across the bed, the smoking pistol, with a jewel on the hilt, still clasped in her hand—the red blood welling over the white laces of her gown—while the two men gaze down upon her cold face with horror in their eyes. Not a bit. Let's end it like this:—

"A shrill despairing cry,—'Ed! Charlie! Come in here quick! Hurry! The steam coil has blown out a plug! You two boys quit talking and come in here, for Heaven's sake, and fix it.'"

And, indeed, if the reader will look back he will see there is nothing in the dialogue to preclude it. He was misled, that's all. I merely said that Mrs. Dangerfield had left her husband a few days before. So she had—to do some shopping in New York. She thought it mean of him to follow her. And I never said that Mrs. Dangerfield had any connection whatever with The Woman with whom Marsden was in love. Not at all. He knew her, of course, because he came from Brick City. But she had thought he was in Philadelphia, and naturally she was surprised to see him back in New York. That's why she exclaimed "Back!" And as a matter of plain fact, you can't pick up a revolver without its pointing somewhere. No one said he meant to fire it.

In fact, if the reader will glance back at the dialogue —I know he has no time to, but if he does—he will see that, being something of a snoopopath himself, he has invented the whole story.

My Affair with My Landlord

As it is now pretty generally known that I have murdered the landlord of our flat, I feel that I should like to make some sort of public explanation of the matter.

I have been assured on all sides that there is no need to do this, but my own feelings on the question were so acute that I felt myself compelled to call upon the Superintendent of Police and offer him an exact account of what I had done. He told me that there is absolutely no need to offer any explanation at all. It is neither customary nor desirable.

"You have killed your landlord," he said, "very good, what of it?" I asked him whether it was not, in a sense, a matter for the law to deal with. But he shook his head. "In what way?" he asked.

I told him that I felt that the affair was putting me in a somewhat false position; that the congratulations that I have been receiving from my friends, and even from strangers, were perhaps, if the full circumstances were known, hardly merited; in short, that I should like a certain publicity given to the whole surroundings of the act.

"Very good," said the Superintendent, "you are entitled to fill out a form if you wish to do so." He searched among his papers.

"Did you say," he asked, "that you *have* killed your landlord, or that you are *going* to kill him?" "I *have* killed him," I said firmly. "Very good," said the officer, "we use separate forms." He gave me a long printed slip with blanks to fill in—my age, occupation, reasons (if any) for the killing, etc.

"What shall I put," I asked, "under the heading of *reasons?*"

"I think," he answered, "that it will be better to put simply, 'no reasons,' or if you like, the 'usual reasons'!" With that he bowed me politely out of his office, expressing, as he did so, the hope that I would bury the landlord and not leave him lying about.

To me the interview was unsatisfactory. I am well aware that the Superintendent was within the strict nicety of the law. No doubt if every case of the shooting of a landlord were made a matter of inquiry the result would be embarrassing and tedious.

The shooting is generally done in connection with a rise of rent, and nothing more needs to be said about it. "I am increasing your rent another $10.00 a month," says the landlord. "All right," says the tenant, "I'll shoot you." Sometimes he does, sometimes he forgets to.

But my own case was quite different. The proposal of the National Tenant League to give me a gold medal next Saturday has brought things to a head and forces an explanation.

I recall distinctly the time, now some five years ago, when my wife and I first took our flat. The landlord showed us over it himself, and I am free to confess that there was nothing in his manner, or very little indeed, to suggest anything out of the normal.

Only one small incident stuck in my mind. He apologized for the lack of cupboard space.

"There are not enough cupboards in this flat," he said.

It made me slightly uncomfortable to hear him speak in this way. "But look," I said, "how large and airy this pantry is. It is at least four feet each way."

He shook his head and repeated that the cupboards were small. "I must build in better ones," he said.

Two months later he built in new cupboards. It gave me a shock of surprise—a touch of the uncanny—to notice that he did not raise the rent. "Are you not raising the rent because of the cupboards?" I asked. "No," he said, "they only cost me fifty dollars." "But, my dear fellow," I objected, "surely the interest of fifty dollars is sixty dollars a year?"

He admitted this, but said that he would rather not raise the rent. Thinking it over, I decided that his conduct might be due to incipient paresis or coagulation of the arteries of the head. At that time I had no idea of killing him. That came later.

I recall no incident of importance till the spring of the year following. My landlord appeared unexpectedly one day with apologies for intruding (a fact which of itself seemed suspicious), and said that he proposed to repaper the entire apartment. I expostulated in vain.

"The paper," I said, "is only ten years old." "It is," he said, "but wall paper has gone up to double its value since that time." "Very good, then," I said firmly, "you must raise the rent twenty dollars a month for the paper." "I shall not," he answered. The incident led to a distinct coolness between us for some months.

The next episodes were of a more pronounced character. Everybody recalls the great increases of rent due to the terrific rise in building costs. My landlord refused to raise the rent of my flat.

"The cost of building," I said, "has increased at least one hundred per cent."

"Very good," he answered, "but I am not building. I have always been getting ten per cent on my investment in this property, and I am still getting it."

"Think of your wife," I said.

"I won't," he answered.

"It is your duty," I went on, "to think of her. Let me tell you that only yesterday I saw in the papers a letter from a landlord, one of the most beautiful letters I ever saw (from a landlord), in which he said the rise in the cost of building materials compelled him to think of his wife and children. It was a touching appeal."

"I don't care," my landlord answered, "I'm not married."

"Ah," I said, "not married." It was, I think, at this moment that the idea first occurred to me that the man might be put out of the way.

There followed the episode of November. My readers will all remember the fifty per cent increase of rents made to celebrate Armistice Day. My landlord refused to join in the celebrations.

This lack of patriotism in the fellow irritated me greatly. The same thing happened at the time of the rise of rents that was instituted to celebrate the visit of Marshal Foch, and the later rise—twenty-five per cent, if I remember rightly—that was made as a tribute to the ex-service men.

It was purely a patriotic movement, done in a spontaneous way without premeditation.

I have heard many of the soldiers say that it was their first welcome home, and that they would never forget it.

It was followed a little later by the rise of rents held as a welcome to the Prince of Wales. No better congratulation could have been planned.

My landlord, alas, remained outside of all this. He made no increase in his rent. "I have," he said, "my ten per cent, and that is enough."

I know now that the paresis or coagulation must have overwhelmed one entire lobe or hemisphere of his head.

I was meditating action.

The crisis came last month. A sharp rise in rent had

been very properly instituted to counterbalance the fall in the German mark. It was based quite evidently on the soundest business reasoning.

If the fall in the mark is not countered in this way, it is plain that we are undone. The cheap German mark will enable the Germans to take away our houses.

I waited for three days, looking in vain for a notice of increase in my rent.

Then I went to visit my landlord in his office. I admit that I was armed, but in extenuation I want to say that I knew that I had to deal with an abnormal, aberrated man, one-half of whose brain was now coagulated.

I wasted no words on preliminaries.

"You have seen," I said, "this fall of the German mark."

"Yes," he answered, "what of it?"

"Simply this," I said. "Are you going to raise my rent or are you not?"

"No," he said doggedly, "I am not."

I raised the revolver and fired. He was sitting sideways to me as I did so. I fired, in all, four shots. I could see through the smoke that one, at least, of the shots had cut his waistcoat into strips, a second had ripped off his collar, while the third and fourth had cut through his braces at the back. He was visibly in a state of collapse. It was doubtful if he could reach the street. But even if he could, it was certain that he couldn't walk upon it.

I left him as he was and reported, as I have said, to the police.

If the Tenant League medal is given to me, I want it to be with full understanding of the case.

The Give and Take of Travel

A Study in Petty Larceny, Pro and Con

I HAVE recently noted among my possessions a narrow black comb and a flat brown hairbrush. I imagine they must belong to the Pullman Car Company. As I have three of the Company's brushes and combs already, I shall be glad to hand these back at any time when the company cares to send for them.

I have also a copy of the New Testament in plain good print which is marked "put here by the Gibbons" and which I believe I got from either the Ritz-Carlton Hotel in Montreal or the Biltmore in New York. I do not know any of the Gibbons. But the hotel may have the book at any time, as I have finished with it. I will bring it to them.

On the other hand, I shall be very greatly obliged if the man who has my winter overshoes (left on the Twentieth Century Limited) will let me have them back again. As the winter is soon coming I shall need them. If he will leave them at any agreed spot three miles from a town I will undertake not to prosecute him.

I mention these matters not so much for their own sake as because they form part of the system of give and take which plays a considerable part in my existence.

Like many people who have to travel a great deal I get absent-minded about it. I move to and fro among trains and hotels shepherded by red-caps and escorted by bell boys. I have been in so many hotels that they all look alike. If there is any difference in the faces of the hotel clerks I can't see it. If there is any way of distinguishing one waiter from another I don't know it. There is the same underground barber surrounded by white marble and carrying on the same conversation all the way from Halifax to Los Angeles. In short I have been in so many towns that I never know where I am.

Under these circumstances a man of careless disposition and absent mind easily annexes and easily loses small items of property. In a Pullman car there is no difficulty whatever, if one has the disposition for it, in saying to a man sitting beside you, "Good morning, sir. It looks like a beautiful day," and then reaching over and packing his hair brush into your valise. If he is the right kind of man he will never notice it, or at best he will say in return, "A beautiful morning," and then take away your necktie.

There is, let it be noticed, all the difference in the world between this process and petty larceny.

The thing I mean couldn't possibly be done by a thief. He wouldn't have the nerve, the quiet assurance, the manner. It is the absolute innocence of the thing that does it.

For example, if a man offers me a cigarette I find that I take his cigarette case and put it in my pocket. When I rise from my hotel dinner I carry away the napkin. When I leave my hotel room I always take away the key.

There is no real sense in this: I have more hotel keys than I can use as it is. But the fault is partly with our hotels. So many of them put up a little notice beside the door that reads, "Have You Forgotten Anything?" Whenever I see this I stand in thought a minute then it occurs to me, "Why, of course, the Key!" and I take it with me.

I am aware that there is a class of persons—women mostly—who carry away spoons and other things deliberately as souvenirs. But I disclaim all connection with that kind of thing. That is not what I meant at all.

I would never take a valuable spoon, unless I happened

to be using it at the table to open the back of my watch, or something of the sort. But when I sign my name on the hotel book I keep the pen. Similarly and in all fairness, I give up my own fountain pen to the telegraph clerk. The theory works both ways.

As a rule, there is nothing more in all this than a harmless give and take, a sort of profit and loss account to which any traveler easily becomes accustomed. But at the same time one should be careful. The theory may go a little too far. I remember not long ago coming home from a theatre in Trenton, New Jersey, with a lady's white silk scarf about my neck.

I had no notion how it had got there. Whether the woman had carelessly wrapped it about my neck in mistake for her own, or whether I had unwound it off her, I cannot say. But I regret the incident and will gladly put the scarf back on her neck at any time. I will also take this occasion to express my regret for the pair of boots which I put on in a Pullman car in Syracuse in the dark of a winter morning.

There is a special arrangement on the New York Central whereby at Syracuse passengers making connections for the South are allowed to get up at four and dress while the others are still asleep. There are signs put up adjuring everybody to keep as quiet as possible. Naturally, these passengers get the best of everything and, within limits, it is fair enough as they have to get up so early. But the boots of which I speak outclass anything I ever bought for myself and I am sorry about them.

Our American railways have very wisely taken firm grounds on this problem of property mislaid or exchanged or lost on the Pullman cars. As everybody knows when one of our trains reaches a depot the passengers leave it with as mad a haste as if it were full of smallpox. In fact, they are all lined up at the door like cattle in a pen ready to break loose before the train stops. What happens to the car itself afterwards they don't care. It is known only to those who have left a hair brush in the car and tried to find it.

But in reality, the car is instantly rushed off to a siding, its number-placard taken out of the window so that it cannot be distinguished, after which a vacuum cleaner is turned on and sucks up any loose property that is left in it. Meantime the porter has avoided all detection by an instantaneous change of costume in which he appears disguised as a member of the Pittsburgh Yacht Club. If he could be caught at this time his pockets would be found to be full of fountain pens, rings and current magazines.

I do not mean to imply for a moment that our railways are acting in a dishonest way in the matter. On the contrary, they have no intention of keeping or annexing their passengers' property. But very naturally they do not want a lot of random people rummaging through their cars. They endeavor, however, through their central offices to make as fair a division of the lost-and-found property as they can. Anyone applying in the proper way can have some of it. I have always found in this respect the greatest readiness to give me a fair share of everything.

A few months ago for example I had occasion to send to the Canadian National Railway a telegram which read, "Have left gray fedora hat with black band on your Toronto-Chicago train." Within an hour I got back a message, "Your gray fedora hat being sent you from Windsor, Ontario." And a little later on the same day I received another message which read, "Sending gray hat from Chicago," and an hour after that, "Gray hat found at Sheboygan, Michigan."

Indeed, I think I am not exaggerating when I say that

any of our great Canadian and American Railways will send you anything of that sort if you telegraph for it. In my own case the theory has become a regular practice. I telegraph to the New York Central, "Please forward me spring overcoat in a light gray or fawn," and they send it immediately; or I call up the Canadian Pacific on the telephone and ask them if they can let me have a pair of tan boots and if possible a suit of golf clothes.

I have found that our leading hotels are even more punctilious in respect to their things than the railways. It is now hardly safe to attempt to leave in their rooms anything that one doesn't want. Last month, having cut my razor strop so badly that it was of no further use, I was foolish enough to leave it hanging in a room in the Biltmore Hotel in New York. On my return home I got a letter which read: "Dear Sir: We beg to inform you that you have left your razor strop in room 2216. We have had your strop packed in excelsior packing and await your instructions in regard to it."

I telegraphed back, "Please keep razor strop. You may have it." After which in due course I got a further letter which said, "We are pleased to inform you that the razor strop which you so generously gave to this Company has been laid before our board of directors who have directed us to express their delight and appreciation at your generous gift. Any time you want a room and bath let us know."

The Retroactive Existence of Mr. Juggins

I FIRST met Juggins,—really to notice him,—years and years ago as a boy out camping. Somebody was trying to nail up a board on a tree for a shelf and Juggins interfered to help him.

"Stop a minute," he said, "you need to saw the end of that board off before you put it up." Then Juggins looked round for a saw, and when he got it he had hardly made more than a stroke or two with it before he stopped. "This saw," he said, "needs to be filed up a bit." So he went and hunted up a file to sharpen the saw, but found that before he could use the file he needed to put a proper handle on it, and to make a handle he went to look for a sapling in the bush, but to cut the sapling he found that he needed to sharpen up the axe. To do this, of course, he had to fix the grindstone so as to make it run properly. This involved making wooden legs for the grindstone. To do this decently Juggins decided to make a carpenter's bench. This was quite impossible without a better set of tools. Juggins went to the village to get the tools required, and, of course, he never came back.

He was re-discovered—weeks later—in the city, getting prices on wholesale tool machinery.

After that first episode I got to know Juggins very well. For some time we were students at college together. But Juggins somehow never got far with his studies. He always began with great enthusiasm and then something happened. For a time he studied French with tremendous eagerness. But he soon found that for a real knowledge of French you need first to get a thorough grasp of Old

247

French and Provençal. But it proved impossible to do anything with these without an absolutely complete command of Latin. This Juggins discovered could only be obtained, in any thorough way, through Sanskrit, which of course lies at the base of it. So Juggins devoted himself to Sanskrit until he realised that for a proper understanding of Sanskrit one needs to study the ancient Iranian, the root-language underneath. This language however is lost.

So Juggins had to begin over again. He did, it is true, make some progress in natural science. He studied physics and rushed rapidly backwards from forces to molecules, and from molecules to atoms, and from atoms to electrons, and then his whole studies exploded backward into the infinities of space, still searching a first cause.

Juggins, of course, never took a degree, so he made no practical use of his education. But it didn't matter. He was very well off and was able to go straight into business with a capital of about a hundred thousand dollars. He put it at first into a gas plant, but found that he lost money at that because of the high price of the coal needed to make gas. So he sold out for ninety thousand dollars and went into coal mining. This was unsuccessful because of the awful cost of mining machinery. So Juggins sold his share in the mine for eighty thousand dollars and went in for manufacturing mining machinery. At this he would have undoubtedly made money but for the enormous cost of gas needed as motive-power for the plant. Juggins sold out of the manufacture for seventy thousand, and after that he went whirling in a circle, like skating backwards, through the different branches of allied industry.

He lost a certain amount of money each year, especially in good years when trade was brisk. In dull times when everything was unsalable he did fairly well.

Juggins' domestic life was very quiet.

Of course he never married. He did, it is true, fall in love several times; but each time it ended without result. I remember well his first love story for I was very intimate with him at the time. He had fallen in love with the girl in question utterly and immediately. It was literally love at first sight. There was no doubt of his intentions. As soon as he had met her he was quite frank about it. "I intend," he said, "to ask her to be my wife."

"When?" I asked. "Right away?"

"No," he said, "I want first to fit myself to be worthy of her."

So he went into moral training to fit himself. He taught in a Sunday school for six weeks, till he realised that a man has no business in Divine work of that sort without first preparing himself by serious study of the history of Palestine. And he felt that a man was a cad to force his society on a girl while he is still only half acquainted with the history of the Israelites. So Juggins stayed away. It was nearly two years before he was fit to propose. By the time he *was* fit, the girl had already married a brainless thing in patent leather boots who didn't even know who Moses was.

Of course Juggins fell in love again. People always do. And at any rate by this time he was in a state of moral fitness that made it imperative.

So he fell in love—deeply in love this time—with a charming girl, commonly known as the eldest Miss Thorneycroft. She was only called eldest because she had five younger sisters; and she was very poor and awfully clever and trimmed all her own hats. Any man, if he's worth the name, falls in love with that sort of thing at first sight. So, of course, Juggins would have proposed to her; only when he went to the house he met her next sister: and of course she was younger still; and, I suppose, poorer: and made not only her own hats but her own blouses. So Juggins fell in love with her. But one night when he went to call, the door was opened by the sister younger still, who not only made her own blouses and trimmed her own hats, but even made her own tailor-made suits. After that Juggins backed up from sister to sister till he went through the whole family, and in the end got none of them.

Perhaps it was just as well that Juggins never married. It would have made things very difficult because, of course, he got poorer all the time. You see after he sold out his last share in his last business he bought with it a diminishing life annuity, so planned that he always got rather less next year than this year, and still less the year after. Thus, if he lived long enough, he would starve to death.

Meantime he has become a quaint-looking elderly man, with coats a little too short and trousers a little above his boots—like a boy. His face too is like that of a boy, with wrinkles.

And his talk now has grown to be always reminiscent. He is perpetually telling long stories of amusing times that he has had with different people that he names.

He says for example—

"I remember a rather queer thing that happened to me in a train one day—"

And if you say, "When was that, Juggins?," he looks at you in a vague way as if calculating and says, "In 1875, or 1876, I think, as near as I recall it—"

I notice, too, that his reminiscences are going further and further back. He used to base his stories on his recollections as a young man; now they are further back.

The other day he told me a story about himself and two people that he called the Harper brothers,—Ned and Joe. Ned, he said was a tremendously powerful fellow.

I asked how old Ned was and Juggins said that he was

three. He added that there was another brother not so old, but a very clever fellow about,—here Juggins paused and calculated—about eighteen months.

So then I realised where Juggins' retroactive existence is carrying him to. He has passed back through childhood into infancy, and presently, just as his annuity runs to a point and vanishes, he will back up clear through the Curtain of Existence and die,—or be born, I don't know which to call it.

Meantime he remains to me as one of the most illuminating allegories I have met.

Homer and Humbug, an Academic Discussion

THE following discussion is of course only of interest to scholars. But, as the public schools returns show that in the United States there are now over a million coloured scholars alone, the appeal is wide enough.

I do not mind confessing that for a long time past I have been very sceptical about the classics. I was myself trained as a classical scholar. It seemed the only thing to do with me. I acquired such a singular facility in handling Latin and Greek that I could take a page of either of them, distinguish which it was by merely glancing at it, and, with the help of a dictionary and a pair of compasses, whip off a translation of it in less than three hours.

But I never got any pleasure from it. I lied about it. At first, perhaps, I lied through vanity. Any coloured scholar will understand the feeling. Lated on I lied through habit; later still because, after all, the classics were all that I had and so I valued them. I have seen thus a deceived dog value a pup with a broken leg, and a pauper child nurse a dead doll with the sawdust out of it. So I nursed my dead Homer and my broken Demosthenes though I knew in my heart that there was more sawdust in the stomach of one modern author than in the whole lot of them. Observe, I am not saying which it is that has it full of it.

So, as I say, I began to lie about the classics. I said to people who knew no Greek that there was a sublimity, a majesty about Homer which they could never hope to grasp. I said it was like the sound of the sea beating against the granite cliffs of the Ionian Esophagus: or words to that effect. As for the truth of it, I might as well have said that it was like the sound of a rum distillery running a night shift on half time. At any rate this is what I said about Homer, and when I spoke of Pindar,—the dainty grace of his strophes,—and Aristophanes, the delicious sallies of his wit, sally after sally, each sally explained in a note calling it a sally—I managed to suffuse my face with an animation which made it almost beautiful.

I admitted of course that Virgil in spite of his genius had a hardness and a cold glitter which resembled rather the brilliance of a cut diamond than the soft grace of a flower. Certainly I admitted this: the mere admission of it would knock the breath out of anyone who was arguing.

From such talks my friends went away sad. The conclusion was too cruel. It had all the cold logic of a syllogism (like that almost brutal form of argument so much admired in the Paraphernalia of Socrates). For if:—

Virgil and Homer and Pindar had all this grace, and pith and these sallies,—
And if I read Virgil and Homer and Pindar,
And if they only read Mrs. Wharton and Mrs. Humphrey Ward
Then where were they?

So continued lying brought its own reward in the sense of superiority and I lied more.

When I reflect that I have openly expressed regret, as a personal matter, even in the presence of women, for the missing books of Tacitus, and the entire loss of the Abacadabra of Polyphemus of Syracuse, I can find no words in which to beg for pardon. In reality I was just as much worried over the loss of the ichthyosaurus. More, indeed:

I'd like to have seen it: but if the books Tacitus lost were like those he didn't, I wouldn't.

I believe all scholars lie like this. An ancient friend of mine, a clergyman, tells me that in Hesiod he finds a peculiar grace that he doesn't find elsewhere. He's a liar. That's all. Another man, in politics and in the legislature, tells me that every night before going to bed he reads over a page or two of Thucydides to keep his mind fresh. Either he never goes to bed or he's a liar. Doubly so: no one could read Greek at that frantic rate: and anyway his mind isn't fresh. How could it be, he's in the legislature. I don't object to this man talking freely of the classics, but he ought to keep it for the voters. My own opinion is that before he goes to bed he takes whiskey: why call it Thucydides?

I know there are solid arguments advanced in favour of the classics. I often hear them from my colleagues. My friend the professor of Greek tells me that he truly believes the classics have made him what he is. This is a very grave statement, if well founded. Indeed I have heard the same argument from a great many Latin and Greek scholars. They all claim, with some heat, that Latin and Greek have practically made them what they are. This damaging charge against the classics should not be too readily accepted. In my opinion some of these men would have been what they are, no matter what they were.

Be this as it may, I for my part bitterly regret the lies I have told about my appreciation of Latin and Greek literature. I am anxious to do what I can to set things right. I am therefore engaged on, indeed have nearly completed, a work which will enable all readers to judge the matter for themselves. What I have done is a translation of all the great classics, not in the usual literal way but on a design that brings them into harmony with modern life. I will explain what I mean in a minute.

The translation is intended to be within reach of everybody. It is so designed that the entire set of volumes can go on a shelf twenty-seven feet long, or even longer. The first edition will be an *édition de luxe* bound in vellum, or perhaps in buckskin, and sold at five hundred dollars. It will be limited to five hundred copies and, of course, sold only to the feeble-minded. The next edition will be the Literary Edition, sold to artists, authors, actors and contractors. After that will come the Boarding House Edition, bound in board and paid for in the same way.

My plan is to so transpose the classical writers as to give, not the literal translation word for word, but what is really the modern equivalent. Let me give an odd sample or two to show what I mean. Take the passage in the First Book of Homer that describes Ajax the Greek dashing into the battle in front of Troy. Here is the way it runs (as nearly as I remember), in the usual word for word translation of the classroom, as done by the very best professor, his spectacles glittering with the literary rapture of it.

"Then he too Ajax on the one hand leaped (or possibly jumped) into the fight wearing on the other hand, yes certainly a steel corselet (or possibly a bronze under tunic) and on his head of course, yes without doubt he had a helmet with a tossing plume taken from the mane (or perhaps extracted from the tail) of some horse which once fed along the banks of the Scamander (and it sees the herd and raises its head and paws the ground) and in his hand a shield worth a hundred oxen and on his knees too especially in particular greaves made by some cunning artificer (or perhaps blacksmith) and he blows the fire and it is hot.

Thus Ajax leapt (or, better, was propelled from behind), into the fight."

Now that's grand stuff. There is no doubt of it. There's a wonderful movement and force to it. You can almost see it move, it goes so fast. But the modern reader can't get it. It won't mean to him what it meant to the early Greek. The setting, the costume, the scene has all got to be changed in order to let the reader have a real equivalent to judge just how good the Greek verse is. In my translation I alter it just a little, not much but just enough to give the passage a form that reproduces the proper literary value of the verses, without losing anything of the majesty. It describes, I may say, the Directors of the American Industrial Stocks rushing into the Balkan War Cloud.—

> Then there came rushing to the shock of war
> Mr. McNicoll of the C. P. R.
> He wore suspenders and about his throat
> High rose the collar of a sealskin coat.
> He had on gaiters and he wore a tie,
> He had his trousers buttoned good and high;
> About his waist a woollen undervest
> Bought from a sad-eyed farmer of the West.
> (And every time he clips a sheep he sees
> Some bloated plutocrat who ought to freeze),
> Thus in the Stock Exchange he burst to view,
> Leaped to the post, and shouted, "Ninety-two!"

There! That's Homer, the real thing! Just as it sounded to the rude crowd of Greek peasants who sat in a ring and guffawed at the rhymes and watched the minstrel stamp it out into "feet" as he recited it!

Or let me take another example from the so-called Catalogue of the Ships that fills up nearly an entire book of Homer. This famous passage names all the ships, one by one, and names the chiefs who sailed on them, and names the particular town or hill or valley that they came from. It has been much admired. It has that same majesty of style that has been brought to an even loftier pitch in the New York Business Directory and the City Telephone Book. It runs along, as I recall it, something like this,—

"And first, indeed, oh, yes, was the ship of Homistogetes the Spartan, long and swift, having both its masts covered with cowhide and two rows of oars. And he, Homistogetes, was born of Hermogenes and Ohpthalmia and was at home in Syncope beside the fast flowing Paresis. And after him came the ship of Preposterus the Eurasian, son of Oasis and Hyteria," . . . and so on endlessly.

Instead of this I substitute, with the permission of the New York Central Railway, the official catalogue of their locomotives taken almost word for word from the list compiled by their superintendent of works. I admit that he wrote in hot weather. Part of it runs:—

Out in the yard and steaming in the sun
Stands locomotive engine number forty-one;
Seated beside the windows of the cab
Are Pat McGaw and Peter James McNab.
Pat comes from Troy and Peter from Cohoes,
And when they pull the throttle off she goes;
And as she vanishes there comes to view
Steam locomotive engine number forty-two.
Observe her mighty wheels, her easy roll,
With William J. Macarthy in control.
They say her engineer some time ago
Lived on a farm outside of Buffalo
Whereas his fireman, Henry Edward Foy,
Attended School in Springfield, Illinois.
Thus does the race of man decay or rot—
Some men can hold their jobs and some can not.

Please observe that if Homer had actually written that last line it would have been quoted for a thousand years as one of the deepest sayings ever said. Orators would have rounded out their speeches with the majestic phrase, quoted in sonorous and unintelligible Greek verse, "some men can hold their jobs and some can not": essayists would have begun their most scholarly dissertations with the words,—"It has been finely said by Homer that (in Greek) 'some men can hold their jobs' ": and the clergy in mid-pathos of a funeral sermon would have raised their eyes aloft and echoed "Some men can not"!

This is what I should like to do. I'd like to take a large stone and write on it in very plain writing,—

"The classics are only primitive literature. They belong in the same class as primitive machinery and primitive music and primitive medicine,"—and then throw it through the windows of a University and hide behind a fence to see the professors buzz!!

"We Have with Us To-Night"

NOT only during my tour in England but for many years past it has been my lot to speak and to lecture in all sorts of places, under all sorts of circumstances and before all sorts of audiences. I say this, not in boastfulness, but in sorrow. Indeed, I only mention it to establish the fact that when I talk of lecturers and speakers, I talk of what I know.

Few people realise how arduous and how disagreeable public lecturing is. The public sees the lecturer step out on to the platform in his little white waistcoat and his long tailed coat and with a false air of a conjurer about him, and they think him happy. After about ten minutes of his talk they are tired of him. Most people tire of a lecture in ten minutes; clever people can do it in five. Sensible people never go to lectures at all. But the people who do go to a lecture and who get tired of it, presently hold it as a sort of a grudge against the lecturer personally. In reality his sufferings are worse than theirs.

For my own part I always try to appear as happy as possible while I am lecturing. I take this to be part of the trade of anybody labelled a humorist and paid as such. I have no sympathy whatever with the idea that a humourist ought to be a lugubrious person with a face stamped with melancholy. This is a cheap and elementary effect belonging to the level of a circus clown. The image of "laughter shaking both his sides" is the truer picture of comedy. Therefore, I say, I always try to appear cheerful at my lectures and even to laugh at my own jokes. Oddly enough this arouses a kind of resentment in some of the audience. "Well, I will say," said a stern-looking woman who spoke to me after one of my lectures, "you certainly do seem to enjoy your own fun." "Madam," I answered, "if I didn't, who would?" But in reality the whole business of being a public lecturer is one long variation of boredom and fatigue. So I propose to set down here some of the many trials which the lecturer has to bear.

The first of the troubles which anyone who begins giving public lectures meets at the very outset is the fact that the audience won't come to hear him. This happens invariably and constantly, and not through any fault or shortcoming of the speaker.

I don't say that this happened very often to me in my tour in England. In nearly all cases I had crowded audiences: by dividing up the money that I received by the average number of people present to hear me I have calculated that they paid thirteen cents each. And my lectures are evidently worth thirteen cents. But at home in Canada I have very often tried the fatal experiment of lecturing for nothing: and in that case the audience simply won't come. A man will turn out at night when he knows he is going to hear a first class thirteen cent lecture; but when the thing is given for nothing, why go to it?

The city in which I live is overrun with little societies, clubs and associations, always wanting to be addressed. So at least it is in appearance. In reality the societies are composed of presidents, secretaries and officials, who want the conspicuousness of office, and a large list of other members who won't come to the meetings. For such an association, the invited speaker who is to lecture for nothing prepares his lecture on "Indo-Germanic Factors in the Current of History." If he is a professor, he takes all the winter at it. You may drop in at his house at any time and his wife will tell you that he is "upstairs working on his lecture." If he comes down at all it is in carpet slippers and dressing gown. His mental vision of his meeting is that of a huge gathering of keen people with Indo-Germanic faces, hanging upon every word.

Then comes the fated night. There are seventeen people present. The lecturer refuses to count them. He refers to them afterwards as "about a hundred." To this group he reads his paper on the Indo-Germanic Factor. It takes him two hours. When he is over the chairman invites discussion. There is *no* discussion. The audience is willing to let the Indo-Germanic factors go unchallenged. Then the chairman makes this speech. He says:

"I am very sorry indeed that we should have had such a very poor 'turn out' to-night. I am sure that the members who were not here have missed a real treat in the delightful paper that we have listened to. I want to assure the lecturer that if he comes to the Owl's Club again we can guarantee him next time a capacity audience. And will any members, please, who haven't paid their dollar this winter, pay it either to me or to Mr. Sibley, as they pass out."

I have heard this speech (in the years when I have had to listen to it) so many times that I know it by heart. I have made the acquaintance of the Owl's Club under so many names that I recognise it at once. I am aware that its members refuse to turn out in cold weather; that they do not turn out in wet weather; that when the weather is really fine, it is impossible to get them together; that the slightest counter-attraction,—a hockey match, a sacred concert,—goes to their heads at once.

There was a time when I was the newly appointed occupant of a college chair and had to address the Owl's Club. It is a penalty that all new professors pay; and the Owls batten upon them like bats. It is one of the compensations of age that I am free of the Owl's Club forever. But in the days when I still had to address them, I used to take it out of the Owls in a speech, delivered, in imagination only and not out loud, to the assembled meeting of the seventeen Owls, after the chairman had made his concluding remarks. It ran as follows:

"Gentlemen—if you are such, which I doubt. I realise that the paper which I have read on "Was Hegel a deist?" has been an error. I spent all the winter on it and now I realise that not one of you pups know who Hegel was or what a deist is. Never mind. It is over now, and I am glad. But just let me say this, only this, which won't keep you a minute. Your chairman has been good enough to say that if I come again you will get together a capacity audience to hear me. Let me tell you that if your society waits for its next meeting till I come to address you again, you will wait indeed. In fact, gentlemen—I say it very frankly—it will be in another world."

But I pass over the audience. Suppose there is a real audience, and suppose them all duly gathered together. Then it becomes the business of that gloomy gentleman—facetiously referred to in the newspaper reports as the "genial chairman"—to put the lecturer to the bad. In nine cases out of ten he can do so. Some chairmen, indeed, develop a great gift for it. Here are one or two examples from my own experience:

"Ladies and gentlemen," said the chairman of a society in a little country town in Western Ontario, to which I had come as a paid (a very humbly paid) lecturer, "we have with us to-night a gentleman" (here he made an attempt to read my name on a card, failed to read it and put the card back in his pocket)—"a gentleman who is to lecture to us on" (here he looked at his card again)—"on Ancient—Ancient—I don't very well see what it is—

Ancient—Britain? Thank you, on Ancient Britain. Now, this is the first of our series of lectures for this winter. The last series, as you all know, was not a success. In fact, we came out at the end of the year with a deficit. So this year we are starting a new line and trying the experiment of cheaper talent."

Here the chairman gracefully waved his hand toward me and there was a certain amount of applause. "Before I sit down," the chairman added, "I'd like to say that I am sorry to see such a poor turn-out to-night and to ask any of the members who haven't paid their dollar to pay it either to me or to Mr. Sibley as they pass out."

Let anybody who knows the discomfiture of coming out before an audience on any terms, judge how it feels to crawl out in front of them labelled *cheaper talent*.

Another charming way in which the chairman endeavours to put both the speaker for the evening and the audience into an entirely good humour, is by reading out letters of regret from persons unable to be present. This, of course, is only for grand occasions when the speaker has been invited to come under very special auspices. It was my fate, not long ago, to "appear" (this is the correct word to use in this connection) in this capacity when I was going about Canada trying to raise some money for the relief of the Belgians. I travelled in great glory with a pass on the Canadian Pacific Railway (not since extended: officials of the road kindly note this) and was most generously entertained wherever I went.

It was, therefore, the business of the chairman at such meetings as these to try and put a special distinction or cachet on the gathering. This is how it was done:

"Ladies and gentlemen," said the chairman, rising from his seat on the platform with a little bundle of papers in his hand, "before I introduce the speaker of the evening,

I have one or two items that I want to read to you." Here he rustles his papers and there is a deep hush in the hall while he selects one. "We had hoped to have with us to-night Sir Robert Borden, the Prime Minister of this Dominion. I have just received a telegram from Sir Robert in which he says that he will not be able to be here" (*great applause*). The chairman puts up his hand for silence, picks up another telegram and continues, "Our committee, ladies and gentlemen, telegraphed an invitation to Sir Wilfred Laurier very cordially inviting him to be here to-night. I have here Sir Wilfred's answer in which he says that he will not be able to be with us" (*renewed applause*). The chairman again puts up his hand for silence and goes on, picking up one paper after another. "The Minister of Finance regrets that he will be unable to come" (*applause*). "Mr. Rodolphe Lemieux (*applause*) will not be here (*great applause*)—the Mayor of Toronto (*applause*) is detained on business (*wild applause*)—the Anglican Bishop of the Diocese (*applause*)—the Principal of the University College, Toronto (*great applause*)—the Minister of Education (*applause*)—none of these are coming." There is a great clapping of hands and enthusiasm, after which the meeting is called to order with a very distinct and palpable feeling that it is one of the most distinguished audiences ever gathered in the hall.

Here is another experience of the same period while I was pursuing the same exalted purpose: I arrived in a little town in Eastern Ontario, and found to my horror that I was billed to "appear" *in a church*. I was supposed to give readings from my works, and my books are supposed to be of a humorous character. A church hardly seemed the right place to get funny in. I explained my difficulty to the pastor of the church, a very solemn looking man. He nodded his head, slowly and gravely, as he grasped my difficulty. "I see," he said, "I see, but I think that I can introduce you to our people in such a way as to make that right."

When the time came, he led me up on to the pulpit platform of the church, just beside and below the pulpit itself, with a reading desk and a big Bible and a shaded light beside it. It was a big church, and the audience, sitting in half darkness, as is customary during a sermon, reached away back into the gloom. The place was packed full and absolutely quiet. Then the chairman spoke:

"Dear friends," he said, "I want you to understand that it will be all right to laugh to-night. Let me hear you laugh heartily, laugh right out, just as much as ever you want to, because" (and here his voice assumed the deep sepulchral tones of the preacher),—"when we think of the noble object for which the professor appears to-night, we may be assured that the Lord will forgive anyone who will laugh at the professor."

I am sorry to say, however, that none of the audience, even with the plenary absolution in advance, were inclined to take a chance on it.

I recall in this same connection the chairman of a meeting at a certain town in Vermont. He represents the type of chairman who turns up so late at the meeting that the committee have no time to explain to him properly what the meeting is about or who the speaker is. I noticed on this occasion that he introduced me very guardedly by name (from a little card) and said nothing about the Belgians, and nothing about my being (supposed to be) a humourist. This last was a great error. The audience, for want of guidance, remained very silent and decorous, and well behaved during my talk. Then, somehow, at the end, while someone was moving a vote of thanks, the chairman discovered his error. So he tried to make it good.

Just as the audience were getting up to put on their wraps, he rose, knocked on his desk and said:

"Just a minute, please, ladies and gentlemen, just a minute. I have just found out—I should have known it sooner, but I was late in coming to this meeting—that the speaker who has just addressed you has done so in behalf of the Belgian Relief Fund. I understand that he is a well-known Canadian humourist (ha! ha!) and I am sure that we have all been immensely amused (ha! ha!). He is giving his delightful talks (ha! ha!)—though I didn't know this till just this minute—for the Belgian Relief Fund, and he is giving his services for nothing. I am sure when we realise this, we shall all feel that it has been well worth while to come. I am only sorry that we didn't have a better turnout to-night. But I can assure the speaker that if he will come again, we shall guarantee him a capacity audience. And I may say, that if there are any members of this association who have not paid their dollar this season, they can give it either to myself or to Mr. Sibley as they pass out."

With the amount of accumulated experience that I had behind me I was naturally interested during my lecture in England in the chairmen who were to introduce me. I cannot help but feel that I have acquired a fine taste in chairmen. I know them just as other experts know old furniture and Pekinese dogs. The witty chairman, the prosy chairman, the solemn chairman,—I know them all. As soon as I shake hands with the chairman in the Committee room I can tell exactly how he will act.

There are certain types of chairmen who have so often been described and are so familiar that it is not worth while to linger on them. Everybody knows the chairman who says,—"Now, ladies and gentlemen, you have not come here to listen to *me*. So I will be very brief; in fact, I will confine my remarks to just one or two very short observations." He then proceeds to make observations for twenty-five minutes. At the end of it he remarks with charming simplicity, "Now I know that you are all impatient to hear the lecturer. . . ."

And everybody knows the chairman who comes to the meeting with a very imperfect knowledge of who or what the lecturer is, and is driven to introduce him by saying:

"Our lecturer of the evening is widely recognised as one of the greatest authorities on,—on,—on his subject in the world to-day. He comes to us from,—from a great distance and I can assure him that it is a great pleasure to this audience to welcome a man who has done so much to,—to, —to advance the interests of,—of,—of everything as he has."

But this man, bad as he is, is not so bad as the chairman whose preparation for introducing the speaker has obviously been made at the eleventh hour. Just such a chairman it was my fate to strike in the form of a local alderman, built like an ox, in one of those small manufacturing places in the north of England where they grow men of this type and elect them into office.

"I never saw the lecturer before," he said, "but I've read his book." (I have written nineteen books.) "The committee was good enough to send me over his book last night. I didn't read it all but I took a look at the preface and I can assure him that he is very welcome. I understand he comes from a college. . . ." Then he turned directly towards me and said in a loud voice, "What was the name of that college over there you said you came from?"

"McGill," I answered equally loudly.

"He comes from McGill," the chairman boomed out.

"I never heard of McGill myself but I can assure him he's welcome. He's going to lecture to us on,—what did you say it was to be about?"

"It's a humorous lecture," I said.

"Ay, it's to be a humorous lecture, ladies and gentlemen, and I'll venture to say it will be a rare treat. I'm only sorry I can't stay for it myself as I have to get back over to the Town Hall for a meeting. So without more ado I'll get off the platform and let the lecturer go on with his humour."

A still more terrible type of chairman is one whose mind is evidently preoccupied and disturbed with some local happening and who comes on to the platform with a face imprinted with distress. Before introducing the lecturer he refers in moving tones to the local sorrow, whatever it is. As a prelude to a humorous lecture this is not gay.

Such a chairman fell to my lot one night before a gloomy audience in a London suburb.

"As I look about this hall to-night," he began in a doleful whine, "I see many empty seats." Here he stifled a sob. "Nor am I surprised that a great many of our people should prefer to-night to stay quietly at home—"

I had no clue to what he meant. I merely gathered that some particular sorrow must have overwhelmed the town that day.

"To many it may seem hardly fitting that after the loss our town has sustained we should come out here to listen to a humorous lecture—"

"What's the trouble?" I whispered to a citizen sitting beside me on the platform.

"Our oldest resident"—he whispered back—"he died this morning."

"How old?"

"Ninety-four," he whispered.

Meantime the chairman, with deep sobs in his voice, continued:

"We debated in our committee whether or not we should have the lecture. Had it been a lecture of another character our position would have been less difficult—"

By this time I began to feel like a criminal.

"The case would have been different had the lecture been one that contained information, or that was inspired by some serious purpose, or that could have been of any benefit. But this is not so. We understand that this lecture which Mr. Leacock has already given, I believe, twenty or thirty times in England—"

Here he turned to me with a look of mild reproval while the silent audience, deeply moved, all looked at me as at a man who went around the country insulting the memory of the dead by giving a lecture thirty times.

"We understand, though this we shall have an opportunity of testing for ourselves presently, that Mr. Leacock's lecture is not of a character which—has not, so to speak, the kind of value—in short, is not a lecture of that class."

Here he paused and choked back a sob.

"Had our poor friend been spared to us for another six years he would have rounded out the century. But it was not to be. For two or three years past he has noted that somehow his strength was failing, that, for some reason or other, he was no longer what he had been. Last month he began to droop. Last week he began to sink. Speech left him last Tuesday. This morning he passed, and he has gone now, we trust, in safety to where there are no lectures."

The audience were now nearly in tears.

The chairman made a visible effort towards firmness and control.

"But yet," he continued, "our committee felt that in another sense it was our duty to go on with our arrangements. I think, ladies and gentlemen, that the war has taught us all that it is always our duty to 'carry on,' no matter how hard it may be, no matter with what reluctance we do it, and whatever be the difficulties and the dangers, we must carry on to the end: for after all there is an end and by resolution and patience we can reach it.

"I will, therefore, invite Mr. Leacock to deliver to us his humorous lecture, the title of which I have forgotten, but I understand it to be the same lecture which he has already given thirty or forty times in England."

But contrast with this melancholy man the genial and pleasing person who introduced me, all upside down, to a metropolitan audience.

He was so brisk, so neat, so sure of himself that it didn't seem possible that he could make any kind of a mistake. I thought it unnecessary to coach him. He seemed absolutely all right.

"It is a great pleasure,"—he said, with a charming, easy appearance of being entirely at home on the platform,— "to welcome here to-night our distinguished Canadian fellow citizen, Mr. Learoyd"—he turned half way towards me as he spoke with a sort of gesture of welcome, admirably executed. If only my name had been Learoyd instead of Leacock it would have been excellent.

"There are many of us," he continued, "who have awaited Mr. Learoyd's coming with the most pleasant anticipations. We seemed from his books to know him already as an old friend. In fact I think I do not exaggerate when I tell Mr. Learoyd that his name in our city has long been a household word. I have very, very great pleasure, ladies and gentlemen, in introducing to you Mr. Learoyd."

As far as I know that chairman never knew his error. At the close of my lecture he said that he was sure that the audience "were deeply indebted to Mr. Learoyd," and then with a few words of rapid, genial apology buzzed off, like a humming bird, to other avocations. But I have amply forgiven him: anything for kindness and geniality; it makes the whole of life smooth. If that chairman ever comes to my home town he is hereby invited to lunch or dine with me, as Mr. Learoyd or under any name that he selects.

Such a man is, after all, in sharp contrast to the kind of chairman who has no native sense of the geniality that ought to accompany his office. There is, for example, a type of man who thinks that the fitting way to introduce a lecturer is to say a few words about the finances of the society to which he is to lecture (for money) and about the difficulty of getting members to turn out to hear lectures.

Everybody has heard such a speech a dozen times. But it is the paid lecturer sitting on the platform who best appreciates it. It runs like this:

"Now, ladies and gentlemen, before I invite the lecturer of the evening to address us there are a few words that I would like to say. There are a good many members who are in arrears with their fees. I am aware that these are hard times and it is difficult to collect money but at the same time the members ought to remember that the expenses of the society are very heavy. The fees that are asked by the lecturers, as I suppose you know, have advanced very greatly in the last few years. In fact I may say that they are becoming almost prohibitive."

This discourse is pleasant hearing for the lecturer. He can see the members who have not yet paid their annual dues eyeing him with hatred. The chairman goes on:

"Our finance committee were afraid at first that we could not afford to bring Mr. Leacock to our society. But fortunately through the personal generosity of two or our members who subscribed ten pounds each out of their own pocket we are able to raise the required sum."

(*Applause: during which the lecturer sits looking and feeling like the embodiment of the "required sum."*)

"Now, ladies and gentlemen," continues the chairman, "what I feel is that when we have members in the society who are willing to make this sacrifice,—because it is a sacrifice, ladies and gentlemen,—we ought to support them in every way. The members ought to think it their duty to turn out to the lectures. I know that it is not an easy thing to do. On a cold night, like this evening, it is hard, I admit it is hard, to turn out from the comfort of one's own fireside and come and listen to a lecture. But I think that the members should look at it not as a matter of personal comfort but as a matter of duty towards this society. We have managed to keep this society alive for fifteen years and, though I don't say it in any spirit of boasting, it has not been an easy thing to do. It has required a good deal of pretty hard spade work by the committee. Well, ladies and gentlemen, I suppose you didn't come here to listen to me and perhaps I have said enough about our difficulties and troubles. So without more ado (this is always a favourite phrase with chairmen) I'll invite Mr. Leacock to address the society,—oh, just a word before I sit down. Will all those who are leaving before the end of the lecture kindly go out through the side door and step as quietly as possible? Mr. Leacock."

Anybody who is in the lecture business knows that that introduction is far worse than being called Mr. Learoyd.

When any lecturer goes across to England from this side of the water there is naturally a tendency on the part of the chairman to play upon this fact. This is especially true in the case of a Canadian like myself. The chairman feels that the moment is fitting for one of those great imperial thoughts that bind the British Empire together. But sometimes the expression of the thought falls short of the full glory of the conception.

Witness this (word for word) introduction that was used against me by a clerical chairman in a quiet spot in the south of England:

"Not so long ago, ladies and gentlemen," said the vicar, "we used to send out to Canada various classes of our community to help build up that country. We sent out our labourers, we sent out our scholars and professors. Indeed we even sent out our criminals. And now," with a wave of his hand towards me, "they are coming back."

There was no laughter. An English audience is nothing if not literal; and they are as polite as they are literal. They understood that I was a reformed criminal and as such they gave me a hearty burst of applause.

But there is just one thing that I would like to chronicle here in favour of the chairman and in gratitude for his assistance. Even at his worst he is far better than having no chairman at all. Over in England a great many societies and public bodies have adopted the plan of "cutting out the chairman." Wearying of his faults, they have forgotten the reasons for his existence and undertaken to do without him.

The result is ghastly. The lecturer steps up on to the platform alone and unaccompanied. There is a feeble ripple of applause; he makes his miserable bow and explains with as much enthusiasm as he can who he is. The atmosphere of the thing is so cold that an Arctic expedition isn't in it with it. I found also the further difficulty that in the absence of the chairman very often the audience, or a large part of it, doesn't know who the lecturer is. On many occasions I received, on appearing, a wild burst of ap

plause under the impression that I was somebody else. I
have been mistaken in this way for Mr. Briand, then Prime
Minister of France, for Charlie Chaplin, for Mrs. Asquith,
—but stop, I may get into a libel suit. All I mean is that
without a chairman "we celebrities" get terribly mixed up
together.

To one experience of my tour as a lecturer I shall always
be able to look back with satisfaction. I nearly had the
pleasure of killing a man with laughing: and this in the
most literal sense. American lecturers have often dreamed
of doing this. I nearly did it. The man in question was
a comfortable apoplectic-looking man with the kind of
merry rubicund face that is seen in countries where they
don't have prohibition. He was seated near the back of
the hall and was laughing uproariously. All of a sudden
I realised that something was happening. The man had
collapsed sideways on to the floor; a little group of men
gathered about him; they lifted him up and I could see
them carrying him out, a silent and inert mass. As in duty
bound I went right on with my lecture. But my heart
beat high with satisfaction. I was sure that I had killed
him. The reader may judge how high these hopes rose
when a moment or two later a note was handed to the
chairman who then asked me to pause for a moment in my
lecture and stood up and asked, "Is there a doctor in the
audience?" A doctor rose and silently went out. The
lecture continued; but there was no more laughter; my
aim had now become to kill another of them and they
knew it. They were aware that if they started laughing
they might die. In a few minutes a second note was
handed to the chairman. He announced very gravely, "A
second doctor is wanted." The lecture went on in deeper
silence than ever. All the audience were waiting for a
third announcement. It came. A new message was

handed to the chairman. He rose and said, "If Mr. Murchison, the undertaker, is in the audience, will he kindly step outside."

That man, I regret to say, got well. Disappointing though it is to read it, he recovered. I sent back next morning from London a telegram of enquiry (I did it in reality so as to have a proper proof of his death) and received the answer, "Patient doing well; is sitting up in bed and reading Lord Haldane's *Relativity*; no danger of relapse."

Caroline's Christmas: or, The Inex-plicable Infant

It was Xmas—Xmas with its mantle of white snow, scintillating from a thousand diamond points, Xmas with its good cheer, its peace on earth—Xmas with its feasting and merriment, Xmas with its—well, anyway, it was Xmas.

Or no, that's a slight slip; it wasn't exactly Xmas, it was Xmas Eve, Xmas Eve with its mantle of white snow lying beneath the calm moonlight—and, in fact, with practically the above list of accompanying circumstances with a few obvious emendations.

Yes, it was Xmas Eve.

And more than that!

Listen to *where* it was Xmas.

It was Xmas Eve on the Old Homestead. Reader, do you know, by sight, the Old Homestead? In the pauses of your work at your city desk, where you have grown rich and avaricious, does it never rise before your mind's eye, the quiet old homestead that knew you as a boy before your greed of gold tore you away from it? The Old Homestead that stands beside the road just on the rise of the hill, with its dark spruce trees wrapped in snow, the snug barns and straw stacks behind it; while from its windows there streams a shaft of light from a coal-oil lamp, about as thick as a slate pencil that you can see four miles away, from the other side of the cedar swamp in the hollow. Don't talk to me of your modern searchlights and your incandescent arcs, beside that gleam of light from the coal-oil lamp in the farmhouse window. It will shine clear to the heart across thirty years of distance. Do you not turn, I say, sometimes, reader, from the roar and hustle of the city with its ill-gotten wealth and its godless creed of mammon, to think of the quiet homestead under the brow of the hill? You don't! Well, you skunk!

It was Xmas Eve.

The light shone from the windows of the homestead farm. The light of the log fire rose and flickered and mingled its red glare on the windows with the calm yellow of the lamplight.

John Enderby and his wife sat in the kitchen room of the farmstead. Do you know it, reader, the room called the kitchen?—with the open fire on its old brick hearth, and the cook stove in the corner. It is the room of the farm where people cook and eat and live. It is the living-room. The only other room beside the bedroom is the small room in front, chill-cold in winter, with an organ in it for playing "Rock of Ages" on, when company came. But this room is only used for music and funerals. The real room of the old farm is the kitchen. Does it not rise up before you, reader? It doesn't? Well, you darn fool!

At any rate there sat old John Enderby beside the plain deal table, his head bowed upon his hands, his grizzled face with its unshorn stubble stricken down with the lines of devastating trouble. From time to time he rose and cast a fresh stick of tamarack into the fire with a savage thud that sent a shower of sparks up the chimney. Across the fireplace sat his wife Anna on a straight-backed chair, looking into the fire with the mute resignation of her sex.

What was wrong with them anyway? Ah, reader, can you ask? Do you know or remember so little of the life of the old homestead? When I have said that it is the Old Homestead and Xmas Eve, and that the farmer is in great trouble and throwing tamarack at the fire, surely you ought to guess!

The Old Homestead was mortgaged! Ten years ago, reckless with debt, crazed with remorse, mad with despair and persecuted with rheumatism, John Enderby had mortgaged his farmstead for twenty-four dollars and thirty cents.

To-night the mortgage fell due, to-night at midnight, Xmas night. Such is the way in which mortgages of this kind are always drawn. Yes, sir, it was drawn with such diabolical skill that on this night of all nights the mortgage would be foreclosed. At midnight the men would come with hammer and nails and foreclose it, nail it up tight.

So the afflicted couple sat.

Anna, with the patient resignation of her sex, sat silent or at times endeavoured to read. She had taken down from the little wall-shelf Bunyan's *Holy Living and Holy Dying*. She tried to read it. She could not. Then she had taken Dante's *Inferno*. She could not read it. Then she had selected Kant's *Critique of Pure Reason*. But she could not read it either. Lastly, she had taken the Farmers' Almanac for 1911. The books lay littered about her as she sat in patient despair.

John Enderly showed all the passion of an uncontrolled nature. At times he would reach out for the crock of buttermilk that stood beside him and drain a draught of the maddening liquid, till his brain glowed like the coals of the tamarack fire before him.

"John," pleaded Anna, "leave alone the buttermilk. It only maddens you. No good ever came of that."

"Aye, lass," said the farmer, with a bitter laugh, as he buried his head again in the crock, "what care I if it maddens me."

"Ah, John, you'd better be employed in reading the

Good Book than in your wild courses. Here take it, father,
and read it"—and she handed to him the well-worn black
volume from the shelf. Enderby paused a moment and
held the volume in his hand. He and his wife had known
nothing of religious teaching in the public schools of their
day, but the first-class non-sectarian education that the
farmer had received had stood him in good stead.

"Take the book," she said. "Read, John, in this hour
of affliction; it brings comfort."

The farmer took from her hand the well-worn copy of
Euclid's *Elements*, and, laying aside his hat with reverence,
he read aloud: "The angles at the base of an isoceles triangle
are equal, and whosoever shall produce the sides, lo, the
same also shall be equal each unto each."

The farmer put the book aside.

"It's no use, Anna. I can't read the good words to-
night."

He rose, staggered to the crock of buttermilk, and before his wife could stay his hand, drained it to the last drop.

Then he sank heavily to his chair.

"Let them foreclose it, if they will," he said; "I am
past caring."

The woman looked sadly into the fire.

Ah, if only her son Henry had been here. Henry, who
had left them three years agone, and whose bright letters
still brought from time to time the gleam of hope to the
stricken farmhouse.

Henry was in Sing Sing. His letters brought news to
his mother of his steady success; first in the baseball nine of
the prison, a favourite with his wardens and the chaplain,
the best bridge player of the corridor. Henry was push-
ing his way to the front with the old-time spirit of the
Enderbys.

His mother had hoped that he might have been with

her at Xmas, but Henry had written that it was practically impossible for him to leave Sing Sing. He could not see his way out. The authorities were arranging a dance and sleighing party for the Xmas celebration. He had some hope, he said, of slipping away unnoticed, but his doing so might excite attention.

Of the trouble at home Anna had told her son nothing. No, Henry could not come. There was no help there. And William, the other son, ten years older than Henry. Alas, William had gone forth from the old homestead to fight his way in the great city! "Mother," he had said, "when I make a million dollars I'll come home. Till then good-bye," and he had gone.

How Anna's heart had beat for him. Would he make that million dollars? Would she ever live to see it? And as the years passed she and John had often sat in the evenings picturing William at home again, bringing with him a million dollars, or picturing the million dollars sent by express with love. But the years had passed. William came not. He did not come. The great city had swallowed him up as it has many another lad from the old homestead.

Anna started from her musing—

What was that at the door? The sound of a soft and timid rapping, and through the glass of the door-pane, a face, a woman's face looking into the fire-lit room with pleading eyes. What was it she bore in her arms, the little bundle that she held tight to her breast to shield it from the falling snow? Can you guess, reader? Try three guesses and see. Right you are. That's what it was.

The farmer's wife went hastily to the door.

"Lord's mercy!" she cried, "what are you doing out on such a night? Come in, child, to the fire!"

The woman entered, carrying the little bundle with her,

and looking with wide eyes (they were at least an inch and a half across) at Enderby and his wife. Anna could see that there was no wedding-ring on her hand.

"Your name?" said the farmer's wife.

"My name is Caroline," the girl whispered. The rest was lost in the low tones of her voice. "I want shelter," she paused, "I want you to take the child."

Anna took the baby and laid it carefully on the top shelf of the cupboard, then she hastened to bring a glass of water and a doughnut, and set it before the half-frozen girl.

"Eat," she said, "and warm yourself."

John rose from his seat.

"I'll have no child of that sort here," he said.

"John, John," pleaded Anna, "remember what the Good Book says: 'Things which are equal to the same thing are equal to one another!'"

John sank back in his chair.

And why had Caroline no wedding-ring? Ah, reader, can you not guess. Well, you can't. It wasn't what you think at all; so there. Caroline had no wedding-ring because she had thrown it away in bitterness, as she tramped the streets of the great city. "Why," she cried, "should the wife of a man in the penitentiary wear a ring."

Then she had gone forth with the child from what had been her home.

It was the old sad story.

She had taken the baby and laid it tenderly, gently on a seat in the park. Then she walked rapidly away. A few minutes after a man had chased after Caroline with the little bundle in his arms. "I beg your pardon," he said, panting, "I think you left your baby in the park." Caroline thanked him.

Next she took the baby to the Grand Central Waiting-room, kissed it tenderly, and laid it on a shelf behind the lunch-counter.

A few minutes later an official, beaming with satisfaction, had brought it back to her.

"Yours, I think, madame," he said, as he handed it to her. Caroline thanked him.

Then she had left it at the desk of the Waldorf Astoria, and at the ticket-office of the subway.

It always came back.

Once or twice she took it to Brooklyn Bridge and threw it into the river, but perhaps something in the way it fell through the air touched the mother's heart and smote her, and she had descended to the river and fished it out.

Then Caroline had taken the child to the country. At first she thought to leave it on the wayside and she had put it down in the snow, and standing a little distance off had thrown mullein stalks at it, but something in the way the little bundle lay covered in the snow appealed to the mother's heart.

She picked it up and went on. "Somewhere," she murmured, "I shall find a door of kindness open to it." Soon after she had staggered into the homestead.

Anna, with true woman's kindness, asked no questions. She put the baby carefully away in a trunk, saw Caroline safely to bed in the best room, and returned to her seat beside the fire.

The old clock struck twenty minutes past eight.

Again a knock sounded at the door.

There entered the familiar figure of the village lawyer. His astrachan coat of yellow dogskin, his celluloid collar, and boots which reached no higher than the ankle, contrasted with the rude surroundings of the little room.

"Enderby," he said, "can you pay?"

"Lawyer Perkins," said the farmer, "give me time and I

will; so help me, give me five years more and I'll clear this debt to the last cent."

"John," said the lawyer, touched in spite of his rough (dogskin) exterior, "I couldn't, if I would. These things are not what they were. It's a big New York corporation, Pinchem & Co., that makes these loans now, and they take their money on the day, or they sell you up. I can't help it. So there's your notice, John, and I am sorry! No, I'll take no buttermilk, I must keep a clear head to work," and with that he hurried out into the snow again.

John sat brooding in his chair.

The fire flickered down.

The old clock struck half-past eight, then it half struck a quarter to nine, then slowly it struck striking.

Presently Enderby rose, picked a lantern from its hook, "Mortgage or no mortgage," he said, "I must see to the stock."

He passed out of the house, and standing in the yard, looked over the snow to the cedar swamp beyond with the snow winding through it, far in the distance the lights of the village far away.

He thought of the forty years he had spent here on the homestead—the rude, pioneer days—the house he had built for himself, with its plain furniture, the old-fashioned spinning-wheel on which Anna had spun his trousers, the wooden telephone and the rude skidway on which he ate his meals.

He looked out over the swamp and sighed.

Down in the swamp, two miles away, could he but have seen it, there moved a sleigh, and in it a man dressed in a sealskin coat and silk hat, whose face beamed in the moonlight as he turned to and fro and stared at each object by the roadside as at an old familiar scene. Round his waist was a belt containing a million dollars in gold coin, and as he halted his horse in an opening of the road he unstrapped the belt and counted the coins.

Beside him there crouched in the bushes at the dark edge of the swamp road, with eyes that watched every glitter of the coins, and a hand that grasped a heavy cudgel of blackthorn, a man whose close-cropped hair and hard lined face belonged nowhere but within the walls of Sing Sing.

When the sleigh started again the man in the bushes followed doggedly in its track.

Meantime John Enderby had made the rounds of his outbuildings. He bedded the fat cattle that blinked in the flashing light of the lantern. He stood a moment among his hogs, and, farmer as he was, forgot his troubles a moment to speak to each, calling them by name. It smote him to think how at times he had been tempted to sell one of the hogs, or even to sell the cattle to clear the mortgage off the place. Thank God, however, he had put that temptation behind him.

As he reached the house a sleigh was standing on the roadway. Anna met him at the door. "John," she said, "there was a stranger came while you were in the barn, and wanted a lodging for the night; a city man, I reckon, by his clothes. I hated to refuse him, and I put him in Willie's room. We'll never want it again, and he's gone to sleep."

"Ay, we can't refuse."

John Enderby took out the horse to the barn, and then returned to his vigil with Anna beside the fire.

The fumes of the buttermilk had died out of his brain. He was thinking, as he sat there, of midnight and what it would bring.

In the room above, the man in the sealskin coat had thrown himself down, clothes and all, upon the bed, tired with his drive.

"How it all comes back to me," he muttered as he fell asleep, "the same old room, nothing changed—except them—how worn they look," and a tear started to his eyes. He thought of his leaving his home fifteen years ago, of his struggle in the great city, of the great idea he had conceived of making money, and of the Farm Investment Company he had instituted—the simple system of applying the crushing power of capital to exact the uttermost penny from the farm loans. And now here he was back again, true to his word, with a million dollars in his belt. "To-morrow," he had murmured, "I will tell them. It will be Xmas." Then William—yes, reader, it was William (see line 503 above) had fallen asleep.

The hours passed, and kept passing.

It was 11.30.

Then suddenly Anna started from her place.

"Henry!" she cried as the door opened and a man entered. He advanced gladly to meet her, and in a moment mother and son were folded in a close embrace. It was Henry, the man from Sing Sing. True to his word, he had slipped away unostentatiously at the height of the festivities.

"Alas, Henry," said the mother after the warmth of the first greetings had passed, "you come at an unlucky hour." They told him of the mortgage on the farm and the ruin of his home.

"Yes," said Anna, "not even a bed to offer you," and she spoke of the strangers who had arrived; of the stricken woman and the child, and the rich man in the sealskin coat who had asked for a night's shelter.

Henry listened intently while they told him of the man, and a sudden light of intelligence flashed into his eye.

"By Heaven, father, I have it!" he cried. Then dropping his voice, he said, "Speak low, father. This man upstairs, he had a sealskin coat and silk hat?"

"Yes," said the father.

"Father," said Henry, "I saw a man sitting in a sleigh in the cedar swamp. He had money in his hand, and he counted it, and chuckled,—five dollar gold pieces—in all, 1,125,465 dollars and a quarter."

The father and son looked at one another.

"I see your idea," said Enderby sternly.

"We'll choke him," said Henry.

"Or club him," said the farmer, "and pay the mortgage."

Anna looked from one to the other, joy and hope struggling with the sorrow in her face. "Henry, my Henry," she said proudly, "I knew he would find a way."

"Come on," said Henry; "bring the lamp, mother, take the club, father," and gaily, but with hushed voices, the three stole up the stairs.

The stranger lay sunk in sleep. The back of his head was turned to them as they came in.

"Now, mother," said the farmer firmly, "hold the lamp a little nearer; just behind the ear, I think, Henry."

"No," said Henry, rolling back his sleeve and speaking with the quick authority that sat well upon him, "across the jaw, father, it's quicker and neater."

"Well, well," said the farmer, smiling proudly, "have your own way, lad, you know best."

Henry raised the club.

But as he did so—stay, what was that? Far away behind the cedar swamp the deep booming of the bell of the village church began to strike out midnight. One, two, three, its tones came clear across the crisp air. Almost at the same moment the clock below began with deep strokes to mark the midnight hour; from the farmyard chicken

coop a rooster began to crow twelve times, while the loud
lowing of the cattle and the soft cooing of the hogs seemed
to usher in the morning of Christmas with its message of
peace and goodwill.

The club fell from Henry's hand and rattled on the
floor.

The sleeper woke, and sat up.

"Father! Mother!" he cried.

"My son, my son," sobbed the father, "we had guessed
it was you. We had come to wake you."

"Yes, it is I," said William, smiling to his parents, "and
I have brought the million dollars. Here it is," and with
that he unstrapped the belt from his waist and laid a million dollars on the table.

"Thank Heaven!" cried Anna, "our troubles are at an
end. This money will help clear the mortgage—and the
greed of Pinchem & Co. cannot harm us now."

"The farm was mortgaged!" said William, aghast.

"Ay," said the farmer, "mortgaged to men who have no
conscience, whose greedy hand has nearly brought us to
the grave. See how she has aged, my boy," and he pointed
to Anna.

"Father," said William, in deep tones of contrition, "I
am Pinchem & Co. Heaven help me! I see it now. I see
at what expense of suffering my fortune was made. I
will restore it all, these million dollars, to those I have
wronged."

"No," said his mother softly. "You repent, dear son,
with true Christian repentance. That is enough. You
may keep the money. We will look upon it as a trust, a
sacred trust, and every time we spend a dollar of it on ourselves we will think of it as a trust."

"Yes," said the farmer softly, "your mother is right,

the money is a trust, and we will restock the farm with it, buy out the Jones's property, and regard the whole thing as a trust."

At this moment the door of the room opened. A woman's form appeared. It was Caroline, robed in one of Anna's directoire nightgowns.

"I heard your voices," she said, and then, as she caught sight of Henry, she gave a great cry.

"My husband!"

"My wife," said Henry, and folded her to his heart.

"You have left Sing Sing?" cried Caroline with joy.

"Yes, Caroline," said Henry. "I shall never go back."

Gaily the reunited family descended. Anna carried the lamp, Henry carried the club. William carried the million dollars.

The tamarack fire roared again upon the hearth. The buttermilk circulated from hand to hand. William and Henry told and retold the story of their adventures. The first streak of the Christmas morn fell through the door-pane.

"Ah, my sons," said John Enderby, "henceforth let us stick to the narrow path. What is it that the Good Book says: 'A straight line is that which lies evenly between its extreme points.'"

Father Knickerbocker—A Fantasy

IT happened quite recently—I think it must have been on April the second of 1917—that I was making the long pilgrimage on a day-train from the remote place where I dwell to the city of New York. And as we drew near the city, and day darkened into night, I had fallen to reading from a quaint old copy of Washington Irving's immortal sketches of Father Knickerbocker and of the little town where once he dwelt.

I had picked up the book I know not where. Very old it apparently was and made in England. For there was pasted across the flyleaf of it an extract from some ancient magazine or journal of a century ago, giving what was evidently a description of the New York of that day.

From reading the book I turned—my head still filled with the vision of Father Knickerbocker and Sleepy Hollow and Tarrytown—to examine the extract. I read it in a sort of half-doze, for the dark had fallen outside, and the drowsy throbbing of the running train attuned one's mind to dreaming of the past.

"The town of New York"—so ran the extract pasted in the little book—"is pleasantly situated at the lower extremity of the Island of Manhattan. Its recent progress has been so amazing that it is now reputed, on good authority, to harbour at least twenty thousand souls. Viewed from the sea it presents, even at the distance of half a mile, a striking appearance owing to the number and beauty of its church spires which rise high above the roofs and foliage and give to the place its characteristically religious aspect. The extreme end of the island is heavily fortified with can-

non, commanding a range of a quarter of a mile, and forbidding all access to the harbour. Behind this Battery a
neat greensward affords a pleasant promenade where the
citizens are accustomed to walk with their wives every
morning after church."

"How I should like to have seen it!" I murmured to
myself as I laid the book aside for a moment—"the Battery, the harbour and the citizens walking with their wives,
their own wives, on the greensward."

Then I read on:

"From the town itself a wide thoroughfare, the Albany
Post Road, runs meandering northward through the fields.
It is known for some distance under the name of the Broad
Way, and is so wide that four moving vehicles are said to
be able to pass abreast. The Broad Way, especially in the
springtime when it is redolent with the scent of clover
and apple-blossoms, is a favourite evening promenade for
the citizens (with their wives) after church. Here they
may be seen any evening strolling toward the high ground
overlooking the Hudson, their wives on one arm, a spy-
glass under the other, in order to view what they can see.
Down the Broad Way may be seen moving also droves of
young lambs with their shepherds, proceeding to the
market, while here and there a goat stands quietly munch-
ing beside the road and gazing at the passers-by."

"It seems," I muttered to myself as I read, "in some
ways but little changed after all."

"The town," so the extract continued, "is not without
its amusements. A commodious theatre presents with
great success every Saturday night the plays of Shakespeare
alternating with sacred concerts; the New Yorker, indeed,
is celebrated throughout the provinces for his love of
amusement and late hours. The theatres do not come out

until long after nine o'clock, while for the gayer habitués two excellent restaurants serve fish, macaroni, prunes and other delicacies till long past ten at night. The dress of the New Yorker is correspondingly gay. In the other provinces the men wear nothing but plain suits of a rusty black, whereas in New York there are frequently seen suits of brown, snuff-colour and even of pepper-and-salt. The costumes of the New York women are equally daring, and differ notably from the quiet dress of New England.

"In fine, it is commonly said in the provinces that a New Yorker can be recognised anywhere, with his wife, by their modish costumes, their easy manners and their willingness to spend money—two, three and even five cents being paid for the smallest service."

"Dear me," I thought, as I paused a moment in my reading, "so they had begun it even then."

"The whole spirit of the place," the account continued, "has recently been admirably embodied in literary form by an American writer, Mr. Washington Irving (not to be confounded with George Washington). His creation of Father Knickerbocker is so lifelike that it may be said to embody the very spirit of New York. The New Yorkers of to-day are accustomed indeed to laugh at Mr. Irving's fancy and to say that Knickerbocker belongs to a day long since past. Yet those who know tell us that the image of the amiable old gentleman, kindly but irascible, generous and yet frugal, loving his town and seeing little beyond it, may be held once and for all to typify the spirit of the place, without reference to any particular time or generation."

"Father Knickerbocker!" I murmured, as a felt myself dozing off to sleep, rocked by the motion of the car. "Father Knickerbocker—how strange if he could be here again and see the great city as we know it now! How different from his day! How I should love to go round New York and show it to him as it is."

So I mused and dozed till the very rumble of the wheels seemed to piece together in little snatches—"Father Knickerbocker—Father Knickerbocker—the Battery—the Battery—the citizens walking with their wives, with their wives—their own wives"—until presently, I imagine, I must have fallen asleep altogether and knew no more till my journey was over and I found myself among the roar and bustle of the concourse of the Grand Central.

And there, lo and behold, waiting to meet me, was Father Knickerbocker himself! I know not how it happened, by what queer freak of hallucination or by what actual miracle—let those explain it who deal in such things—but there he stood before me, with an outstretched hand and a smile of greeting—Father Knickerbocker himself, the Embodied Spirit of New York.

"How strange," I said. "I was just reading about you in a book on the train and imagining how much I should like actually to meet you and to show you round New York."

The old man laughed in a jaunty way.

"Show *me* round?" he said. "Why, my dear boy, I *live* here."

"I know you did long ago," I said.

"I do still," said Father Knickerbocker. "I've never left the place. I'll show *you* around. But wait a bit—don't carry that handbag. I'll get a boy to call a porter to fetch a man to take it."

"Oh, I can carry it," I said; "it's a mere nothing."

"My dear fellow," said Father Knickerbocker, a little testily I thought, "I'm as democratic and as plain and simple as any man in this city. But when it comes to carrying a handbag in full sight of all this crowd, why, as I said to Peter Stuyvesant about—about"—here a misty look seemed to come over the old gentleman's face—"about two hundred years ago—I'll be hanged if I will. It can't be done. It's not up to date."

While he was saying this, Father Knickerbocker had beckoned to a group of porters. "Take this gentleman's handbag," he said, "and you carry his newspapers, and you take his umbrella. Here's a quarter for you and a quarter for you and a quarter for you. One of you go in front and lead the way to a taxi."

"Don't you know the way yourself?" I asked in a half-whisper.

"Of course I do, but I generally like to walk with a boy in front of me. We all do. Only the cheap people nowadays find their own way."

Father Knickerbocker had taken my arm and was walking along in a queer, excited fashion, senile and yet with a sort of forced youthfulness in his gait and manner.

"Now then," he said, "get into this taxi."

"Can't we *walk?*" I asked.

"Impossible," said the old gentleman. "It's five blocks to where we are going."

As we took our seats I looked again at my companion, this time more closely. Father Knickerbocker he certainly was, yet somehow strangely transformed from my pictured fancy of the Sleepy Hollow days. His antique coat with its wide skirt had, it seemed, assumed a modish cut as if in imitation of the bell-shaped spring overcoat of the young man about town. His three-cornered hat was set at a rakish angle till it looked almost like an up-to-date fedora. The great stick that he used to carry had somehow changed itself into the curved walking-stick of a Broadway lounger. The solid old shoes with their wide buckles were gone. In their place he wore narrow slippers of patent leather of which he seemed inordinately proud, for he had stuck his feet up ostentatiously on the seat opposite. His eye followed my glance toward his shoes.

"For the fox-trot," he said, "the old ones were no good. Have a cigarette? These are Armenian, or would you prefer a Honoluluan or a Nigerian? Now," he resumed, when we had lighted our cigarettes, "what would you like to do first? Dance the tango? Hear some Hawaiian music, drink cocktails, or what?"

"Why, what I should like most of all, Father Knickerbocker—"

But he interrupted me. "There's a devilish fine woman! Look, the tall blonde one! Give me blondes every time!" Here he smacked his lips. "By gad, sir, the women in this town seem to get finer every century. What were you saying?"

"Why, Father Knickerbocker," I began, but he interrupted me again.

"My dear fellow," he said. "May I ask you not to call me *Father* Knickerbocker?"

"But I thought you were so old," I said humbly.

"Old! Me *old!* Oh, I don't know. Why, dash it, there are plenty of men as old as I am dancing the tango here every night. Pray call me, if you don't mind, just Knickerbocker, or simply Knicky—most of the other boys call me Knicky. Now what's it to be?"

"Most of all," I said, "I should like to go to some quiet place and have a talk about the old days."

"Right," he said. "We're going to just the place now— nice quiet dinner, a good quiet orchestra—Hawaiian, but quiet—and lots of women." Here he smacked his lips again, and nudged me with his elbow. "Lots of women, bunches of them. Do you like women?"

"Why, Mr. Knickerbocker," I said hesitatingly, "I suppose—I—"

The old man sniggered as he poked me again in the ribs.

"You bet you do, you dog!" he chuckled. "We *all* do. For me, I confess it, sir, I can't sit down to dinner without plenty of women, stacks of them, all round me."

Meantime the taxi had stopped. I was about to open the door and get out.

"Wait, wait,' said Father Knickerbocker, his hand upon my arm, as he looked out of the window. "I'll see somebody in a minute who'll let us out for fifty cents. None of us here ever get in or out of anything by ourselves. It's bad form. Ah! Here he is!"

A moment later we had passed through the portals of a great restaurant, and found ourselves surrounded with all the colour and tumult of a New York dinner *à la mode*. A burst of wild music, pounded and thrummed out on ukuleles by a group of yellow men in Hawaiian costumes, filled the room, helping to drown or perhaps only serving to accentuate the babel of talk and the clatter of dishes that arose on every side. Men in evening dress and women in all the colours of the rainbow, *décolleté* to a degree, were seated at little tables, blowing blue smoke into the air, and drinking green-and-yellow drinks from glasses with thin stems. A troupe of cabaret performers shouted and leaped on a little stage at the side of the room, unheeded by the crowd.

"Ha! ha!" said Knickerbocker, as we drew in our chairs to a table, "some place, eh? There's a peach! Look at her! Or do you like better that lazy-looking brunette next to her?"

Mr. Knickerbocker was staring about the room, gazing at the women with open effrontery, and a senile leer upon his face. I felt ashamed of him. Yet, oddly enough, no one about us seemed in the least disturbed.

"Now, what cocktail will you have?" said my companion. "There's a new one this week—The Fantan, fifty cents each—will you have that? Right! Two Fantans. Now to eat—what would you like?"

"May I have," I said, "a slice of cold beef and a pint of ale?"

"Beef!" said Knickerbocker contemptuously. "My dear fellow, you can't have that. Beef is only fifty cents. Do take something reasonable. Try Lobster Newburg—or no, here's a more expensive thing—Filet Bourbon à la something—I don't know what it is, but by gad, sir, it's three dollars a portion anyway."

"All right," I said. "You order the dinner." Mr. Knickerbocker proceeded to do so, the head-waiter obsequiously at his side, and his long finger indicating on the menu everything that seemed most expensive and that carried the most incomprehensible name.

When he had finished he turned to me again. "Now," he said, "let's talk."

"Tell me," I said, "about the old days and the old times on Broadway."

"Ah, yes," he answered, "the old days—you mean ten years ago before the Winter Garden was opened. We've been going ahead, sir, going ahead. Why, ten years ago there was practically nothing, sir, above Times Square, and look at it now."

I began to realise that Father Knickerbocker, old as he was, had forgotten all the earlier times with which I associated his memory. There was nothing left but the cabarets, and the Gardens, the Palm Rooms and the ukuleles of to-day. Behind that his mind refused to travel.

"Don't you remember," I asked, "the apple orchards

and the quiet groves of trees that used to line Broadway long ago?"

"Groves!" he said. "I'll show you a grove, a cocoanut grove"—here he winked over his wineglass in a senile fashion—"that has appletrees beaten from here to Honolulu." Thus he babbled on.

All through our meal his talk continued—of cabarets and dances, of fox-trots and midnight suppers, of blondes and brunettes, "peaches" and "dreams," and all the while his eye roved incessantly among the tables, resting on the women with a bold stare. At times he would indicate and point out for me some of what he called the "representative people" present.

"Notice that man at the second table," he would whisper across to me; "he's worth all the way to ten millions: made it in government contracts; they tried to send him to the penitentiary last fall but they can't get him—he's too smart for them! I'll introduce you to him presently. See the man with him? That's his lawyer—biggest crook in America, they say—we'll meet him after dinner." Then he would suddenly break off and exclaim: "Egad, sir, there's a fine bunch of them," as another bevy of girls came trooping out upon the stage.

"I wonder," I murmured, "if there is nothing left of him but this? Has all the fine old spirit gone? Is it all drowned out in wine and suffocated in the foul atmosphere of luxury?"

Then suddenly I looked up at my companion, and I saw to my surprise that his whole face and manner had altered. His hand was clenched tight on the edge of the table. His eyes looked before him—through and beyond the riotous crowd all about him—into vacancy, into the far past, back into memories that I thought forgotten. His face had altered. The senile, leering look was gone, and in its place the firm-set face of the Knickerbocker of a century ago.

He was speaking in a strange voice, deep and strong. "Listen," he said, "listen. Do you hear it—there—far out at sea—ships' guns—listen—they're calling for help— ships' guns—far out at sea!" He had clasped me by the arm. "Quick, to the Battery, they'll need every man to-night, they'll . . ."

Then he sank back into his chair. His look changed again. The vision died out of his eyes.

"What was I saying?" he asked. "Ah, yes—this old brandy—a very special brand. They keep it for me here —a dollar a glass. They *know* me here," he added in his fatuous way—"all the waiters know me. The headwaiter always knows me the minute I come into the room—keeps a chair for me. Now try this brandy and then presently we'll move on and see what's doing at some of the shows."

But somehow, in spite of himself, my companion seemed to be unable to bring himself fully back into the consciousness of the scene before him. The far-away look still lingered in his eyes.

Presently he turned and spoke to me in a low, confidential tone. "Was I talking to myself a moment ago?" he asked. "Yes? Ah! I feared I was. Do you know, I don't mind telling it to you—lately I've had a strange, queer feeling that comes over me at times, as if *something were happening*—something, I don't know what. I suppose," he continued, with a false attempt at resuming his fatuous manner, "I'm going the pace a little too hard, eh! Makes one fanciful . . . but the fact it, at times"—he spoke gravely again—"I feel as if there were something happening, something coming . . ."

"Knickerbocker," I said earnestly, "Father Knickerbocker, don't you know that something *is* happening— that this very evening as we are sitting here in all this riot, the President of the United States is to come before Congress on the most solemn mission that ever . . ."

But my speech fell unheeded. Knickerbocker had picked up his glass again and was leering over it at a bevy of girls dancing upon the stage.

"Look at that girl," he interrupted quickly, "the one dancing at the end—what do you think of her, eh? Some peach!"

Knickerbocker broke off suddenly. For at this moment our ears caught the sound of a noise, a distant tumult, as it were, far down the street and growing nearer. The old man had drawn himself erect in his seat, his hand to his ear, listening as he caught the sound.

"Out on the Broad Way," he said, instinctively calling it by its ancient name as if a flood of memories were upon him. "Do you hear it?—listen—listen—what is it? I've heard that sound before—I've heard every sound on the Broad Way these two centuries back—what is it? I seem to know it!"

The sound and tumult as of running feet and of many voices crying came louder from the street. The people at the tables had turned in their seats to listen. The music of the orchestra had stopped. The waiters had thrown back the heavy curtains from the windows and the people were crowding to them to look out into the street. Knickerbocker had risen in his place, his eyes looked toward the windows, but his gaze was fixed on vacancy as with one who sees a vision passing.

"I know the sound," he cried. "I see it all again. Look, can't you see them? It's Massachusetts soldiers marching South to the war—can't you hear the beating of the drums and the shrill calling of the fife—the regiments from the North, the first to come. I saw them pass, here where we are sitting, sixty years ago—"

Knickerbocker paused a moment, his hand still extended in the air, and then with a great light upon his face he cried:

"I know it now! I know what it meant, the feeling that has haunted me—the sounds I kept hearing—the guns of the ships at sea and the voices calling in distress! I know now. It means, sir, it means . . ."

But as he spoke a great cry came up from the street and burst in at the doors and windows, echoing in a single word:

WAR! WAR! The message of the President is for WAR!

"War!" cried Father Knickerbocker, rising to his full height, stern and majestic and shouting in a stentorian tone that echoed through the great room.

"War! War! To your places, every one of you! Be done with your idle luxury! Out with the glare of your lights! Begone you painted women and worthless men! To your places every man of you! To the Battery! Man the guns—stand to it, every one of you for the defence of America—for our New York, New York—"

Then with the sound "New York, New York" still echoing in my ears I woke up. The vision of my dream was gone. I was still on the seat of the car where I had dozed asleep, the book upon my knee. The train had arrived at the dépôt and the porters were calling into the doorway of the car—"New York, New York."

All about me was the stir and hubbub of the great dépôt. But loud over it all was heard the call of the newsboys crying "WAR! WAR! The President's message is for WAR! Late extra! War! War!"

And I knew that a great nation had cast aside the bonds of sloth and luxury, and was girding itself to join in the fight for the free democracy of all mankind.

Simple Stories of Success or How to Succeed in Life

LET me begin with a sort of parable.

Many years ago when I was on the staff of a great public school, we engaged a new swimming master.

He was the most successful man in that capacity that we had had for years.

Then one day it was discovered that he couldn't swim.

He was standing at the edge of the swimming tank explaining the breast stroke to the boys in the water.

He lost his balance and fell in. He was drowned.

Or no—he wasn't drowned—I remember—he was rescued by some of the pupils whom he had taught to swim.

After he was resuscitated by the boys—it was one of the things he had taught them—the school dismissed him.

Then some of the boys who were sorry for him taught him how to swim, and he got a new job as a swimming master in another place.

But this time he was an utter failure. He swam well, but they said he couldn't *teach*.

So his friends looked about to get him a new job. This was just at the time when the bicycle craze came in. They soon found the man a position as an instructor in bicycle riding. As he had never been on a bicycle in his life, he made an admirable teacher. He stood fast on the ground and said, "Now then, all you need is confidence."

Then one day he got afraid that he might be found out. So he went out to a quiet place and got on a bicycle, at the top of a slope, to learn to ride it. The bicycle ran away with him. But for the skill and daring of one of his pupils, who saw him and rode after him, he would have been killed.

This story, as the reader sees, is endless. Suffice it to say that the man I speak of is now in an aviation school teaching people to fly. They say he is one of the best aviators that ever walked.

According to all the legends and story books, the principal factor in success is perseverence. Personally, I think there is nothing in it. If anything, the truth lies the other way.

There is an old motto that runs, *"If at first you don't succeed, try, try again."* This is nonsense. It ought to read—"If at first you don't succeed, quit, quit, at once."

If you can't do a thing, more or less, the first time you try, you will never do it. Try something else while there is yet time.

Let me illustrate this with a story.

I remember, long years ago, at a little school that I attended in the country, we had a schoolmaster, who used perpetually to write on the blackboard, in a copperplate hand, the motto that I have just quoted:—

> *"If at first you don't succeed,*
> *Try, try, again."*

He wore plain clothes and had a hard, determined face. He was studying for some sort of preliminary medical examination, and was saving money for a medical course. Every now and then he went away to the city and tried the examination: and he always failed. Each time he came back, he would write up on the blackboard—

> *"Try, try, again."*

And always he looked grimmer and more determined than before. The strange thing was that with all his industry and determination, he would break out every now and then into drunkenness, and lie round the tavern at the crossroads, and the school would be shut for two days. Then he came back, more fiercely resolute than ever. Even children could see that the man's life was a fight. It was like the battle between Good and Evil in Milton's epics.

Well, after he had tried it four times, the schoolmaster at last passed the examination; and he went away to the city in a suit of store clothes, with eight hundred dollars that he had saved up, to study medicine. Now it happened that he had a brother who was not a bit like himself, but was a sort of ne'er-do-well, always hard-up and sponging on other people, and never working.

And when the schoolmaster came to the city and his brother knew that he had eight hundred dollars, he came to him and got him drinking and persuaded him to hand over the eight hundred dollars and to let him put it into the Louisiana State lottery. In those days the Louisiana Lottery had not yet been forbidden the use of the mails, and you could buy a ticket for anything from one dollar up. The Grand Prize was two hundred thousand dollars, and the Seconds were a hundred thousand each.

So the brother persuaded the schoolmaster to put the money in. He said he had a system for buying only the tickets with prime numbers, that won't divide by anything, and that it must win. He said it was a mathematical certainty, and he figured it out with the schoolmaster in the back room of a saloon, with a box of dominoes on the table to show the plan of it. He told the schoolmaster that he himself would only take ten per cent of what they made, as a commission for showing the system, and the schoolmaster could have the rest.

So in a mad moment, the schoolmaster handed over his roll of money, and that was the last he ever saw of it.

The next morning when he was up he was fierce with rage and remorse for what he had done. He could not go back to the school, and he had no money to go forward. So he stayed where he was in the little hotel where he had got drunk, and went on drinking. He looked so fierce and unkempt, that in the hotel they were afraid of him, and the bartenders watched him out of the corners of their eyes wondering what he would do: because they knew that there was only one end possible, and they waited for it to come. And presently it came. One of the bartenders went up to the schoolmaster's room to bring up a letter, and he found him lying on the bed with his face grey as ashes, and his eyes looking up at the ceiling. He was stone dead. Life had beaten him.

And the strange thing was that the letter that the bartender carried up that morning was from the management of the Louisiana Lottery. It contained a draft on New York, signed by the treasurer of the State of Louisiana, for two hundred thousand dollars. The schoolmaster had won the Grand Prize.

The above story, I am afraid, is a little gloomy. I put it down merely for the moral it contained, and I became so absorbed in telling it that I almost forgot what the moral was that it was meant to convey. But I think the idea is that if the schoolmaster had long before abandoned the study of medicine, for which he was not fitted, and gone in, let us say, for playing the banjo, he might have become end-man in a minstrel show. Yes, that was it.

Let me pass on to other elements in success.

I suppose that anybody will admit that the peculiar

quality that is called initiative,—the ability to act promptly on one's own judgment,—is a factor of the highest importance.

I have seen this illustrated two or three times in a very striking fashion.

I knew, in Toronto,—it is long years ago,—a singularly bright young man whose name was Robinson. He had had some training in the iron and steel business, and when I knew him was on the lookout for an opening.

I met him one day in a great hurry, with a valise in his hand.

"Where are you going?" I asked.

"Over to England," he said. "There is a firm in Liverpool that have advertised that they want an agent here, and I'm going over to apply for the job."

"Can't you do it by letter?" I asked.

"That's just it," said Robinson, with a chuckle, "all the other men will apply by letter. I'll go right over myself and get there as soon or sooner than the letters. I'll be the man on the spot, and I'll get the job."

He was quite right. He went over to Liverpool, and was back in a fortnight with English clothes and a big salary.

But I cannot recommend his story to my friends. In fact, it should not be told too freely. It is apt to be dangerous.

I remember once telling this story of Robinson to a young man called Tomlinson, who was out of a job. Tomlinson had a head two sizes too big, and a face like a bun. He had lost three jobs in a bank and two in a broker's office, but he knew his work, and on paper he looked a good man.

I told him about Robinson, to encourage him, and the story made a great impression.

"Say, that was a great scheme, eh?" he kept repeating. He had no command of words, and always said the same thing over and over.

A few days later I met Tomlinson on the street with a valise in his hand.

"Where are you going?" I asked.

"I'm off to Mexico," he answered. "They're advertising for a Canadian teller for a bank in Tuscapulco. I've sent my credentials down, and I'm going to follow them right up in person. In a thing like this, the personal element is everything."

So Tomlinson went down to Mexico and he travelled by sea to Mexico City, and then with a mule train to Tuscapulco. But the mails, with his credentials went by land and got there two days ahead of him.

When Tomlinson got to Tuscapulco he went into the bank and he spoke to the junior manager and told him what he came for. "I'm awfully sorry," the junior manager said, "I'm afraid that this post has just been filled." Then he went into an inner room to talk with the manager. "The tellership that you wanted a Canadian for," he asked, "didn't you say that you have a man already?"

"Yes," said the manager, "a brilliant young fellow from Toronto; his name is Tomlinson, I have his credentials here —a first class man. I've wired him to come right along, at our expense, and we'll keep the job open for him ten days."

"There's a young man outside," said the junior, "who wants to apply for the job."

"Outside?" exclaimed the manager. "How did he get here?"

"Came in on the mule train this morning: says he can do the work and wants the job."

"What's he like?" asked the manager.

The junior shook his head. "Pretty dusty-looking customer," he said; "shifty-looking."

"Same old story," murmured the manager. "It's odd how these fellows drift down here, isn't it? Up to something crooked at home, I suppose. Understands the working of a bank, eh? I guess he understands it a little too well for my taste. No, no," he continued, tapping the papers that lay on the table, "now that we've got a first class man like Tomlinson, let's hang on to him. We can easily wait ten days, and the cost of the journey is nothing to the bank as compared with getting a man of Tomlinson's stamp. And, by the way, you might telephone to the Chief of Police and get him to see to it that this loafer gets out of town straight off."

So the Chief of Police shut up Tomlinson in the calaboose and then sent him down to Mexico City under a guard. By the time the police were done with him he was dead broke, and it took him four months to get back to Toronto; when he got there, the place in Mexico had been filled long ago.

But I can imagine that some of my readers might suggest that I have hitherto been dealing only with success in a very limited way, and that more interest would lie in discussing how the really great fortunes are made.

Everybody feels an instinctive interest in knowing how our great captains of industry, our financiers and railroad magnates made their money.

Here the explanation is really a very simple one. There is, in fact, only one way to amass a huge fortune in business or railway management. One must begin at the bottom. One must mount the ladder from the lowest rung. But this lowest rung is everything. Any man who can stand upon it with his foot well poised, his head erect, his arms braced and his eye directed upward, will inevitably mount to the top.

But after all—I say this as a kind of afterthought in conclusion. Why bother with success at all? I have observed that the successful people get very little real enjoyment out of life. In fact the contrary is true. If I had to choose—with an eye to having a really pleasant life— between success and ruin, I should prefer ruin every time. I have several friends who are completely ruined—some two or three times—in a large way of course; and I find that if I want to get a really good dinner, where the champagne is just as it ought to be, and where hospitality is unhindered by mean thoughts of expense, I can get it best at the house of a ruined man.

Historical Drama

AFTER all there is nothing like the Historical Drama! Say what you will about moving pictures or high-speed vaudeville they never have the same air and class to them. For me as soon as I see upon the program "A tucket sounds!" I am all attention, and when it says "Enter Queen Elizabeth to the sound of Hoboes," I am thrilled. What does it matter if the queen's attendants seem to speak as if they came from Yonkers? There is dignity about it all the same. When you have, moving in front of you on the stage, people of the class of Louis Quatorze, Henry Quinze, Arthur Cromwell and Mary of Roumania, you feel somehow as if they were distinctly superior to such characters as Big-hearted Jim, and Shifty Pete and Meg of the Bowery and Inspector Corcoran. Perhaps they are!

But of all the characters that walk upon the stage, commend me to Napoleon. What I don't know about that man's life, from seeing him on the boards is not worth discussing. I have only to close my eyes and I can see him before me as depicted by our greatest actors, with his one lock of hair and his forehead like a door knob, his melancholy eyes painted black and yellow underneath. And as for his family life, his relations with Josephine, his dealings with the Countess Skandaliska, I could write it all down if it was lost.

There is something about that man,—I don't mind admitting it,—that holds me. And he exercises the same fascination over all our great actors. About once in every ten years some one of them, intoxicated by success, decides that he wants to be Napoleon. It is a thing that happens to all of them. It is something in their brain that breaks.

Every time that this happens a new Napoleonic play is produced. That is, it is called *new* but it is really the same old play over again. The title is always entirely new but that is because it is a convention that the title of a Napoleon play is never a straight-out statement of what it means such as "Napoleon, Emperor of France" or "Napoleon and Josephine." It is called, let us say, "Quinze Pour Cent" or "Mille Fois Non" or "Des Deux Choses L'Une"—that sort of thing. And after it is named it is always strung together in the same way and it is always done in little fits and starts that have no real connection with one another but are meant to show Napoleon at all the familiar angles. In fact, here is how it goes:—

"DES DEUX CHOSES L'UNE"

A DRAMA OF THE FIRST EMPIRE

Adapted from the French of Dumas, Sardou, Hugo, Racine, Corneille, and all others who ever wrote of Napoleon.

The opening part of the play is intended to show the extraordinary fidelity towards the Emperor on the part of the marshals of France whom he had created.

SCENE ONE

The ball room of the palace of the Tuileries. Standing around are ladies in directoire dresses, brilliant as rainbows. Up right beside them are the marshals of France. There is music and a buzz of conversation.

Enter Napoleon followed by Talleyrand in black, and two secretaries carrying boxes. There is silence. The Emperor seats himself at a little table. The secretaries place on it two black despatch boxes.

The Emperor speaks: Marshal Junot.

The Marshal steps forward and salutes.

THE EMPEROR: Marshal: I have heard strange rumours and doubts about your fidelity. I wish to test it. I have here,—he opens one of the boxes,—a vial of poison. Here, —drink it.

JUNOT: With pleasure, Sire.

Junot drinks the poison and stands to attention.

THE EMPEROR: Go over there and stand beside the Comtesse de la Polissonerie till you die.

JUNOT (*saluting*): With pleasure, Sire.

NAPOLEON (*turns to another marshal*): Berthier?

Here, Sire!

Berthier steps out in front of the Emperor.

THE EMPEROR (*rising*): Ha! Ha! Is it you,—he reaches up and pinches Berthier's ear,—*Vieux paquet de linge sale!*

Berthier looks delighted. It is amazing what a French marshal will do for you if you pinch his ear. At least it is a tradition of the stage. In these scenes Napoleon always pinched the Marshals' ears and called them,—*Vieux paquet de linge sale,* etc.

The Emperor turns stern in a moment.

Marshal Berthier!

Sire!

Are you devoted to my person?

Sire, you have but to put me to the test.

Very well. Here, Marshal Berthier (Napoleon reaches into the box), is a poisoned dog biscuit. Eat it.

BERTHIER (*saluting*): With pleasure, Sire. It is excellent.

NAPOLEON: Very good, *Mon Vieux trait d'union.* Now go and talk to the Duchesse de la Rotisserie till you die.

Berthier bows low.

THE EMPEROR: Marshal Lannes! You look pale. Here is a veal chop. It is full of arsenic. Eat it.

Marshal Lannes bows in silence and swallows the chop in one bite.

The Emperor then gives a paquet of prussic acid to Marshal Soult, one pill each to Marshals Ney and Augereau, then suddenly he rises and stamps his foot.

No, Talleyrand, no! The farce is finished! I can play it no longer. Look, *les braves enfants!* They have eaten poison for me. *Ah non, mes amis, mon vieux.* Reassure yourselves. You are not to die. See, the poison was in the other box.

TALLEYRAND (*shrugging his shoulders*): If your Majesty insists upon spoiling everything.

NAPOLEON: Yes, yes, those brave fellows could not betray me. Come, Berthier. Come, Junot, come and let us cry together—

The Emperor and his marshals all gather in a group, sobbing convulsively and pulling one another's ears.

But one must not think that the Imperial Court was all sentiment. Ah, no! The great brain of the Emperor could be turned in a moment to other concerns and focused into a single point of concentrated efficiency. As witness:—

SCENE TWO
Showing how Napoleon used to dictate a letter, carry on a battle, and Reveal Business Efficiency at the Acme.

Napoleon in a room in a château, announced to be somewhere near a battle, striding up and down, dictating a letter with his hat on. On the stage the great Emperor always dictates through his hat. A secretary sitting at a table is vainly trying to keep pace with the rush of words.

Now are you ready, de Meneval. Have you written that last sentence?

DE MENEVAL (*writing desperately*): In a moment, Sire, in a moment.

Imbecile, write this then, "The Prefect of Lyons is ordered to gather all possible cannon for the defense of Toulon . . . He is reminded that there are six cannon on the ramparts of Lyons which he has apparently forgotten. The Emperor orders him to pass them forward at once—" Have you written that, imbecile?

In a moment, Sire, in a moment.

"To have them forwarded to Toulon. He is reminded that there are six more in the back garden of the Ministry of the Marine, and two put away in the basement of the Methodist Church."

The Secretary collapses. Napoleon stamps his foot. A terrible looking Turkish attendant, Marmalade the Mameluke, comes in and drags him out by the collar, and then drags in another secretary and props him up in a chair where he at once commences to write furiously.

Napoleon never stops dictating,—

"There are two more cannons in the garage of the Prefect of Police. One has a little piece knocked out of the breech—"

THE SECRETARY (*pausing in surprise*): Mon Dieu!

THE EMPEROR: Eh, what, mon enfant. What surprises you?

THE SECRETARY: Ah, Sire, it is too wonderful. How can you tell that a piece is out of the breeches?

NAPOLEON (*pinching his ear*): Ha! You think me wonderful!

THE SECRETARY: I do.

NAPOLEON (*pulling his hair*): I am. And my cannon!

I know them all. That one with the piece knocked out of the breech shall I tell you how I know it?

THE SECRETARY: Ah, Sire!

Marmalade, the Mameluke comes in and salaams to the ground.

THE EMPEROR: Well, what is it? *Vieux fromage de cuir!*

The Mameluke gurgles about a pint of Turkish.

THE EMPEROR: Ha! Bring her in (*to the secretary*). You may go. You, Marmalade, after she enters, stand behind that curtain, so,—your scimitar so,—if I stamp my left foot—you understand.

MARMALADE (*with a salaam*): Zakouski, Anchovi.

EMPEROR: Good. Show her in.

There enters with a rush a beautiful half Polish Countess Skandaliska. She throws herself at the Emperor's feet.

Sire, Sire, my husband! I crave his life.

NAPOLEON (*taking her by the chin and speaking coldly*): You are very beautiful.

Sire! My husband. I ask his life. He is under orders to be shot this morning.

THE EMPEROR (*coldly*): Let me feel your ears.

Ah! Sire. In pity, I beg you for his life.

THE EMPEROR (*absently*): You have nice fat arms. Let me pinch them.

Sire! My husband. . . .

THE EMPEROR (*suddenly changing his tone*): Yes, your husband. Did you think I did not know. I have it here. (*He turns his back on the Countess, picks up a document from the table and reads*):

"Scratchitoff Skandaliska, Count of Poland, Baron of Lithuania, Colonel of the Fifth Lancers, reported by the Imperial police as in the pay of the Czar of Russia—" Ha! Did you think I did not know that?—

His back is still turned. The Countess is standing up-right. Her face is as of stone. Slowly she draws from her bodice a long poniard, slowly she raises it above the Emperor's back.

Napoleon goes on reading.

"—conspired with seven others, since executed, to take the life of the Emperor, and now this 5th day of September . . ."

The Countess has raised the poniard to its height. As she is about to stab the Emperor, he taps slightly with his foot. Marmalade, the Mameluke, has flung aside the curtain and grasps the Countess from behind by both wrists. The poniard rattles to the floor. The Emperor turns and goes on calmly reading the document.

"This 5th day of September, pardoned by the clemency of the Emperor and restored to his estates."

The Countess released by Marmalade, falls weeping at the Emperor's feet.

Ah! Sire, you are indeed noble.

NAPOLEON: Am I not? Take her out, Marmalade. (*The Mameluke bows, takes out the weeping Countess and returns with a renewed salaam*):

THE EMPEROR (*dreamily*): We know how to treat them, don't we? old trognan de chou. Let no one disturb that mirror. It may serve us again. And now, bring me a secretary, and I will go on dictating.

In this way did the great Emperor transact more business in a week than most men would get through in a day.

*   *   *   *   *   *   *

But in this very same play of *Des Deux Choses L'Une,* we have to remember that while all these other things are happening Napoleon is also fighting a battle.

In fact hardly is the Countess Skandaliska well off the premises before a military aide-de-camp comes rattling into the room. The great Brain is in full operation again in a second.

Ha! Colonel Escargot. What news?

Bad news, Sire. Marshal Masséna reports the battle is lost.

THE EMPEROR (*frowning*): Bad news. The battle lost? Do you not know, Colonel Escargot, that I do not permit a battle to be lost? How long have you been in my service? Let me see, you were at Austerlitz?

I was, Sire.

And you were afterwards in Cantonments at Strasburg?

It is true, Sire.

I saw you there for five minutes on the afternoon of the 3rd of November of 1810.

Sire! It is wonderful.

Tut, tut, it is nothing. You were playing dominoes. I remember you had just thrown a double three when I arrived.

COLONEL ESCARGOT (*falling on his knees*): Sire, it is too much. You are inspired.

THE EMPEROR (*smiling*): Perhaps. But realize then, that I do not allow a battle to be lost. Get up, *mon vieux bonnet de coton*, let me pinch your ear. Now then, this battle, let us see. You, the secretary, give me a map.

The secretary unfolds a vast map on the table. The Emperor stands in deep thought regarding it. Presently he speaks:

Where is Masséna?

COLONEL ESCARGOT (*indicating a spot*): He is here, Sire.

What is his right resting on?

His right, Sire, is extended here. It is endangered. (*The Emperor remains a moment in thought.*)

How is his centre?

His centre is solid.

And where has he got his rear?

His rear, Sire, is resting on a thorn hedge.

THE EMPEROR: Ha! Ride to Masséna at once. Tell him to haul in his centre and to stick out his rear. The battle will be won in two hours.

ESCARGOT (*saluting*): Sire. It is wonderful. (*He clatters out.*)

Napoleon sinks wearily into a chair. His head droops in his hands. "Wonderful!" he broods, "and yet the one thing of all things that I want to do, I can't do."

Indeed the man is really up against it. He can remember cannons and win battles and tell Masséna where to put his rear, but when it comes to Josephine, he is no better than the rest of us.

The Emperor rings the bell.

The secretary comes in.

Listen, I have taken a decision. I am going to divorce Josephine.

The secretary bows.

Go to her at once and tell her that she is divorced.

The secretary bows again.

If she asks why, say that it is the Emperor's command. You understand.

I do.

If she tries to come here, do not permit it. Stop her, if need be with your own hands. Tell Marmalade she is not to pass. Tell him to choke her. Tell the guard outside to stop her. Tell them to fire a volley at her. Do you understand? She is *not* to come.

Alas, Sire, it is too late. She is here now. I hear her voice.

One can hear outside the protests of the guards.

The Empress Josephine, beautiful and disheveled and streaming with tears pushes Marmalade aside with an imperious gesture and dashes into the room. She speaks:—

Napoleon, what is this? What does it mean? Tell me it is not true? You could not dare?

NAPOLEON (*timidly*): I think there is some mistake. Not dare what?

JOSEPHINE: To divorce me? You could not? You would not? Ah! heartless one, you could not do it.

She falls upon Napoleon's neck weeping convulsively.

THE EMPEROR: Josephine, there has been a delusion, a misunderstanding, of course I would not divorce you. Who dares hint at such a thing?

JOSEPHINE: Outside, in the waiting room, in the court they are all saying it.

NAPOLEON: Ha! Let them dare! They shall answer with their heads.

JOSEPHINE: Ah, now, you are my own dear Napoleon. Let me fold you in my arms. Let me kiss you on the top of the head. (*She hugs and kisses the Emperor with enthusiasm.*)

NAPOLEON: Ah, Josephine, how much I love you.

A voice is heard without. Colonel Escargot enters rapidly. He is deadly pale but has a triumphant look on his face. He salutes.

Sire, everything is saved.

NAPOLEON: Ah! So the battle was not lost after all.

No, Sire, your orders were sent by semaphore telegraph. Masséna withdrew his rear and thrust out his centre. A panic broke out in the ranks of the enemy.

Ha! The enemy? Who are they?

We are not sure. We think Russians. But at least, Sire, they are fleeing in all directions. Masséna is in pursuit. The day is ours.

THE EMPEROR: It is well. But you Colonel Escargot, you are wounded!

THE COLONEL (*faintly*): No, Sire, not wounded.

NAPOLEON: But, yes,—

COLONEL ESCARGOT: Not wounded, Sire, killed, I have a bullet through my heart.

He sinks down on the carpet.

The Emperor bends over him.

ESCARGOT (*feebly*): *Vive l'Empereur.* (*He dies.*)

NAPOLEON (*standing for a moment and looking at the body of Colonel Escargot*): Alas! Josephine, all my victories cannot give me back the life of one brave man. I might have known it at the start.

He remains in reflection. "I should have chosen at the beginning. Tranquillity or conquest, greatness or happiness,—*Des Deux Choses L'Une.*"

And as he says that the curtain slowly sinks upon the brooding Emperor. The play is over. In fact there is no need to go on with it. Now that the audience know why it is called *Des Deux Choses L'Une*, there is no good going any further. All that is now needed is the usual Transfiguration Scene.

Napoleon, dying at St. Helena, seen in a half light with a vast net curtain across the stage and a dim background of storm, thunder, and the armies of the dead—

That, with a little rumbling of cannon—the distant rolling of a South Atlantic storm—

And then,—the pomp has passed,—turn up the lamps and let the matinée audience out into the daylight.

.   .   .   .

But we must not suppose for a minute that French history has any monopoly of dramatic interest. Oh, dear, no. We have recently discovered that right here on the North American continent there is material teeming with dramatic interest. Any quantity of it. In fact it begins right at the start of our history and goes right on. Consider the aboriginal Indian; what a figure for tragedy. Few people perhaps realize that no less than seventeen first-class tragedies, each as good as Shakespeare's, and all in blank verse, have been written about the Indians. They have to be in blank verse. There was something about the primitive Indian that invited it. It was the real way to express him.

Unfortunately these Indian tragedies cannot be produced on the stage. They are ahead of the age. The managers to whom they have been submitted say that as yet there is no stage suitable for them, and no actors capable of acting them, and no spectators capable of sitting for them. Here is a sample of such a tragedy.

METTAWAMKEAG

An Indian Tragedy

The scene is laid on the shores of Lake Mettawamkeag near the junction of the Peticodiac and the Passamoquidiac Rivers. The sun is rising.

Enter *Areopagitica*, an Indian chief.

With *The Encyclopedia*—a brave of the Appendixes.

And *Pilaffe de Volaille*, a French Coureur des bois.

· · · · · · · ·

AREOPAGITICA:
Hail, vernal sun, that thus with trailing beam
Illuminates with gold the flaming east,
Hail, too, cerulean sky that touched with fire
Expels th' accumulate cloud of vanished night.
THE ENCYCLOPEDIA: Hail! Oh! Hail.
PILAFFE DE VOLAILLE: Hêle! Oh, hêle.
AREOPAGITICA:

All nature seems to leap with morn to song,
Tempting to gladness the awakening bird,
E'en the dark cedar feels the gladsome hour
And the light larch pulsates in every frond.
Who art thou? Whence? And whither goest thou?
  PILAFFE DE VOLAILLE:
Thrice three revolving suns have waxed and waned
Since first I wended hither from afar,
Nor knowing not, nor caring aught, if here or there,
Who am I? One that is. Whence come I? From beyond,
The restless main whose hyperboreal tide
Laves coast and climes unknown, Oh, Chief, to thy
      sagacity.
                    From France I came.
  AREOPAGITICA: Hail!
  (*What Pilaffe de Volaille means is that he has been out
here for nine years and lives near Mettawamkeag. But
there is such a size and feeling about this other way of
saying it, that it seems a shame that dramas of this kind
can't be acted.*)
  After they have all said, "Oh, hail!" and "Oh, hêle," as
many times as is necessary, Areopagitica and The Ency-
clopedia take Pilaffe de Volaille to the Lodge of the Ap-
pendixes.
  There he is entertained on hot dog. And there he meets
Sparkling Soda Water, the daughter of Areopagitica.
  After the feast the two wander out into the moonlight
together beside the waterfall. Love steals into their hearts.
Pilaffe de Volaille invokes the moon.
"Thou silver orb whose incandescent face
Smiles on the bosom of the turgid flood
Look deep into mine heart and search if aught
Less pure than thy white beam inspires its love,
Soda, be mine!"

Soda Water speaks:

Alas! What words are these! What thought is this!
Thy meaning what? Unskilled to know,
My simple words can find no answer to the heart's appeal,
Where am I at?

PILAFFE DE VOLAILLE: Flee with me.

SODA WATER: Alas!

PILAFFE: Flee.

SODA WATER (*invoking the constellations of the Zodiac*):

Ye glimmering lights that from the Milky Way
To the tall zenith of the utmost pole
Illume the vault of heaven and indicate
The inclination of the axis of the earth
Showing sidereal time and the mean measurement
Of the earth's parallax,
Help me.

PILAFFE DE VOLAILLE (*in despair*): "Oh, hêle!"

Both the lovers know that their tragic love is hopeless.
For them, marriage is out of the question. De Volaille is
sprung from an old French family, with eight quarters of
noble birth, a high average even at a time when most
people were well born. He cannot ally himself with anything less white than himself. On the other hand Sparkling Soda knows that, after the customs of her time, her
father has pledged her hand to the Encyclopedia. She
cannot marry a pale face.

Thus, what might have been a happy marriage, is
queered from the start. Each is too well born to stoop
to the other. This often happens.

Standing thus in the moonlight beside the waterfall the
lovers are surprised by Areopagitica and The Encyclopedia.
In despair Sparkling Soda leaps into the flood. The noble
Encyclopedia plunges headlong after her into the boiling
water and is boiled. De Volaille flees.

Areopagitica vows vengeance. Staining himself with grape juice he declares a war of extermination against the white race. The camp of the French is surprised in a night attack. Pilaffe de Volaille, fighting with the courage of his race, is pierced with an Indian arrow. He expires on the spot, having just time before he dies to prophesy in blank verse the future greatness of the United States.

Areopagitica, standing among the charred ruins of the stockaded fort and gazing upon the faces of the dead, invokes the nebular Hypothesis and prophesies clearly the League of Nations.

· · · · · · ·

The same dramatic possibilities seem to crop up all through American history from Christopher Columbus to President Hoover.

But to see the thing at its height it is better to skip about three hundred years in one hop and come down to what is perhaps the greatest epic period in American history,—the era of the Civil War.

This great event has been portrayed so often in the drama and the moving pictures that everybody knows just how it is dealt with. It is generally put on under some such title as the Making of the Nation, or The Welding of the Nation, or the Riveting of the Nation,—or, The Hammering, or the Plastering,—in short, a metaphor taken from the building and contracting trades. Compare this:—

FORGING THE FIFTEENTH AMENDMENT

A Drama of the Civil War

The scene is laid in the Council room of the White House. There are present Abraham Lincoln, Seward.

Staunton, Artemus Ward, and the other members of the cabinet.

LINCOLN (*speaking very gravely*): Mr. Secretary, what news have you from the Army of the Potomac?

STAUNTON: Mr. President, the news is bad. General Halleck has been driven across the Rappahannock, General Pope has been driven across the Roanoke, and General Burnside has been driven across the Pamunkey.

LINCOLN (*with quiet humour*): And has anybody been driven across the Chickahominy?

STAUNTON: Not yet.

LINCOLN: Then it might be worse. Let me tell you a funny story that I heard ten years ago.

SEWARD (*with ill-disguised impatience*): Mr. President, this is no time for telling stories ten years old.

LINCOLN (*wearily*): Perhaps not. In that case fetch me the Constitution of the United States.

The Constitution is brought and is spread out on the table, in front of them. They bend over it anxiously.

LINCOLN (*with deep emotion*): What do you make of it?

STAUNTON: It seems to me, from this, that all men are free and equal.

SEWARD (*gravely*): And that the power of Congress extends to the regulation of commerce between the States, with foreign states, and with Indian Tribes.

LINCOLN (*thoughtfully*): The price of liberty is eternal vigilance.

(In the printed text of the play there is a note here to the effect that Lincoln did not on this particular occasion use this particular phrase. Indeed it was said by someone else on some other occasion. But it is such a good thing for anyone to say on any occasion, that it is the highest dramatic art to use it.)

LINCOLN (*standing up from the table to his full height and speaking as one who looks into the future*): Gentlemen, I am prepared to sacrifice any part of this Constitution to save the whole of it, or to sacrifice the whole of it to save any part of it, but what I will not do is to sacrifice all of it to save none of it.

There is a murmur of applause. But at this very moment, a messenger dashes in.

THE MESSENGER: Mr. President, telegraphic news from the seat of war. General Grant has been pushed over the Chickahominy.

LINCOLN: Pushed backwards or pushed forwards?

THE MESSENGER: Forwards.

LINCOLN (*gravely*): Gentlemen, the Union is safe.

Humour As I See It

IT is only fair that at the back of this book I should be allowed a few pages to myself to put down some things that I really think.

Until two weeks ago I might have taken my pen in hand to write about humour with the confident air of an acknowledged professional.

But that time is past. Such claim as I had has been taken from me. In fact I stand unmasked. An English reviewer writing in a literary journal, the very name of which is enough to put contradiction to sleep, has said of my writing, "What is there, after all, in Professor Leacock's humour but a rather ingenious mixture of hyperbole and myosis?"

The man was right. How he stumbled upon this trade secret, I do not know. But I am willing to admit, since the truth is out, that it has long been my custom in perparing an article of a humorous nature to go down to the cellar and mix up half a gallon of myosis with a pint of hyperbole. If I want to give the article a decidedly literary character, I find it well to put in about half a pint of paresis. The whole thing is amazingly simple.

But I only mention this by way of introduction and to dispel any idea that I am conceited enough to write about humour, with the professional authority of Ella Wheeler Wilcox writing about love, or Eva Tanguay talking about dancing.

All that I dare claim is that I have as much sense of humour as other people. And, oddly enough, I notice that everybody else makes this same claim. Any man will admit, if need be, that his sight is not good, or that he cannot swim, or shoots badly with a rifle, but to touch upon his sense of humour is to give him a mortal affront.

"No," said a friend of mine the other day, "I never go to Grand Opera," and then he added with an air of pride—"You see, I have absolutely no ear for music."

"You don't say so!" I exclaimed.

"None!" he went on. "I can't tell one tune from another. I don't know *Home Sweet Home* from *God, Save the King*. I can't tell whether a man is tuning a violin or playing a sonata."

He seemed to get prouder and prouder over each item of his own deficiency. He ended by saying that he had a dog at his house that had a far better ear for music than he had. As soon as his wife or any visitor started to play the piano the dog always began to howl—plaintively, he said, as if it were hurt. He himself never did this.

When he had finished I made what I thought a harmless comment.

"I suppose," I said, "that you find your sense of humour deficient in the same way: the two generally go together."

My friend was livid with rage in a moment.

"Sense of humour!" he said. "My sense of humour! Me without a sense of humour! Why, I suppose I've a keener sense of humour than any man, or any two men, in this city!"

From that he turned to bitter personal attack. He said that *my* sense of humour seemed to have withered altogether.

He left me, still quivering with indignation.

Personally, however, I do not mind making the admission, however damaging it may be, that there are certain forms of so-called humour, or, at least, fun, which I am quite unable to appreciate. Chief among these is that ancient thing called the Practical Joke.

"You never knew McGann, did you?" a friend of mine asked me the other day. When I said, "No, I had never known McGann," he shook his head with a sigh, and said:

"Ah, you should have known McGann. He had the greatest sense of humour of any man I ever knew—always full of jokes. I remember one night at the boarding house where we were, he stretched a string across the passageway and then rang the dinner bell. One of the boarders broke his leg. We nearly died laughing."

"Dear me!" I said. "What a humourist! Did he often do things like that?"

"Oh, yes, he was at them all the time. He used to put tar in the tomato soup, and beeswax and tin-tacks on the chairs. He was full of ideas. They seemed to come to him without any trouble.

McGann, I understand, is dead. I am not sorry for it. Indeed I think that for most of us the time has gone by when we can see the fun of putting tacks on chairs, or thistles in beds, or live snakes in people's boots.

To me it has always seemed that the very essence of good humour is that it must be without harm and without malice. I admit that there is in all of us a certain vein of the old original demoniacal humour or joy in the misfortune of another which sticks to us like our original sin. It ought not to be funny to see a man, especially a fat and pompous man, slip suddenly on a banana skin. But it is. When a skater on a pond who is describing graceful circles and showing off before the crowd, breaks through the ice and gets a ducking, everybody shouts with joy. To the original savage, the cream of the joke in such cases was found if the man who slipped broke his neck, or the man who went through the ice never came up again. I can imagine a group of prehistoric men standing round the ice-hole where he had disappeared and laughing till their sides split. If there had been such a thing as a prehistoric newspaper, the affair would have been headed up: *"Amusing Incident. Unknown Gentleman Breaks Through Ice and Is Drowned."*

But our sense of humour under civilisation has been weakened. Much of the fun of this sort of thing has been lost on us.

Children, however, still retain a large share of this primitive sense of enjoyment.

I remember once watching two little boys making snowballs at the side of the street and getting ready a little store of them to use. As they worked there came along an old man wearing a silk hat, and belonging by appearance to the class of "jolly old gentlemen." When he saw the boys his gold spectacles gleamed with kindly enjoyment. He began waving his arms and calling, "Now, then, boys, free shot at me! free shot!" In his gaiety he had, without noticing it, edged himself over the sidewalk on to the street. An express cart collided with him and knocked him over on his back in a heap of snow. He lay there gasping and trying to get the snow off his face and spectacles. The boys gathered up their snow-balls and took a run towards him. "Free shot!" they yelled. "Soak him! Soak him!"

I repeat, however, that for me, as I suppose for most of us, it is a prime condition of humour that it must be without harm or malice, nor should it convey even incidentally any real picture of sorrow or suffering or death. There is a great deal in the humour of Scotland (I admit its general merit) which seems to me, not being a Scotchman, to sin in this respect. Take this familiar story (I quote it as something already known and not for the sake of telling it).

A Scotchman had a sister-in-law—his wife's sister—with whom he could never agree. He always objected to going anywhere with her, and in spite of his wife's entreaties always refused to do so. The wife was taken mortally ill and as she lay dying, she whispered, "John, ye'll drive Janet with you to the funeral, will ye no?" The Scotchman, after an internal struggle, answered, "Margaret, I'll do it for ye, but it'll spoil my day."

Whatever humour there may be in this is lost for me by the actual and vivid picture that it conjures up—the dying wife, the darkened room and the last whispered request.

No doubt the Scotch see things differently. That wonderful people—whom personally I cannot too much admire—always seem to me to prefer adversity to sunshine, to welcome the prospect of a pretty general damnation, and to live with grim cheerfulness within the very shadow of death. Alone among the nations they have converted the devil—under such names as Old Horny—into a famaliar acquaintance not without a certain grim charm of his own. No doubt also there enters into their humour something of the original barbaric attitude towards things. For a primitive people who saw death often and at first hand, and for whom the future world was a vivid reality, that could be *felt*, as it were, in the midnight forest and heard in the roaring storm—for such a people it was no doubt natural to turn the flank of terror by forcing a merry and jovial acquaintance with the unseen world. Such a practice as a wake, and the merrymaking about the corpse, carry us back to the twilight of the world, with the poor savage in his bewildered misery, pretending that his dead still lived. Our funeral with its black trappings and its elaborate ceremonies is the lineal descendant of a merrymaking. Our undertaker is, by evolution, a genial master of ceremonies, keeping things lively at the death-dance. Thus have the ceremonies and the trappings of death been transformed in the course of ages till the forced gaiety is gone, and the black hearse and the gloomy mutes betoken the cold dignity of our despair.

But I fear this article is getting serious. I must apologise.

I was about to say, when I wandered from the point, that there is another form of humour which I am also quite unable to appreciate. This is that particular form of story which may be called, par excellence, the English Anecdote. It always deals with persons of rank and birth, and, except for the exalted nature of the subject itself, is, as far as I can see, absolutely pointless.

This is the kind of thing that I mean.

"His Grace the Fourth Duke of Marlborough was noted for the openhanded hospitality which reigned at Blenheim, the family seat, during his régime. One day on going in to luncheon it was discovered that there were thirty guests present, whereas the table only held covers for twenty-one. 'Oh, well,' said the Duke, not a whit abashed, 'some of us will have to eat standing up.' Everybody, of course, roared with laughter."

My only wonder is that they didn't kill themselves with it. A mere roar doesn't seem enough to do justice to such a story as this.

The Duke of Wellington has been made the storm-centre of three generations of wit of this sort. In fact the typical Duke of Wellington story had been reduced to a thin skeleton such as this:

"A young subaltern once met the Duke of Wellington coming out of Westminster Abbey. 'Good morning, your Grace,' he said, 'rather a wet morning.' 'Yes,' said the

Duke, with a very rigid bow, 'but it was a damn sight wetter, sir, on the morning of Waterloo.' The young subaltern, rightly rebuked, hung his head."

Nor is it only the English who sin in regard to anecdotes.

One can indeed make the sweeping assertion that the telling of stories as a mode of amusing others, ought to be kept within strict limits. Few people realise how extremely difficult it is to tell a story so as to reproduce the real fun of it—to "get it over" as the actors say. The mere "facts" of a story seldom make it funny. It needs the right words, with every word in its proper place. Here and there, perhaps once in a hundred times, a story turns up which needs no telling. The humour of it turns so completely on a sudden twist or incongruity in the dénouement of it that no narrator however clumsy can altogether fumble it.

Take, for example, this well known instance—a story which, in one form or other, everybody has heard.

"George Grossmith, the famous comedian, was once badly run down and went to consult a doctor. It happened that the doctor, though, like everybody else, he had often seen Grossmith on the stage, had never seen him without his make-up and did not know him by sight. He examined his patient, looked at his tongue, felt his pulse and tapped his lungs. Then he shook his head. 'There's nothing wrong with you, sir,' he said, 'except that you're run down from overwork and worry. You need rest and amusement. Take a night off and go and see George Grossmith at the Savoy.'

"'Thank you,' said the patient, 'I *am* George Grossmith.'"

Let the reader please observe that I have purposely told this story all wrongly, just as wrongly as could be, and yet there is something left of it. Will the reader kindly look back to the beginning of it and see for himself just how it ought to be narrated and what obvious error has been made. If he has any particle of the artist in his make-up, he will see at once that the story ought to begin:

"One day a very haggard and nervous-looking patient called at the office of a fashionable doctor, etc., etc."

In other words, the chief point of the joke lies in keeping it concealed till the moment when the patient says, "Thank you, I am George Grossmith." But the story is such a good one that it cannot be completely spoiled even when told wrongly. This particular anecdote has been variously told of George Grossmith, Coquelin, Joe Jefferson, John Hare, Cyril Maude, and about sixty others. And I have noticed that there is a certain type of man who, on hearing this story about Grossmith, immediately tells it all back again, putting in the name of somebody else, and goes into new fits of laughter over it, as if the change of name made it brand new.

But few people, I repeat, realise the difficulty of reproducing a humorous or comic effect in its original spirit.

"I saw Harry Lauder last night," said Griggs, a Stock-Exchange friend of mine, as we walked up town together the other day. "He came onto the stage in kilts" (here Griggs started to chuckle) "and he had a slate under his arm" (here Griggs began to laugh quite heartily), "and he said, 'I always like to carry a slate with me' (of course he said it in Scotch, but I can't do the Scotch the way he does it) 'just in case there might be any figures I'd be wanting to put down'" (by this time Griggs was almost suffocated with laughter)—"and he took a little bit of chalk out of his pocket, and he said" (Griggs was now almost hysterical), "'I like to carry a wee bit chalk along because I find the slate is (Griggs was now faint with laughter), "'the slate is—is—not much good without the chalk.'"

Griggs had to stop, with his hand to his side and lean

against a lamp post. "I can't, of course, do the Scotch the way Harry Lauder does it," he repeated.

Exactly. He couldn't do the Scotch and he couldn't do the rich mellow voice of Mr. Lauder and the face beaming with merriment, and the spectacles glittering with amusement, and he couldn't do the slate, nor the "wee bit chalk" —in fact he couldn't do any of it. He ought merely to have said, "Harry Lauder," and leaned up against a post and laughed till he had got over it.

Yet in spite of everything, people insist on spoiling conversation by telling stories. I know nothing more dreadful at a dinner table than one of these amateur raconteurs— except perhaps, two of them. After about three stories have been told, there falls on the dinner table an uncomfortable silence, in which everybody is aware that everybody else is trying hard to think of another story, and is failing to find it. There is no peace in the gathering again till some man of firm and quiet mind turns to his neighbour and says—"But after all there is no doubt that whether we like it or not prohibition is coming." Then everybody in his heart says, Thank Heaven! and the whole tableful are happy and contented again, till one of the story tellers "thinks of another," and breaks loose.

Worst of all perhaps is the modest story teller who is haunted by the idea that one has heard his story before. He attacks you after this fashion:

"I heard a very good story the other day on the steamer going to Bermuda"—then he pauses with a certain doubt in his face—"but perhaps you've heard this?"

"No, no, I've never been to Bermuda. Go ahead."

"Well, this is a story that they tell about a man who went down to Bermuda one winter to get cured of rheumatism—but you've heard this?"

"No, no."

"Well, he had rheumatism pretty bad and he went to Bermuda to get cured of it. And so when he went into the hotel he said to the clerk at the desk—but, perhaps you know this."

"No, no, go right ahead."

"Well, he said to the clerk I want a room that looks out over the sea—but perhaps—"

Now the sensible thing to do is to stop the narrator right at this point. Say to him quietly and firmly, "Yes, I have heard that story. I always liked it ever since it came out in *Titbits* in 1878, and I read it every time I see it. Go on and tell it to me and I'll sit back with my eyes closed and enjoy it."

No doubt the story-telling habit owes much to the fact that ordinary people, quite unconsciously, rate humour very low: I mean, they underestimate the difficulty of "making humour." It would never occur to them that the thing is hard, meritorious and dignified. Because the result is gay and light, they think the process must be. Few people would realise that it is much harder to write one of Owen Seaman's "funny" poems in *Punch* than to write one of the Archbishop of Canterbury's sermons. Mark Twain's *Huckleberry Finn* is a greater work than Kant's *Critique of Pure Reason*, and Charles Dickens' creation of Mr. Pickwick did more for the elevation of the human race —I say it in all seriousness—than Cardinal Newman's *Lead, Kindly Light, Amid the Encircling Gloom*. Newman only cried out for light in the gloom of a sad world. Dickens gave it.

But the deep background that lies behind and beyond what we call humour is revealed only to the few who, by instinct or by effort, have given thought to it. The world's humour, in its best and greatest sense, is perhaps the highest product of our civilisation. One thinks here not of the mere spasmodic effects of the comic artist or the blackface expert of the vaudeville show, but of the really great humour which, once or twice in a generation at best, illuminates and elevates our literature. It is no longer dependent upon the mere trick and quibble of words, or the odd and meaningless incongruities in things that strike us as "funny." Its basis lies in the deeper contrasts offered by life itself: the strange incongruity between our aspiration and our achievement, the eager and fretful anxieties of to-day that fade into nothingness to-morrow, the burning pain and the sharp sorrow that are softened in the gentle retrospect of time, till as we look back upon the course that has been traversed we pass in view the panorama of our lives, as people in old age may recall, with mingled tears and smiles, the angry quarrels of their childhood. And here, in its larger aspect, humour is blended with pathos till the two are one, and represent, as they have in every age, the mingled heritage of tears and laughter that is our lot on earth.

L'Envoi

The Faded Actor

I CAN call him to my mind as I have seen him burlesqued and parodied a hundred times—The Faded Actor. There he stands in his bell-shaped coat drawn at the waist and ample in the skirt. The battered hat that he handles in his elaborate gestures, and holds against his heart as he bows, is but the wreck of a hat that was. His faded trousers are tight upon his leg, drawn downwards with a strap, and carrying some lingering suggestion of the days of Beau Brummel and George the Fourth. His ample buttons are pierced out with string. His frilled cuffs are ostentatious in their raggedness.

From top to toe his creators have made a guy of him, a mean parody of forgotten graces. When he speaks his voice is raucous and rotund. There is something of Shakespeare in it, and something of gin. His face is a blossom that has bloomed overmuch. His feet move in long shoes, fitless, and so worn that he slides noiselessly across the stage. Beneath his arm, as if to complete the pathos of his figure, is the rolled up manuscript of the play that he has composed and that the managers, shame be to them, refuse to produce.

In a thousand plays and parodies you shall see this figure of the Faded Actor, a stock abject of undying ridicule. It is a signal for our laughter when he takes a drink, fawning to get it and swallowing it as if into a funnel; it is a signal for our laughter when he cadges for a coin, the smallest not coming amiss; when he arranges with elaborate care upon his uplifted wrist the ruins of his cuff; and most of all when he draws forth from beneath his arm his manuscript and stands forth to read what none will hear except in mockery, with his poor self carried away unconscious with the art of it.

Mark him now as he strikes his attitude to read. Hear the full voice, deep and resonant for all the gin that is in it. No parody can quite remove the majesty of that, nor the grace that has once lived in those queer gestures. Let us temper our laughter, as we look upon him, with something kindlier than mockery, something nearer to respect; for in the Faded Actor with his strange twists and graces, his futile manuscript, his blighted hopes, his unredeemed ambitions, we are looking upon all that is best in the great traditions of the stage. That thick deep voice—comic now, but once revered—that is the surviving tradition of the Elizabethan tragedy, declaimed as a Shakespeare or a Marlowe would have had it. That sliding step so funny to our eye, is all that lingers of the dainty grace of the eighteenth century when dance and stage were one; or that dragging limp with which the poor Faded Actor crosses the stage—he does not know it, but that has come to him from Garrick; or see that long gesticulation of the hand revealing the bare wrist below the cuff, there was a time when such gesticulation was the admired model of a Fox or a Sheridan, and held, even at second hand, the admiration of a senate.

Nay more, there is a thing in the soul of the Faded Actor that all may envy who in this life are busied with the æsthetic arts. For after all what does he want, poor battered guy, with his queer gestures and his outlandish graces? Money? Not he. He has never had, nor ever dreamed of it. A coin here, and there, enough to buy a dram of gin or some broad cheap writing paper on which to enscribe his thoughts—that much he asks; but beyond that his ambition never goes, for it travels elsewhere and by another road. His soul at least is pure of the taint that is smeared across the arts by the money rewards of a commercial age. He lived too soon to hear of the millions a year that crown success and kill out genius; that substitute publicity for fame; that tempt a man to do the work that pays and neglect the promptings of his soul, and that turn the field of the arts into one great glare of notoriety and noise. Not so worked and lived a Shakespeare or a Michael Angelo; and the Faded Actor descends directly from them. Art for Art's sake, is his whole creed, unconscious though it be. Someone to listen to his lines, an audience though only in a barn or beside the hedge row, a certain mead of praise that is the breath of art and the inspiration of effort; this he asks and no more. A yacht, a limousine, a palace beside the sea—of these things the Faded Actor has never heard. A shelter in someone else's premises, enough gin to keep his voice as mellow as Shakespeare would have wished it, and with that, permission to recite his lines, and to stand forth in his poor easy fancy as a King of Carthage, or a Sultan of Morocco. Such is the end and aim of his ambition. But out of such forms of ambition has been built up all that is best in art.

To him, therefore, I dedicate this book. He will never read it, and I easily forgive him that. His brain has long since acquired a delicacy of adjustment that renders reading a superfluity. But I make the dedication all the same as a humble tribute to those high principles of art which are embodied in the Faded Actor.

THE END